M000235500

Enoch at 100

Enoch at 100

A re-evaluation of the life, politics and philosophy of
ENOCH POWELL

Edited by
Lord Howard of Rising

Biteback Publishing

First published in Great Britain in 2012 by
Biteback Publishing Ltd
Westminster Tower
3 Albert Embankment
London SE1 7SP
'Immigration' chapter © Tom Bower.
All other material, unless otherwise stated, copyright © The J. Enoch Powell
Literary Trust.

The individual contributors have asserted their rights under the Copyright,
Designs and Patents Act 1988 to be identified as the authors of this work.

All rights reserved. No part of this publication may be reproduced, stored in
a retrieval system or transmitted, in any form or by any means, without the
publisher's prior permission in writing.

This book is sold subject to the condition that it shall not, by way of trade
or otherwise, be lent, resold, hired out or otherwise circulated without the
publisher's prior consent in any form of binding or cover other than that in
which it is published and without a similar condition, including this condition,
being imposed on the subsequent purchaser.

Every reasonable effort has been made to trace copyright holders of material
reproduced in this book, but if any have been inadvertently overlooked the
publishers would be glad to hear from them.

ISBN 978-1-84954-310-1

10 9 8 7 6 5 4 3 2 1

A CIP catalogue record for this book is available from the British Library.

Set in Old Standard and Adobe Caslon Pro

Printed and bound in Great Britain by
CPI Group (UK) Ltd, Croydon CR0 4YY

About the Authors

Lord Norton of Louth
Philip Norton, Lord Norton of Louth, is an author, academic and Conservative peer. He is Professor of Government in the Department of Politics and International Studies at the University of Hull, and since 1992 has been the Director of the Centre for Legislative Studies.

Lord True, CBE
Nicholas True was nominated as a member of the House of Lords in 2010. After holding various posts in government he served as Deputy Head of the Prime Minister's Policy Unit from 1991 to 1995. From 1997 to 2010 he was Private Secretary to the Leader of the Opposition in the House of Lords. He has been a local councillor since 1986 and has served as Leader of Richmond Council in London since 2010.

The Rt Hon. Frank Field
Frank Field has been the Member of Parliament for Birkenhead since 1979. He was nominated to the Privy Council in 1997. From 1997 to 1998 he served as Minister of Welfare Reform. After Labour's defeat in the 2010 election, he was given the role of 'poverty czar' in the coalition government.

The Rt Hon. Lord Forsyth of Drumlean
Michael Forsyth was MP for Stirling from 1983 until 1997. He served in government for more than ten years as Secretary of State for Scotland, as a Minister of State at the Home Office and Department of Employment and as Parliamentary Private Secretary to the Foreign Secretary. He was nominated to the Privy Council in 1995, Knighted in 1997 and appointed to the House of Lords in 1999. He is a non-executive Director of NBNK Investments Plc, J&J Denholm Ltd and of the Centre for Policy Studies.

Dr Simon Heffer

Simon Heffer writes a weekly political column for the *Daily Mail* and edits the paper's political comment website, RightMinds. He has been deputy editor of both the *Daily Telegraph* and *The Spectator*. He has written books on, among others, Thomas Carlyle and Ralph Vaughan Williams, and a guide to written English, *Strictly English*. His definitive biography of Enoch Powell, *Like the Roman*, was published in 1998.

Professor Roger Scruton

Roger Scruton is a philosopher and writer, currently holding the post of Visiting Professor in the School of Philosophical, Anthropological and Film Studies at the University of St Andrews. He is the author of over thirty books, as well as two operas, and has written articles in the press on both political and cultural issues. He is a Fellow of the Royal Society of Literature and a Fellow of the British Academy.

Dr Andrew Roberts

Andrew Roberts is a historian and journalist. He is the author of numerous books, including biographies of the Earl of Halifax and the 3rd Marquess of Salisbury and *A History of the English–Speaking Peoples since 1900*. *The Storm of War*, published in 2009, is Roberts' bestselling title to date and reached number two in the *Sunday Times* bestseller list.

Anne Robinson

Journalist and broadcaster.

Andrew Alexander

Andrew Alexander is an award-winning journalist whose column appears weekly in the *Daily Mail*, where since 1972 he has variously held the posts of sketch writer, City Editor and Director of Associated Newspapers. He was previously a leader writer and parliamentary sketch writer for the *Daily Telegraph*, where he is thought to have invented the tradition of reporting irreverently on the House of Commons. His devastating analysis of the Cold War, *America and the Imperialism of Ignorance*, was published in 2011.

Richard Ritchie

Richard Ritchie served as archivist for Enoch Powell, as well as editing two books of Enoch Powell's speeches (*A Nation or No Nation*; *Enoch Powell on 1992*). He stood as a Conservative Parliamentary Candidate in the elections of 1974 and 1979. He is Director, UK Government Relations at BP and is also an actor and composer of several musicals and songs.

Tom Bower

Tom Bower is an award-winning TV documentary producer, noted for his revelatory investigative work, who has written twenty-one books, including four which featured at the top of the *Sunday Times* bestseller list. In particular, he is known for his unauthorised biographies of Gordon Brown, Richard Branson, Robert Maxwell, Mohamed Fayed, Conrad Black, Bernie Ecclestone and, most recently, Simon Cowell.

Lord Lexden OBE

Alistair Cooke was political adviser to Airey Neave from 1977 to 1979, working in the Conservative Research Department of which he was later Deputy Director. He was Chairman of the Friends of the Union, established by Ian Gow, from 1995 to 2003. His publications include *Ulster: The Origins of the Problem* and *Ulster: The Ulster Options* published by the Conservative Political Centre in 1988 and 1990 respectively. He speaks frequently on Northern Ireland issues in the House of Lords. Further information can be found on his website, www.alistairlexden.org.uk

Dr Margaret Mountford

Dr Margaret Mountford is a lawyer and businesswoman. She was a non-executive director of Amstrad plc for a number of years. From 2005 to 2009 she starred as one of Lord Sugar's advisers in the TV hit *The Apprentice*. She has recently completed a Ph.D. in Papyrology at University College London.

Contents

Powell's place in history

For those who saw and heard Enoch Powell, the memory is indelible – the black moustache, the burning eyes, the hypnotic, metallic voice, the precision of language, the agility in debate. These will be largely lost to future generations. But, in a more important respect, Powell will survive more surely than any other British politician of the 20th century except Winston Churchill. His speeches and writings will be read so long as there exists a political and parliamentary culture in which speaking and writing matter. And if there comes a time when such a culture is all but destroyed, those brave few who wish to restore it will find in the thoughts of Enoch Powell something approaching their Bible.

Daily Telegraph, 9 February 1998

Editor's Note

This volume has been produced to mark the one hundredth anniversary of the birth of John Enoch Powell. Whatever views may be held about him he was a towering figure in British politics in the second half of the twentieth century. He achieved this not because of having held office, he was only in government for a limited period of time, but because of the force of his intellect and the clarity with which he articulated his ideas.

Although best known to the wider public for his speech on immigration in Birmingham in 1968 he was not only a significant figure in politics but a classical scholar, an historian, a theologian and a poet.

In political terms he remains an enigma to many who find it difficult to reconcile seeming contradictions. How could the man who electrified the House of Commons defending the treatment of Africans at Hola Camp go on to make the 'Rivers of Blood' speech? How could the politician who resigned over too much government spending initiate the first ten-year hospital building programme for the NHS? How could a man who twice refused high office out of loyalty to his colleagues come to be regarded as disloyal and an opportunist? What comes through clearly is that for Enoch Powell principle was more important than personal advancement.

In this book various authors were asked to look at subjects Enoch Powell spoke about in the context of his own words:

> At the end of a lifetime in politics, when a man looks back, he discovers that the things he most opposed have come to pass and that nearly all the objects he set out with are not merely not accomplished, but seem to belong to a different world from the one he lives in.

The Trustees of The J. Enoch Powell Literary Trust may not agree with all that the authors say in this book but it was never intended to be a hagiography; it was meant to be an objective look at how the views and concerns Enoch Powell expressed, some as long as half a century ago, are relevant today.

Included loosely are snippets of some of Enoch Powell's interests outside of politics, and twelve poems published for the first time. There is also the first interview given by his widow Pam.

One would need Enoch Powell's mastery of the English language properly to express the debt of gratitude owed to the authors who have given their time and taken the trouble to make this book possible. The preparation, and the immense amount of reading required, make that generosity all the greater: from all Enoch Powell's Literary Trustees – unreserved thanks. Thanks are also due to Katharine Thomson of the Churchill archive for her invaluable assistance and for always being so willing to help, however demanding the request.

Finally, a very special thank you must be given to Richard Ritchie without whom this book would never have appeared. It was his idea and he has generously given of his time and immense knowledge, not only to make his own contribution, but in research and assistance to other authors.

Greville Howard
June 2012

Foreword

I was surprised when Greville Howard asked me to write the foreword to this book as I am from the generation that entered Parliament after Enoch had left. I did not have the opportunity to hear him speak in Parliament or to see him in his heyday, holding forth in a House of Commons filled with political giants such as Michael Foot, Tony Benn and Iain Macleod. Yet I did not hesitate in accepting for I feel it is important for a politician from my generation to acknowledge the influence of this remarkable man, often remembered, as the essays in the book evidence, for the wrong reason.

Although not in Parliament, I did have one final opportunity to hear him in debate and years later I remember it vividly. It was at the Cambridge Union on 2 May 1995. As one of the invited speakers, I had rushed from the House of Commons to take part in a debate on the European Union. Arriving slightly late after having struggled into a dinner jacket on a slow train from London, I tumbled into the pre-debate dinner to find myself sitting near Enoch. He acknowledged me with the faintest of nods. I fancied he remembered that we had both spoken two years before in Oxford at a small conference on the same subject and I later had volunteered to drive him back to London. It was not an auspicious journey as I tried in vain to engage him in conversation and not concentrating missed the main turning to London. Staring straight ahead he intoned sharply, 'I think, young man, you will find that the road you seek is not the one you are on.'

Nonetheless, I was one of four speakers and Enoch was the last on our side, opposing the motion. I had rebelled over the Maastricht treaty and in so doing had stored up all the key arguments against the new European Union, so on the train I had penned a number of the principal ones and felt comfortable that I had enough time to make them all. As we filed in to the chamber, I was struck by the size of the audience; the place was packed to overflowing, and I assumed that a number of them were in the audience to cause trouble because of Enoch's presence and I expected we would get a rough ride. I was wrong. While interventions from the floor were rowdy and I recall feeling a little dissatisfied after my speech, that perhaps I had included too many points. Then Enoch stood and the whole place fell silent; not one person in the crowded chamber uttered a word or even a sound. In intense tones, his voice pitched higher than of old, he set out his argument with precision. All could see that his sharp and agile brain was no longer as flexible as it had been, as his pauses between phrases seemed to last for an age. Yet long though some of the pauses were, no one broke the silence, people even leaning forward in their seats, willing him to find the words he sought so that he could continue, their eyes fixed upon him. Ramrod straight, without any facial inflection, Enoch delivered his words. The passion of earlier days was no longer evident in his gestures, yet his eyes flashed as he challenged us all to refute his logic. In so doing he taught me the most vital lesson of debating; people listening to debates do not remember lists of facts or numerous arguments, so the speaker must choose the one thing he wants them to remember and have the courage to challenge them to agree with him. He did so that evening with this simple question: who should govern Britain, a government elected by the British people in Parliament or the institutions of the European Union? He made the same point three different ways and then sat down to huge applause. I, fresh from my Maastricht rebellion, found it profoundly moving.

Yet perhaps even more challenging was a chance encounter on the return train to London. I found myself sitting opposite a man in his fifties, who recognised me from the earlier debate. We exchanged pleasantries and then I asked him what he did for a living. 'I am at the Foreign Office,' he replied and sighed. He went on to explain that his daughter was at Cambridge and he had come to hear Enoch speak for what he felt might be the last time. I was intrigued that someone from the Foreign Office should want to come to hear such a political maverick voice such anti-EU arguments. 'Because,' he replied, 'he was right about the whole European project. We are losing our ability to govern ourselves.' With a shake of his head, he then explained that agreeing with Enoch Powell was

severely frowned on at the Foreign Office, for the European orthodoxy was so overwhelmingly strong in that most integrationist of
British institutions that no one would be allowed to achieve high
office, were such views to be known. 'Watching that remarkable
man tonight made me wish I had been braver.'

As one reads through the essays in the book, the complexity of
the man comes through. The essays paint a personal picture of this
one time 25-year-old professor of Greek, Biblical scholar, Brigadier,
poet, economic liberal, passionate parliamentarian and dedicated
family man, shedding light on a life full of bravery, power and
contradiction. From Simon Heffer we read how Enoch brought
his huge intellect to bear on the growing problem of inflation. He
realised early on that government had to tackle the problem of
our lax control on money supply. This led to his resignation from
Macmillan's government in 1958 and his later fallout with Heath,
whose retreat from 'Selsdon man' into an expansion of the money
supply many believe laid the grounds for the start of the UK's later
inflation problems. Heath's reactive prices and incomes policy
caused them to clash in the Commons – all of this as a forerunner
to Margaret Thatcher's economic policy.

Michael Forsyth reminds us how relevant he is today on the constitution. Those of us who sit in Parliament have long worried about
how the power of the Commons has shrunk over the years. Enoch
Powell laid the blame at Parliament's door. He spoke of the way
in which the Commons had willingly surrendered power to the UN,
the European Court of Human Rights and the EU. So many of
these issues dominate our discussions today, one only has to think
of the coalition proposal for an elected Upper House and the debate
about Scottish independence. Andrew Roberts takes this further and
shows that the sovereign right of nation states to govern themselves
was for Powell the only way to ensure proper accountable government. What is also interesting is that such was the esteem in which
he was held in the House of Commons, he was able to scupper the
Labour government's plans for Lords reform by joining forces with
Michael Foot in 1969. They were to join forces again in opposition
to the European Common Market (EU).

What is fascinating as one reads through these contributions
is the way in which Enoch was so determined to challenge the

orthodoxy of the day, whether it was on economic policy, self-government or the European Union. Yet in that also lay a contradiction.
Early on in his career, the uncompromising and unbending Enoch
of reputation did in fact compromise and accommodate. Although
opposed to our joining the Coal and Steel community in 1950, later
little was heard from him and in 1967 he even voted for Wilson's
formal application for entry into the Common Market. Early on
he even stayed in the government despite the disaster of Suez and
sat on his hands as his government at first flirted with an incomes
policy. Perhaps for a period Powell saw possession of high office
the best way to advance his ideas and, to achieve this, political
accommodation was required. However, later he was to find such
accommodation an anathema and by the advent of Heath's government he was determined not to repeat such tactics again. It was
perhaps this moment that above all else explains why someone of
such intellect and talent had so few Parliamentary triumphs to his
name. In a career spanning thirty-seven years, only fifteen months
were spent in office, with little of historic substance bearing his name
on the statute book. It is from the late 1960s that the Enoch Powell
who still excites commentators and politicians alike originated, not
as a creature of government but as a man of Parliament and more
often alone. That he chose this path was to many a cause of regret but
it was, as this book illustrates, his assault on Ted Heath in opposition
and government that was to shape popular memory of the man.

On Saturday 20 April 1968, Powell delivered his speech on immigration to the AGM of the West Midlands Conservative Area and
nothing in his political life was ever to be the same. Tom Bower's
essay both seeks to put the speech in context and using hindsight he
evaluates whether with our experience of the last forty years what
Powell forecast was in any way accurate. The backdrop to the speech
was the Labour government's Race Relations Bill going through
Parliament. Of all that Powell did it is this speech that lives on, still
causing controversy even among those who weren't born when he
delivered the speech. Almost since that time any attempt to enter
the debate in a rational and measured way has been met with the
allegation of racism, and it has only been in recent years that politicians have engaged with this topic again. However, what is clear
from Bower's essay is that this fear that politicians would be charged

with racism if they entered the debate was already there. After all this fear was one of the reasons Ted Heath chose to seek some sort of consensus with the Labour government for immigration policy. Notwithstanding that however, what Tom Bower concludes I feel is persuasive, which is that as a result of the injudicious use of such inflammatory language proper mainstream debate of the issue became much more difficult as both extremes were able to use the speech to attack rational debate. Yet I do not believe Enoch Powell himself was a racist; such a concept could never have been tolerated in such a rational mind as his, I am sure, a charge also rejected by others with impeccable credentials such as Michael Foot.

Yet what sets this speech apart is not the arguments for integration or tighter control of the numbers, it is the pointed language used to illustrate his concerns. The emotive references to the views and fears of two people he recounted and of course the reference to the Tiber '... foaming with much blood'.

There exists the strong likelihood that Enoch Powell, since his earlier well reported but far less emotive Walsall speech on immigration, now saw an opportunity to use the immigration issue to do Heath as much damage as possible – by making a speech to rock the Tory establishment. I wonder if his low opinion of Ted Heath distorted his judgement on the speech and I feel that he was also influenced by a false sense of his own security in the shadow Cabinet, believing he was, in effect, unsackable. What is certain is that he of all people must have realised how emotive his language was. He, as a first-rate speaker who measured every word, understood the power of language. That is why I believe that in focusing so fiercely on Ted Heath, Enoch Powell suspended his political judgement. For I do not believe he had for one moment anticipated the scale of the attack on him that followed, with its attendant charge of racism, or that it would lead to the end of his career in government. I am sure he assumed the anger would be directed at the leadership of the party for, in his belief, they had failed to deal with the issue. I also don't believe, as some have argued, that he chose this as the issue to leave the front bench over. This book shows that to be justification after the event, for as Pam Powell says in her interview, '... he [Enoch] was very surprised [to be sacked] and he thought what a bloody fool Ted Heath had been.' Not the words of a man determined to step down from the Front Bench at all costs.

Yet in discussing this issue it is important to remember how Powell was regarded by the public. Perhaps on that, the last word should go to Anne Robinson and her mother. Anne writes that her mother taught her from when she was a small child that it was far more instructive to listen to Enoch Powell or Michael Foot than either of their leaders as they had advocacy, oratory and flair that were second to none. Anne goes on to conclude about his immigration speech after getting to know him that 'Yes, Enoch was a controversial figure. His language was ill judged ... But to ascribe racist motives to a politician simply because he used language which for many of his listeners was normal is sloppy logic. Enoch deserves better. My mother was right. He was a worthy hero.'

The irony of all of this is that far from damaging Ted Heath, Enoch Powell's speech almost certainly ensured a Conservative election victory and a Heath government. It was this that was to lead to his break with the Conservative Party and his final furious attack on Heath, as he recommended Conservatives should not vote for Heath in 1974 because of Heath's pro-European policies.

A balanced analysis of this book leaves the reader in no doubt that Enoch Powell was one of the most significant British political figures of the post-war era. Even today, in so many areas his views continue to resonate and influence. He influenced a generation of politicians such as Margaret Thatcher, who in turn recognised that Enoch Powell and Keith Joseph were the two biggest influences on her political thinking, not least in the reshaping of Britain's failing economy.

But for me it is Powell's belief in the importance of the democratic nation state as the source of political power and his fight to ensure the British people did not lose their sovereignty to supranational institutions which carry the greatest weight. I cut my political teeth during the fierce debates over the Maastricht treaty and understand why such debates remain relevant today. As we watch the crisis in the eurozone and are often confounded by the judgments made in the European Court of Human Rights, Powell's view that our freedoms rest on our ability to defend our nation state and its democratic institutions is as important today as it was when he first advanced it. For at the heart of Powell's thinking was a profound attachment to the institution of Parliament and its important role in shaping our island history and our future. He deplored the reduction of this power through the 1972 act and other amendments. His words still remind and rebuke us for the casual way we have traded Parliament's supremacy to others, whether to foreign institutions or to the British judiciary. As Andrew Roberts writes, 'Powell's challenge is for us now to articulate the role of the nation state in the twenty-first century and by so doing enhance and protect it.'

When Powell said he admired Mrs Thatcher for her ability to put up with things even though she didn't agree with them until the time came when she could deal with them, he recognised his own weakness as a politician, in that he had little capacity to operate in the same way. It was this that ensured above all else that Enoch Powell would never be Prime Minister. Yet too often in British politics we think only in terms of careers. I believe in politics the power to shape thoughts and ideas and through them deeds is often more important than political position. Powell is a constant reminder for us that we do poor service to our countrymen and women if we sacrifice all belief to party advancement. In the cockpit of debate that is the Commons, ideas must excite and drive us, even if they create deep disagreement.

That is why Simon Heffer is right in saying that it is as a philosopher, rather than as a practical politician, that Powell has enjoyed continuing influence on Conservative thinking.

Through this study of Enoch Powell's life I hope this book helps a new generation of politicians understand why politics is the poorer without the clash of ideas and people of courage and stature to advance them.

Rt Hon. Iain Duncan Smith MP

Biographical Note

Philip Norton

John Enoch Powell was born on 16 June 1912, the son of Albert Enoch Powell (1872–1956), a primary school head teacher, and Ellen Mary, née Breese (1886–1953), a teacher, of Stechford, Warwickshire. His mother gave up teaching in order to learn Greek and impart it to her son. He was educated at King Edward's High School, Birmingham and Trinity College, Cambridge: an outstanding student, he achieved sufficient scholarships to cover the cost of his education. While at Cambridge, he was much influenced by the professor of Latin, the poet A. E. Housman. (He was later to publish four volumes of poetry.) He married Margaret Pamela (Pam), daughter of Lieutenant-Colonel L. E. Wilson, in 1952; they had two daughters.

He was a Fellow of Trinity College, Cambridge from 1934 to 1938 and was then appointed professor of Greek at the University of Sydney, making him the youngest professor in the British Empire. He published *A Lexicon to Herodotus* in 1938 followed by *The History of Herodotus* in 1939. He returned to England on the outbreak of war in order to serve in the Army. He served from 1939 to 1945 in the Royal Warwickshire Regiment (when he could not join as an Englishman, because he had no previous military service, he joined as an Australian) and on the General Staff. He rose rapidly through the ranks, exceptionally (though not uniquely) from private to brigadier, and at the age of thirty-two was one of the youngest brigadiers in the British army. He was awarded the MBE (military) in 1943 for 'gallant and distinguished services in the Middle East'. His task was to assess intelligence reports and contribute to military planning – in effect to anticipate Rommel's actions. He was then posted to India to serve on the South-East Command planning staff and fell in love with the country.

After his wartime service, Powell decided to pursue a career in politics – essentially to fight for the Empire and especially India. By the time he entered the House of Commons the cause for which he wanted to fight had been lost, but he was already in love with the House of Commons. He served in the Conservative Parliamentary Secretariat and then the Research Department from 1945 until 1951, working alongside Reginald Maudling and Iain Macleod. His first candidacy was in the 1947 Normanton by-election. After nineteen unsuccessful attempts to be selected in other seats, he was adopted as the Conservative candidate for Wolverhampton South West; he was elected in the 1950 general election with a majority of 691 and served as the Member for the seat until February 1974. He enjoyed his highest majority, of 14,467, in the 1970 general election. He was a director of the London Municipal Society between 1952 and 1955.

After initially declining office, he accepted in 1955 the post of parliamentary secretary at the Ministry of Housing and Local Government and two years later was promoted to Financial Secretary to the Treasury. One year after taking up the post, he resigned – along with the Chancellor of the Exchequer, Peter Thorneycroft, and the Economic Secretary to the Treasury, Nigel Birch, over the Cabinet's failure to support cuts in public expenditure. The following year, he declined a junior post in the Ministry of Education (because nothing had been offered to Thorneycroft) but returned to government in 1960 as Minister of Health and in 1962 was advanced to the Cabinet.

His Cabinet career was short lived. Along with Iain Macleod, he refused to serve in 1963 under Sir Alec Douglas-Home, believing that his support for Rab Butler made it too dishonourable to accept office in Douglas-Home's government. Powell also believed that the way in which the outgoing premier, Harold Macmillan, had engineered the succession was essentially dishonest. When Douglas-Home resigned the party leadership in 1965, and new rules were introduced for the election of the leader, Powell put himself forward as a candidate, garnering fifteen votes. He served under the new leader, Edward Heath, as shadow Defence Secretary.

On 20 April 1968 he addressed a meeting of the West Midlands Conservative Political Centre, of which he was president – his speech was circulated in advance by the West Midlands CPC and not the party Central Office – and delivered an attack on unchecked immigration from the Commonwealth to the United Kingdom. He used a classical allusion to Virgil, declaring, 'Like the Roman, I seem to see "the river Tiber foaming with much blood".' Though the script, typed by his wife, had the quotation in Latin, he delivered it in English and it was soon dubbed the 'Rivers of Blood' speech. It was immediately denounced in the media and by party leaders: Heath sacked him from the shadow Cabinet. However, there were marches by workers in support of his stance, and opinion polls showed majority support for his views. It was a speech that both made him and destroyed him. Overnight, he became a national figure and a political pariah. He never held office again but spent the rest of his life as one of the nation's most controversial politicians.

During the 1970–74 parliament, Powell was the leading Conservative critic of the Heath government, voting against it on 115 occasions. He opposed especially the U-turns on the economy and industry in 1971 and the European Communities Bill 1972, seeing the bill as a betrayal of British sovereignty. He was one of fifteen Tory MPs to vote against the government in 1972 in a vote of confidence on the second reading of the bill. The party leadership considered withdrawing the party whip from him, but concluded that this would simply give him added publicity as well as be counter-productive, given that he was so well entrenched in his constituency.

He declined to seek re-election in the February 1974 general election, regarding the premature election as 'essentially fraudulent', and recommended that voters give their support to whatever party had committed itself to renegotiating the Treaty of Rome and submitting it to the British people: in effect, the Labour Party. Having been credited with contributing to, or even being responsible for, the Conservative Party's surprise win in the 1970 general election, he was now credited with helping defeat it in 1974.

A dedicated Unionist, he was adopted as the Ulster Unionist candidate for South Down and was elected in the general election of October 1974. He held the seat until 1987, narrowly holding on in the by-election in 1986, triggered when Unionist MPs resigned to force and fight by-elections in opposition to the Anglo-Irish Agreement. He lost the seat by 731 votes in 1987. His time as an

Ulster Unionist MP was somewhat fraught, the integrationist Powell clashing at times with his devolutionist Ulster colleagues.

The loss of his seat left him with no clear sense of purpose and no dedicated routine. He worked on a book on St Matthew's Gospel, *The Evolution of the Gospel*, which appeared in 1994, and began work on a study of St John's Gospel. He continued in public life with a range of speeches and articles – especially on the issue of European integration – but in 1992 was diagnosed as suffering from Parkinson's disease. Towards the end of his life, he suffered a number of falls. He died on 8 February 1998.

A distinguished academic and soldier, Powell was an outstanding debater. His speeches were honed and compelling. His speech, delivered in the early hours of 28 July 1959, on the deaths of Mau Mau detainees in the Hola camp in Kenya, was one of the most outstanding delivered in the House of Commons in the latter half of the twentieth century. Denis Healey described it as 'the greatest parliamentary speech I have ever heard'. His reputation after he returned to the back benches in 1968 was such that MPs would fill the chamber to hear his speeches.

He was noted for taking an independent line, even when in the shadow Cabinet. He opposed holding nuclear weapons and maintaining a presence east of Suez. His views were distinctive, at times verging on the extreme: his acute distrust of the USA, acquired during the war, led him to see the hand of the CIA in the death of Lord Mountbatten; he believed the Earl of Oxford penned the works of Shakespeare. Though he advanced powerful arguments in support of his beliefs, he made no effort to craft a body of supporters. He relied on eloquence rather than organisation. Though he drew other Conservative MPs into the lobby with him on most occasions that he opposed the Heath government, he never generated a coherent political philosophy. There were Powellites – MPs who agreed with him on a good many (though not all) issues – but no Powellism. He was, in essence, a Tory neo-liberal, wedded to institutions but believing in economic and social freedom.

His advocacy, not least of the free market, influenced others (including Margaret Thatcher), but he had few political achievements to his name. His greatest was in joining with Michael Foot to frustrate and eventually destroy the Parliament (No. 2) Bill in

1969 to reform the House of Lords. Powell – who co-authored *The House of Lords in the Middle Ages* – was a passionate supporter of the Upper House, the product of prescription. Though a great parliamentarian, he recognised his limitations as a politician. He admired the skills of Margaret Thatcher and her ability 'to put up with things and go along with them, even though she doesn't agree with them, until the time comes when they can be dealt with. Now not possessing that quality myself – having the loquacity which always impels me to say "I don't agree" – I admire this.' It made Thatcher, in his view, a superb politician. As Simon Heffer observed, Powell occupied the place of a philosopher rather than a practitioner, 'a role for which baser skills are required'. Enoch Powell operated on a different plane.

European Union

Nicholas True

'The euro is much, much more than a currency ... The euro is the guarantee of a united Europe. If the euro fails, then Europe fails.' So Mrs Merkel told the Bundestag on 9 September 2011. She repeated this in starker terms on 26 October. The German Chancellor, like the ancient Roman, now seemed to see the Tiber foaming with much blood:

> Another half-century of peace and prosperity in Europe is not to be taken for granted. If the euro fails, Europe fails. We have a historical obligation: to protect by all means Europe's unification process [*Einigungswerk*] begun by our forefathers after centuries of hatred and blood spill. None of us can foresee what the consequences would be if we were to fail.[†]

Historical determinism is never appealing, generally coercive and rarely borne out by events. The agony of the euro, aggravated by unsustainable public spending in a hatful of EU countries (including the UK), has allowed the leaders of the unification process to press down upon the brows of the south ever more 'historical obligation' – a single currency sustained from Lisbon to Lesbos and Lapland to Lampedusa by supranational means that constrain the

---

[†] 'Niemand sollte glauben, dass ein weiteres halbes Jahrhundert Frieden und Wohlstand in Europa selbstverständlich ist. Es ist es nicht. Deshalb sage ich: Scheitert der Euro, dann scheitert Europa.... Wir haben eine historische Verpflichtung, das Einigungswerk Europas, das unsere Vorfahren nach Jahrhunderten des Hasses und des Blutvergießens vor über 50 Jahren auf den Weg gebracht haben, mit allen uns zur Verfügung stehenden verantwortbaren Mitteln zu verteidigen und zu schützen. Die Folgen, wenn das nicht gelänge, kann niemand von uns absehen.'

basic fiscal policies of elected governments, policed by the European Court of Justice and an 'automatic correction mechanism' defined by an unelected Brussels Commission.[†] Twenty-five nation states have agreed to it.

What would Enoch Powell have said to those government leaders, who, unlike Mr Cameron, so far, have bound their peoples to this new *Verpflichtung* (obligation) to protect a single currency? He had this simple advice for the English people thirty years ago:

> If the United Kingdom and Germany ... were part of a single unit with a single currency, then of course the less efficient producers would be knocked out. That is why Germany is so keen for Britain to go into the European Monetary System, so that it can wipe out the British industries with which it is in competition ... What we need not fear, however so long as we remain a nation with our own currency and allow the exchange rate of that currency to move freely, is that our inferior productivity ... will drive us out of international trade or impoverish us, de-industrialise us, or leave us without the means to import food. All these are bogies to be relegated to the world of Hans Andersen.[‡]

Between 2005 and 2010 Germany ran a current balance of payments surplus of 6.1 per cent of GDP; Spain ran a deficit of 7.6 per cent, Portugal 10.8 per cent, Greece 11.7 per cent. The euro blocks the floating exchange rate adjustments that would correct this. Instead, EU leaders are creating political structures to impose punishing austerity on the Mediterranean nations and defend the

---

† 'This balanced budget rule must be incorporated into the member states' national legal systems, preferably at constitutional level, within one year after the entry into force of the treaty. In the event of deviation from this rule, an automatic correction mechanism will be triggered. It will be defined by each member state on the basis of principles proposed by the European Commission. The EU Court of Justice will be able to verify national transposition of the balanced budget rule. Its decision is binding, and can be followed up with a penalty of up to 0.1 per cent of GDP, payable to the European Stability Mechanism in the case of euro area member states.' EU Presidency press release, 2 March 2011.

‡ London, 21 March 1980.

comfortable economic space that the eurozone provides for the north. Meanwhile, Italy, whose small industries managed well with a declining lira, and Greece have even suffered the humiliation of political *coups d'état* dictated by foreign powers. Enoch Powell forecast such compulsion long ago:

> A common currency means common government; the one is meaningless and impossible without the other. Accept common money and you have accepted common government ... If one threatens to diverge, what happens? ... They order it to alter its ways and dictate to it how to do so. Who then is going to do the dictating? Where will be that common government which a common currency implies? ... France and Germany, who hatched and willed this business, will see to it they rule the roost: a Franco-German hegemony to begin with and afterwards we shall see whether it will be French hegemony, as France intends, or a German hegemony ... All this has nothing to do with common markets or freedom of trade or all the alleged ideals of the EEC. Quite the reverse. This is not about freedom; it is about compulsion.[†]

For the purposes of this chapter, the success or otherwise of the latest attempt to prevent a shipwreck of the euro does not matter. But it would be polite to note that some do sleep better knowing there are ravens (with clipped wings) in the Tower of London, for, of course, if the ravens fail, the United Kingdom will fail.

The 2011–2012 euro crisis has again laid bare a never hidden, but often dissembled, end game of a united 'Europe' and the binding of the eccentric, and astonishingly creative, variety of Europe's nation states to the pillars of a temple of rationalist, bureaucratic uniformity. Whether or not the successive 'bail-outs' prove to be more than the dipping of rusty buckets in an ocean of debt, there has over

---

† Newbury, 3 October 1978. The hegemony is German, as France seems incapable of matching long-term German productive power. France's admirable sense of national pride and the convenience to Germany of tying France into her orbit will require the fiction of parity to be displayed for as long as it might. The Francophile Powell, in his last speeches in the 1990s, expressed sympathy for France's national interest and called attention to the need to help her sustain a European balance of power.

the last two generations come into being a structure of control in Europe, a legal entity, driven by a Franco-German alliance, with far-reaching powers over nation states, directed by a Commission all too prone, as Mr Hurd acknowledged in 1991, to insert itself in 'every nook and cranny of daily life'. Over that time the 300-year-old supremacy of the Westminster Parliament and the domestic rule of law, hard won in the travails of civil wars, army dictatorship and revolution, has evaporated.

For some in the 1960s, that was necessary. Britain could no longer 'stand alone'. It must 'find a new role'. For them, the real zealots in this great matter, political and economic salvation would be guaranteed by a 'united Europe', though they rarely laid this particular titbit at the front of their political stalls. For most, the far distant, or carefully veiled, objective of a European unity beyond free trade was unnoticed, uninteresting (if instinctively unappealing) and, critically, as a result, unthreatening. Enoch Powell sought to tear away the veil and reveal a present danger. But his brilliant speeches between 1969 and 1975 overestimated the British people's readiness to be stirred to stop a surrender of sovereignty. What is more, in a period whose elite discourse did, and does, sloppily equate 'modern' with 'good', and 'modernising' with imposing the smug perceptions of an erosive relativism and an increasingly intolerant 'liberalism', appeals to the 'past', to the accumulated wisdom of constitution and tradition, to the call of nation, have often fallen on doubting ears. So it was with Powell on 'Europe'. But his compelling sense of nation made the issue of the EEC one that for him came to override all others. It led him to give up his safe seat as a Conservative in 1974 and to urge his fellow Tories to vote for the socialist foe.

Powell did oppose British entry to the European Coal and Steel Community in 1950. Yet the charge is that in the 1950s and 1960s he did not throw at the EEC any of the kind of rhetoric he was to use in the 1970s and 1980s.[†] Powell did not deny his 'mistake' in the early 1960s in seeing the 'Common Market' chiefly in the context of trade. Mr Heath opened talks in October 1961, only for General de Gaulle to veto UK entry in January 1963. Addressing his

---

† Explored, for example, in Robert Shepherd, *Enoch Powell* (Pimlico, 1997), pp. 248–50.

constituency AGM in 1963 Powell noted 'setbacks' to free trade policy 'in our relations with the Common Market'.[†] During the 1966 election he said it was only 'fear that whispers to us that we would not be able to compete or keep our identity in the thriving, jostling market of western Europe'.[‡] When Mr Wilson sought Commons support for a formal application for entry on 10 May 1967, Powell voted for it. As it was, de Gaulle's continuing hostility resulted in a second French veto. The UK application lay like a deflated balloon until Heath's government pumped it up.

Only after Heath sacked him from the shadow Cabinet, the charge goes on, did Powell voice opposition to that idealistic cause of European unity with which Heath, above all, was identified. Hatred of the man was a goad to his hostility to the EEC. True or false, that charge is an irrelevance. High politics is as often shaped by enmities as affinities. Sometimes enmities have beneficial consequence.[§] And Powell's critique was, from the outset, intellectual, not *ad hominem*. But if he could save the English nation from the folly, as he came to see it, of signing the Treaty of Rome *and* hang Heath at the yardarm as well, that was worth a *Te Deum* indeed.

If Powell's view did change on Europe, and, as noted, he offered an explanation of the change, which will be read as evidence of honesty or dissimulation, according the predisposition of the reader, what occasioned it? In late 1967 de Gaulle's second veto, coupled with the devaluation of 18 November and retrenchment in defence, provoked Powell to pose questions about the nature of the country Britain now was. He spoke indignantly of Britain's 'orgy of self-abasement'. It had 'gulped down the dish of humble pie which General de Gaulle served up to us … and came back asking for more'. It was being brainwashed into thinking itself the sick man of Europe.[¶]

---

† Wolverhampton, 13 December 1963. Earlier he characterised Labour opposition as resulting from their wish for centralised economic planning: Bromley, 24 October 1963.

‡ Wolverhampton, 30 March 1966.

§ Thus, a useful aspect of Mr Brown's hatred of Mr Blair was to stop Blair taking the UK into the euro.

¶ London, 30 November 1967.

Eloquent as few could be in his love of country,[†] Powell had yet warned for some time about the danger of the delusions, or 'myths', that Britain no longer mattered as it was no longer an imperial power or 'workshop of the world'. He dissociated himself from the 1960s quest to answer Mr Acheson's gibe by finding a 'new role' for post-imperial Britain. 'Happiness and success,' Powell observed, 'are likeliest to come to the nations which know themselves as they really are.'[‡] 'A healthy, self-confident, self-knowing nation no more keeps telling itself that it is great, or asking how great it is, than a healthy person keeps taking his temperature.'[§]

After Powell's ejection from the shadow Cabinet his counterblast to the assault he saw on national substance and self-confidence intensified. 'The time has come', he wrote above a typescript for a speech in June 1968, 'when this conspiracy, like other conspiracies against common sense, must be ended.' He scorned claims of Franco-German superiority in economic performance based on undervalued currencies: 'I say we have had enough of this. It is time we stood up and told our accusers where they get off.'[¶] The startling demotic that broke into the intense, academic nature of his discourse reflected more than Powell's eye for a headline, or cry for attention. He had a respect for working-class opinion and an ability to popularise with which he thought to sustain the old alliance between the Conservative Party and a mass of patriotic, self-reliant voters, in a way that social condescension, the elitist liberalism of the 'superior people'[**] or modernising managerialism never would or could.

In March 1969 Powell publicly recanted and warned of the dangers of entry to the EEC. He again set his speech in the context of the 'sense of humiliation' and a 'mood somewhere between dejection and desperation'. He declared: 'We do not need ... to be

---

† Classically expressed in his St George's Day address, 1961, quoted in full elsewhere in this book.

‡ For example, Dublin, 13 November 1964.

§ Hanwell, 25 May 1967; the metaphor of temperature was used also in a Waterloo Day address at Weybridge, 18 June 1968.

¶ High Wycombe, 21 June 1968.

** 'So easy and so dangerous to liberty is it to allow the clever people who despise you to pull the wool over your eyes.' Exeter, 23 October 1968.

tied up with anybody.' UK trade with western Europe had grown despite an EEC tariff wall.[†] 'Membership of a protectionist group is not ideal for Britain', but, in 1961, it had seemed desirable to try for 'freedom of trade with as many countries as possible'. That attempt had failed. Now, Powell observed, de Gaulle's recent talk of an *'Europe des patries'* was 'profoundly congenial to the British outlook': 'A Europe of Nations, of sovereign nations, is the only Europe to which Britain, so long as she herself remains a nation, could belong.'

Powell called the aspiration for European 'unity' 'a chimera which the people of Britain find not so much undesirable as inconceivable'. Indeed, he felt any move to 'development of supra-national, not to say federal, institutions and authority' was 'likely to be arrested' by nation states.[‡]. He derided the view that creating a directly elected European Parliament could ever create a 'politically united nation':

> This is the same fallacy as to suppose that, as rich people frequent nightclubs, we ourselves have only to go to a nightclub in order to become rich … Unless and until the inhabitants of different parts of Europe are so penetrated with a sense of their ultimate common interest that they will accept burdens and disadvantages for the benefit of the whole or of other parts, the attempt to create an elective assembly or parliament would be foredoomed not merely to disappointment but to ridicule and mutual recrimination.[§]

Powell swiftly drove past the economic case for the Common Market, which he had now discarded, to examine the critical institutional implications for Parliament and nation. In hand-written notes on the typescript of the speech, he wrote that the 'only way of protecting ourselves against this sort of jumping to conclusions is to get the basic simplicities right'. Against the oft-used phrase 'going into Europe', he wrote: '<u>but what is Europe</u>'. He noted on defence: 'no reason why area of alliance should coincide with political, not to

---

[†] He again cited proof that trade with western Europe could grow outside the EEC as a reason to change his mind in his 'Man in the News' interview, London Weekend Television, 8 February 1970.

[‡] Clacton, 21 March 1969.

[§] Market Drayton, 6 June 1969.

say, economic union'. Looking back, on the economy, he drew attention to the 'non-fulfilment of our fears'. He underlined the 'growing
importance of Europe' in trade, but added that this was 'not artificial,
but natural'. 'Political union', he scribbled in pencil, 'not implicit in
free trade – the purposes are political and not economic, concerned
with the pursuit of power.' 'What should policy be?' 'We have to
face issue of the application and not be saddled with the answer
to a question ten years out of date. Self-confidence based on national
self-knowledge – myth of Empire and Commonwealth – pity if
succeeded by the myth of European union. Nothing to lead us to
suppose that loss or disaster would attend on non-participation in
the present form of the Common Market of the Six'.

I do not claim that this vivid insight into Powell's 'basic
simplicities' in 1969, scraps of marble from which carefully polished
criticism would be sculpted, marks any turning moment in his thinking. However, it does show that his Tory instincts and search for a
language of self-confident, but realistic, nationalism were snagging
on and jarring against the emerging political purposes of the EEC.

At Smethwick on 5 September Powell's attack attracted wider
attention. He said he detected a change in national mood. 'It is
to demand that a clear, definite and cast-iron case be made out
before Britain is again committed to accede to the Treaty of Rome.
People are … no longer prepared to be led blind, as they might have
been seven or eight years ago, on a general hunch.' He repeated that
the UK's trade with Western Europe had grown and questioned if
there was evidence that a larger, protected market had improved the
performance of the Six:

> Of course, the economic production of certain goods implies a large
> market for them; but it does not follow either that those products
> offer the most advantageous use for a particular nation's resources,
> or that the large market in question must be a domestic market. The
> argument, so far as it is one, dissolves again into the case for free, or
> freer, trade all round.

Powell warned that the EEC was not in any case a free trade area.
It was a managed market, with an aspiration to widen competences
and with an interventionist and uneconomic agricultural policy.

'This is the result not of free trade but of politics in the Community, and one which brings us naturally to the political side.'

> I want to concentrate upon one facet only of the political case for accession to the Rome Treaty. This is the argument that only a big country can have 'a voice' or 'an influence in the world', and that as some countries, such as Russia and America, are very big, we ought therefore to club together to form another one of comparable size. You may think I have put the point crudely and thus unfairly; but the whole argument is crude, astonishingly crude, as well as transparently unsound.

Ruling out the idea that by 'influence in the world' was meant military force, for the EEC did not design conquest or the acquisition of nuclear weapons, and defence was best accomplished 'in alliance with others who are threatened at that time by the same danger', Powell tackled the concept of 'influence in the world':

> Once a military meaning is eliminated, however, it is impossible to find any sense in which 'influence' depends on size. 'Influence' must mean persuading others to do what one thinks they ought. I question anyhow whether this is a proper ambition for one nation in relation to others; but if it is, then there are only two methods available, physical force (which we have agreed to rule out), and force of reason for example. But as good and laudable an example can be set by a small nation as by a large one, and history to this present day is full of the instances which prove it.[†]

For all Powell's conviction that the case was astonishingly crude, he was right to single out this recurrent desire to be 'influential', 'at the top table' or, in more modern parlance, to be 'at the heart of Europe' or to 'punch above our weight', as one of the most seductive arguments of the pro-EU lobby. It still is today. The converse is the parrot's cry that the UK would 'be isolated', 'left on the side-lines', unless it tagged along with the rest of the class. Heath's Central Office kept saying just that:

---

† Smethwick, 5 September 1969.

Whatever the present shortcomings of the Community our withdrawal from it would face us with an unattractive choice between
almost total dependence on the United States and a dangerous drift
into weak neutralism ... It would reduce this country to the status of
a relatively insignificant offshore island and would leave any British
government markedly less able to defend our national interests
than is the case now that Britain is a full and effective member of
the Community.[†]

It is unfortunate that Powell's arguments, consistently pressed,
against the 'offshore island' delusion of the need to 'act', even as a
bit part, on a larger stage in order to have 'influence' failed to find
purchase. The cost of this failure has been seen not only in Brussels,
Strasbourg and Lisbon, but in Basra and Kabul.[‡] Doing something
to please others is not necessarily congruent with personal, or
national, interest.

Powell now turned to 'another area of dangerous vagueness', the
phrase 'European unity', which 'is being abused if it conveys any
less connotation than in "United Kingdom" or "United States",
namely, that of a single, independent, sovereign state':

Whatever is meant by 'unity' in the context of Britain and the
European Economic Community must imply that, within that meaning, the views and wishes of the majority are accepted by the minority
or the minorities. The precondition for any political unity is the subordination of the parts to the whole. Short of force, this can only come
about through a settled, deep and instinctive conviction felt by those
concerned that they belong first and foremost to the whole and that its
interests override those of the parts. Unless and until this conviction

---

† Conservative Central Office, *The Campaign Guide 1974: Supplement*, p. 107.
‡ The 'influence' argument convinced Mr Blair: 'He passionately believed if we
  went in, we would change the European Union quickly and for the better.
  There was a lot we could do out, but a lot more we could do in ... If we wait
  four or five years we will not be able to extract as good a deal and we will have
  less influence. So ... the national interest may be best served by joining early.'
  Alastair Campbell, *The Blair Years* (London: Hutchinson, 2007), pp. 552–3.
  Doubtless the same argument is urged by those wanting more EU integration
  today. Mr Cameron will have to display great toughness to resist it.

exists, democratic or representative institutions are unworkable. On the other hand, without such institutions, the acts of sovereignty, which a political unit must perform, on behalf of all its members and binding upon all its members, would be intolerable and unacceptable ...

If therefore we are to contemplate accession to the Treaty of Rome on political grounds, we must put this solemn question to ourselves. Do we see, or do we foresee, a single electorate, comprising the Six, the United Kingdom and any other countries which might accede? It must be a single electorate in the sense that decisions taken by the majority would be accepted by the minority, that divisions would be on the basis of party, and not nationality, that the local electorate of any one nation or country would take for granted that a majority consisting of other nationalities would overrule its wishes and its interests. If the answer to that question is 'No', and if we cannot envisage democratic institutions, then we dare not advocate on political grounds the accession of Britain to the European Economic Community.

Powell, with striking prescience, had seen, as does Mrs Merkel, the inexorable logic whereby economic unity and a common currency meant European political unification. Yet, at this stage, his conviction of the centrality of the Queen in Parliament to the very being of Britain seems to have led him to conclude that the British people were unlikely ever to agree to control by a European government in a European parliament, and this would be fatal to UK participation in the EEC. It was the gravamen of his political argument, since, for him, authority with consent could only be exercised through a parliament. If there could be no such parliament, there could be no such political unit. He could not then foresee that the House of Commons and House of Lords would consent to transfer their functions elsewhere. Nor could he envisage that this simulacrum of a sovereign parliament would be quietly accepted by the British people because they neither knew nor cared very much about it, thinking, rightly in many respects, that its members were slow to pass the gravy, and that the views of MEPs didn't amount to a hill of beans with the people making the decisions in Britain or Berlaymont.

The real challenge to national self-determination that concerned Powell was to stem not so much from a common parliament, sustaining as he posited (while thinking it, in fact, inconceivable) a common 'European' government, but from other collective instruments of the *Einigungswerk* – the Commission, the Council of Ministers (increasingly hobbled as defenders of the national interest by qualified majority voting) and the courts. In tilting at the European Parliament and a putative government of the future drawn from it, which he was probably correct to say the British people would not accept, Powell at first stuck a tail on the wrong donkey. As he himself noted: 'Across the Channel in western Europe, there is being erected in the European Common Market an international bureaucracy which aspires to manage and to organise the entire economy of half a continent.'[†] It proved to be a bureaucratic ('technocratic', if one must please the imposed Prime Minister of Italy), not a democratic, project all along.

In his speeches in early 1970 Powell pressed more determinedly his warning that the British people must not be lulled, or gulled, by the feeling that 'unification' was something remote and theoretical. As a textual critic, he examined the texts and the reading of the text was clear. Not for him the insouciance of Mr Clarke, who boasted of never having read the Maastricht Treaty he advocated. The creation of common institutions was the crux of the matter, as Powell argued, after predictions by the Commission President that the EEC would have a common currency and a common parliament in ten years. Unification remains the crux of the matter in 2012.

A common currency means a common government; and if anybody should say that 'this is Enoch being too logical again', let me quote to you what the Netherlands Foreign Minister said to his parliament two or three weeks ago: 'Europe (he meant the Common Market) cannot realise a monetary unity before having succeeded in realising political unity.' That's Dutch for 'common currency means common government'. It is a great pity we have got into the habit of using this term 'Common Market' instead of the clumsier but correct description 'European Economic Community'; for 'economic community' is something which not merely implies common economic policy, but is synonymous with it ...

---

† Dorking, 21 February 1970.

A common economic policy in its turn does not exist in the void: it is the policy of a common government – not just a provisional or skeleton government, but a government which exercises continuing authority throughout the greater part of the whole spectrum of government – from taxation to economic controls, from public expenditure to employment …

It is well that we should be confronted with all this. As Mr Heath said a few months ago: 'The greatest possible mistake would be for the British people to go into this without themselves realising the full implications of what the European policy meant.' Well, here are, perhaps not the full implications, but at any rate *some* of the implications; and they are profound, and they are political … The economic presupposes the political and is meaningless without it. Too long there has been loose and empty talk about 'unity', the benefits of 'European unity', and about 'unifying' Europe; and when anybody ventured to point out that unity means just what it says, that was treated with levity as a frightfully funny remark. And now here, as a New Year's gift from the Commission itself, comes the meaning of unity writ large …

We do have to decide whether unity is imaginable or is desired by *us*; and we cannot shrug off the question as one which will gradually get itself worked out as we go along … To knock on the door again or to enter the portals without that question clearly answered, and answered *ex animo* by the British people … is to court humiliation and perhaps disaster.[†]

Powell's deployment of this case for the first time in the Commons was not his most successful, as he concluded with the claim that Britain would have been defeated in 1940 had it been part of a larger political unit: 'I ask: does anyone suppose that the force which saved this country and saved liberty would not have been thrown into the lost battle by that unit and swallowed up in defeat?'[‡] This irritated some MPs who, like Powell, had seen active service.[§] They, as millions of ordinary people who also served, hoped this

---

[†] Kingston-on-Thames, 12 January 1970.
[‡] Hansard, HC Deb, 25 February 1970, vol. 796, col. 1270.
[§] Shepherd, *Enoch Powell*, pp. 389–90.

coming together might avoid a return to the disastrous European conflicts of 1914–1918 and 1939–1945. (It was a sentiment strongly held by many of the then Tory leaders, including Mr Heath, Lord Carrington and Mr Whitelaw, who had fought in the Second World War; it is the same sentiment appealed to by Mrs Merkel in evoking centuries of *Blutvergiessen* (spilt blood)). Whereas now, war on the European landmass seems to most, rightly or not, incredible, forty years ago its experience had been cruel reality.

Powell did confront this argument, for he realised that it could be a Trojan horse to the surrender of sovereignty. 'Many people', he acknowledged,

find that for them the heart of the whole matter lies in the hope of peace, and I know those whose whole instinct and reasoning say no to British entry but who in the end conclude: 'But if it means peace in my children's and my children's children's time, I will acquiesce in it.' This is not an ignoble sentiment, and those who hold it have the right to be seriously heard...

If that could be demonstrated, or even shown to be probable, then many might reasonably think it again worth purchasing, even if a high price had to be paid for it. Alas, the proposition is not only not demonstrable or probable: it can without much difficulty be shown to be improbable and even absurd.

May I take as typical of the proposition the form in which it was recently put by an English bishop to his diocese. 'If we are to avoid a third conflict', he wrote, 'we must turn Europe into a family. In the past Europe has been a group of independent warring states at the cost of thousands of lives. Had there been a genuine fraternity of nations, these terrible tragedies might have been avoided. Thank God, Germany and France, together with four other countries, are now within a single community. They may not have achieved complete reconciliation, but at least the chances of war are infinitely less. If Britain joins they will be even better.'

Obviously, there is a certain element of special pleading here. If nations are 'genuinely fraternal' or 'completely reconciled', they don't go to war ... The question is whether the chance of hostility and thus of war is diminished by political unification, either in general or in the case of western Europe ...

The first fact that confronts us is that civil war – war within a political unit – is not only not unknown, but frequently as terrible as international war. The first great war of modern times happens to have been a civil war; America suffered more casualties in it than in the First and Second World Wars put together. In the history of mankind's sanguinary conflicts as many wars have been fought to break existing political units up as to settle scores between independent nations or to produce political units by force.

The second fact is that large or composite political units have not proved more pacific or immune from wars than small ones. On the contrary, it would be much easier to argue that the larger and more powerful a political unit is, the more likely it is to be involved in major warfare. The only general conclusion we can draw is that the existence of a large political unit affords no special protection or guarantee against war, internal or external, but rather the contrary. So if there is any virtue such as is claimed in the political unification of western Europe, that virtue must lie in circumstances special to western Europe. It is not a consequence of large size or political unification as such …

Well then, let us take a look at Europe as it is today. Fear of war there is and has been, but we rub our eyes with astonishment! With whom was war feared? With whom is war feared to this moment? Not with Germany; not between Germany and France, though they 'have not achieved complete reconciliation'. No; with a power outside western Europe altogether. With Russia. So what has political unification to do with that, the most eminent fear and danger of war?

We shall not, I presume, be told that the EEC is the transitional stage towards a political unit which would include Russia. I confess to insurmountable personal difficulty in imagining a political unit – 'family', the bishop called it – from the North Cape to Sicily, from the Shannon to the Elbe; but only a lunatic could imagine a political unit from the Shannon to Vladivostok. No; the answer we receive is that a politically united western Europe will be more capable of waging war successfully with Russia and her allies and therefore arguably is less likely to be involved in it.

By now we are a long way from banishing war by 'turning Europe into a family'. We are back in the old familiar world of force; but even in that world the answer carries little conviction, because for twenty-five years we have been protesting that the only defence against Russian attack is the American nuclear armoury. So our European 'family of nations' would have to be furnished with its nuclear arsenal on an American scale; and I wonder whether anyone thinks that would enable them or their children or their children's children to sleep more soundly in their beds. No doubt a western Europe politically united, with a single policy and a single will, could be a great military power. What is improbable, to put it mildly, is that the creation and existence of such a military power would maximize the hopes of peace.[†]

Powell was no doubt right that the attempt to sustain or to break up a political unit could cause war, as Yugoslavia reminded us in the 1990s and Libya more lately. The violent resistance in Greece to EU-imposed austerity to protect its politico-economic project has, so far, stopped at social strife. That cannot be guaranteed. But Powell's argument of reason failed and, perhaps, with millions of well-remembered dead, it was then bound to do so. It is beyond doubt that the sentiment that it might 'put an end to war' was, along with a sentiment that it would 'help' industry and jobs, one pre-eminent reason why so many in the UK accepted the EEC in 1975. Whether the same sentiments put today – as the living memory of world war slips into extreme old age and the 'obligation' of a common currency wreaks daily havoc with jobs and industry in southern Europe – would again carry a referendum is improbable.

Powell's election address in 1970 was stonily hostile to the EEC:

The community is designed to be a political unit, with common internal and external policies: the same tax system, the same laws, the same economic policies, the same currency, the same treaties. All this means a single government, and therefore a common parliament based on one electorate. For my part I do not believe the British people should consent to be a minority in a European electorate. I do not want to see this country give its political independence away.

---

† West Ham, 13 September 1971.

The Conservatives' 1970 election manifesto, *A Better Tomorrow*, was considerably less direct. It said they believed membership of the EEC was in the long-term interest of the British people but they would negotiate, 'no more, no less'.[†] But, after preparatory talks, Mr Heath met President Pompidou in Paris where the two leaders made a joint declaration of agreement on 21 May 1971. On 7 July Heath published a White Paper setting out the basis for UK accession to the EEC.[‡] Since his government was formed with a majority of just thirty, and lost a by-election to Labour in May, Labour's view was crucial.[§] Mr Gaitskell had once said that to turn our backs on the Commonwealth was something 'for which history would not forgive us', warning of the EEC's constitutional implications. He had said he could foresee the end to 'a thousand years of history': 'If we go into this we are no more than a state … in the United States of Europe, such as Texas or California.' For Mr Wilson, by contrast, the EEC was not an issue of principle; instead, like much else, it was an instrument of his unending manoeuvres to hold together a party that already held within it the seeds and

---

[†] 'If we can negotiate the right terms, we believe that it would be in the long-term interest of the British people for Britain to join the European Economic Community, and that it would make a major contribution to both the prosperity and the security of our country. The opportunities are immense. Economic growth and a higher standard of living would result from having a larger market.

'But we must also recognise the obstacles. There would be short-term disadvantages in Britain going into the European Economic Community which must be weighed against the long-term benefits. Obviously there is a price we would not be prepared to pay. Only when we negotiate will it be possible to determine whether the balance is a fair one, and in the interests of Britain. Our sole commitment is to negotiate; no more, no less. As the negotiations proceed we will report regularly through Parliament to the country.

'A Conservative Government would not be prepared to recommend to Parliament, nor would Members of Parliament approve, a settlement which was unequal or unfair. In making this judgment, Ministers and Members will listen to the views of their constituents and have in mind, as is natural and legitimate, primarily the effect of entry upon the standard of living of the individual citizens whom they represent.'

[‡] *The United Kingdom and the European Community*, Cmnd. 4715.

[§] Conservative & Unionist 330 (+77), Labour 287 (–76), Liberal 6 (–6), SNP 1 (+1), Others 6 (+4).

personalities of the great split of 1981. So, although he had applied
for entry himself in 1966–7, as his party swung against entry, Wilson
too moved. He told a special party conference in July 1971 that the
'terms' were poor. Heath countered by offering his MPs a free vote
on the principle of entry on 28 October 1971. Labour declined to
do the same, but sixty-nine Labour MPs nonetheless voted with
the government, which won a majority of 112. Heath signed the
Accession Treaty on 22 January 1972.

Enoch Powell fought to prevent all of this happening. In January
1971 he warned that the negotiators were behaving as if the principle were already agreed. Heath had indeed accepted that the UK
must agree the established treaty and *Acquis* (including the recently
negotiated Common Agricultural Policy), if it were to join the
unity process:

> The great issues, the obstacles, the doubts, the anxieties – they would
> seem to be about no more than the difference of a year or two in
> the transition period, or the difference between one percentage and
> another of the Community's budget to be contributed by Britain.
> The prior questions: transition to what? budget for what? and other
> questions greater still are treated as if they had already been answered
> … In fact the prior questions, the great questions have not even been
> properly asked, let alone debated, let alone answered. It is as if there
> were a conspiracy to be silent about them, in the hope that no one
> would notice that they exist.

Powell noted the inescapability of a programme of regulation, later
infamous as 'harmonisation', being advanced supposedly to deliver
a 'common market'. The 'price', just as he foresaw, was to be the
enhanced interventionism that followed the Single European
Act in 1986, or the persistence with which the EU Commission
exploited QMV procedure, on the pretext of 'health and safety', to
get round Mr Major's opt-out from the Social Chapter in 1991:

> We have already in microcosm broached the central question of
> sovereignty; but let us, for the moment, follow the argument from
> balance of advantage which the negotiators advance. In return,
> say they, for the admitted disadvantage of joining a self-sufficient

agricultural community, there is the advantage of joining a large market in non-agricultural goods and services, and the one more than outweighs the other. That non-agricultural market is not, however, a free trade area; it is an economic community, in which the same rules must apply to all parts, and in which, therefore, as now within the United Kingdom, laws, systems of taxation and economic policies, so far as they affect the movement of goods, services, capital and labour – and that is very far indeed – must be uniform. So the price of whatever are the advantages of membership of that non-agricultural market is the acceptance of common economic regulation in a community of which the United Kingdom would be permanently a minority.

Developing the point of the disadvantage of regulation, Powell warned of:

> ... the effect of the common policies of the Community itself in the future, in so far as they might tend to regulation and restriction and to the distortion of market forces; and it is impossible to overlook the fact that the traditions and outlook of government in most of the Community are interventionist, even measured by British standards.[†]

In the same speech Powell argued that entry into the Community would, inevitably, impair Britain's sovereignty. This issue was persistently dismissed by the pro-EEC camp, as either far off and theoretical, or else countered by the circular argument that by 'pooling its sovereignty' the UK would gain more 'influence':

> The assertion that, with Britain part of the European Economic Community, we – you and I – would belong, or be well on the way to belonging, to just such a large and powerful political entity, is often in the mouth of those who would have Britain join the Common Market, and in no one's mouth more often or more emphatically than that of Mr Heath himself.
>
> The condition of an entity being large and politically powerful is precisely – to *be* an entity, to have a single will, a single policy and

---

† Banbridge, 16 January 1971.

a single voice which speaks unequivocally for it, as HMG speaks for the United Kingdom or the President speaks for the United States. In all relevant matters there must be sovereignty, such as Her Majesty's Government exercises in a unitary state or the United States government in a federal state. It is in these terms and no lesser – unless we aim to deceive ourselves or others – that we must envisage a European community whose people would be 'citizens of no mean city'. Moreover, we must envisage it not as a distant and optional ideal but as the precondition of anything solid which the European Economic Community has to offer.

The question, then, of membership resolves itself, not ultimately but immediately and on the very threshold, into the most basic of all possible questions which can be addressed to the people of any nation: can they, and will they, so merge themselves with others that, in face of the external world, there is no longer 'we' and 'they', but only 'we'; that the interests of the whole are instinctively seen as overriding those of any part; that a single political will and authority, which must necessarily be that supported by the majority, is unconditionally accepted as binding upon all? That is the question. That is what the real debate is about.

Early 1971 he took his case to the EEC itself, with speeches in Lyons (in French),[†] Frankfurt (in German),[‡] Turin (in Italian)[§] and The Hague.[¶] Few politicians have been capable of such versatility, but Powell was no 'little Englander'. 'There is', he said, 'no more ignorant vulgarity than to treat language as an impediment to intercourse, which education, habit, travel, trade abolish and remove'. He addressed the issue of sovereignty with deep respect for the nationhood of others and in the knowledge that the historic experience of other nations had been diverse. The constitutional development of most European nations has been interrupted, violently, by revolution, conquest or civil war, in modern times; in England, since 1689, an immemorial parliament enabled the peaceful evolution and

---

† 12 February 1971. Text reproduced in full in this volume.
‡ 29 March 1971.
§ 4 May 1971.
¶ 17 May 1971.

transformation of the nation and has been the basis of its being. European constitutions and legal codes were rationalist products; they had less to give up in a rationalist construct like the EEC.

Powell saw, rightly, that the forefathers of the EEC, and their inheritors, like Mrs Merkel today, intended what they said and intended the process to be irreversible:

There is no need to tie ourselves into juristic knots over the meaning of the 'unlimited duration' for which the Treaty of Rome is concluded. The Community itself, and the proposition that we should join it, make no sense except on the basis that it is meant to be for good and all. The decision must be understood as irrevocable in intention. The Heath–Pompidou declaration, asserting the right of veto on common decisions where the vital national interest is involved, does not permit us the luxury of indulging in double-think about political unity. No doubt, each additional area of policy would only pass within the realm of common decision as and when all members were ready to accept that; but once there, it would be there to stay. The practical necessity of compliance as the alternative to sabotaging the principle of the Community itself has already – even at an early stage – proved to be a powerful lever. It would become progressively stronger with the process of time ...

There is no need to deny or dispute, as if it were something shameful or dishonest that had to be kept out of sight, the fact that entry signifies deliberate decision to surrender sovereignty to another and much larger political entity. There is nothing abstract or theoretical about the sovereignty which would be surrendered; it is a plain matter which any elector can readily see and understand. Parliament, and in particular the House of Commons, would no longer be the body which took more and more of the decisions which govern the economic and social life of the people of this country and which determine its safety and even its existence. If membership of the Community does not mean this, it means nothing.

This deliberate surrender of sovereignty would be something new not merely in degree but in kind ... It is merely quibbling to confuse it with the fact that circumstances always have, and always will, circumscribe the freedom of decision of every sovereign state, large or small. The answer to the simple question 'By whom are the people

of Britain taxed?' would cease to be, what it indubitably is today, 'By
Parliament' ...

Surely the advocates of British membership have no need to
dispute this? The dispute is not whether it would be so, but whether
we wish it so. They need not stoop either to the pretence that a
nation has not ceased to be sovereign when its sovereignty is shared
or pooled in a larger political unit. Britain of course ... would have
a voice in the decisions of the Community – call it, if you will, in a
common phrase, which seems to give some people great satisfaction
and comfort, a 'full voice'. The Greater London constituencies have a
'voice' in the decisions of Parliament, a 'full voice' no doubt, approximately the same proportionately as the United Kingdom would have
in the council of the enlarged Community; but nobody imagines
this means that Greater London possesses sovereignty ...

The decision, then, is one no less solemn than this: whether the
sovereign government and parliament of this country should engage
themselves, deliberately and progressively, to give that sovereignty
up; and the true debate turns on what we are to receive in return that
would be sufficient for that sacrifice ...

I will make a confession. I can myself imagine no gain so great,
nor danger so threatening, that it should persuade us to part with
what we have held for so long and defended so dearly.[†]

For the Tory Powell, with his what now seems – considering what it
has become, with its IPSA and its regulators and its don't-have-any-
job-outside-politics and its passing of power to others – poignant,
if not pathetic, reverence for the House of Commons, the essence
of sovereignty lay in the Queen in Parliament. Shortly before battle
on the Bill was joined, unsheathing his sabre in the face of the
tanks arrayed ahead, he forecast the future stripping-away of
the authority of the Commons:

No such legislation has ever been laid before the House of Commons
as that which is proposed to it for the ratification of the Treaty of
Brussels ... There are at least two respects in which that legislation
is without precedent. First, the House of Commons will be told

---

† Beckenham, 17 September 1971.

that, of all the multitude of changes in our laws which the legislation makes or which it enables to be made, not a jot or tittle can be altered or deleted or amended: the House of Commons in effect will be told that it may debate if it pleases, but decide it cannot – short of the great decision itself – one way or the other. That is language which has not been used to the House of Commons these many hundred years.

Let us suppose that the House of Commons might wish to do what it is free to do with any other Bills submitted to it and often does – to alter what stands in the Bill. There is one argument, and one argument only, which the Government not only can but must use. Of the merits and the reasons they need say nothing; indeed they waste time if they do so. Their sole but sufficient reply is: 'This is necessary in order to ratify and fulfil the treaty which we have signed; otherwise we would not have bothered to put it in the Bill.'

Imagine, however, that, greatly presuming, the House of Commons were to say to the government: 'Yes; but suppose we do reject or amend this provision, what then? Will you go back to Brussels and start negotiating again? Or will you give the whole thing up?' ... The government's reply would be as follows. They might not give it at the first or second time of asking; but in the end it would be given. 'No, of course we should not, and we could not, reopen negotiations. Nevertheless we shall still go ahead and ratify. Naturally, we have discussed all this with our friends in the Commission at Brussels, and we have decided what to do. When the treaty is in force, the Commission will trot along to the Court of Justice, and lay a complaint that in that or any other matter over which you might be tempted to be recalcitrant the UK is not fulfilling its obligations; then of course they will get an order from the Court and you will be obliged to put back anything which you have altered or left out.'

When this lesson has been taught, not once but over and over again, the House of Commons, and through the House of Commons the British people, will have begun to understand what it means to be a subordinate legislature. The House of Commons will have been told for the first time in its history: 'You must do this; you cannot do that.' The public will begin, too, to understand their own part of the bargain. Whatever law is made by or under this legislation, it will be no use constituents writing to their MPs or lobbying them and saying 'Change this law, we do not like it' or 'Make us another law instead of this one.' Wearily the MPs will reply: 'We are sorry, dear friends; the House of Commons did not make this law because it wanted to, but because it had to; and we are not allowed to change it now if we wished.' ...

Thus will the House of Commons be required publicly to divest itself of its own supreme and exclusive right to make law for the people of this kingdom, and to acknowledge the overriding competence of an external authority in spheres of law-making which, according to the declared intention, are to be progressively extended. The House may think itself lucky to escape being made to wear a sanbenito and walk barefoot with a candle in its hand...

It will not be the House of Commons which will decide how and whether to tax the people by placing duties and levies on this country's imports and exports: that power is gone from the start. Nor will it be the House of Commons which will decide in what form indirect taxation is to be imposed upon the goods and services of use and of consumption: no longer will the budget be the House of Commons' exclusive right and business. Some of the contents of Mr Gladstone's despatch box will have been put there (to quote again) 'by instruments issued by the Community's institutions', and the remainder of the contents must accommodate themselves to those.

The loss of legislative competence is not the only derogation which the House of Commons will be asked to accept. It will also be stripped of a considerable and ever-increasing part of its practical right to criticise and call to account the executive. Membership of the Community brings with it an immense exaltation of the power of the executive in the member states, and a corresponding diminution in the power of Parliament. 'But we', say the apologists of membership, 'we shall be able to influence the common decisions; we shall have a voice along with the rest in the Council of Ministers; we shall, if the worst comes to the worst, be able, wherever the rule of unanimity applies, to impose our veto.' Who is this 'we'? It is not Parliament; it is not the House of Commons; it is the executive, and it is the executive acting not as heretofore in a sphere where it is fully responsible to Parliament and through Parliament to the people – it is the executive acting outside the sphere of parliamentary challenge.

When this executive 'we' return from Brussels to Westminster and proceed to put the new decrees into effect, they demand of Parliament the necessary compliance even more imperiously than the passage of this initial legislation is demanded: Parliament is told, 'You cannot do otherwise, or you break the rules and decisions by which this country is now bound.' If Parliament should presume to complain, to criticise the executive, to ask: 'Why did you agree to this? Why did you not veto it?', Parliament is promptly and conclusively told: 'But we are few among many, and the majority went the other way; we could not use our veto because the consequences would have been even more disagreeable.'

There is moreover a parting shot, which brooks no argument. The executive says to the House of Commons: 'Censure us, if you please; defeat us, if you can; force a general election, and turn us out. It will all be to no effect. You cannot alter what is done, because it is not we who did it.' ...

It is for or against this revolution that the people of Britain are able to decide and are called upon to decide. The people of this country ... have to say whether or not they are content no longer to be governed, taxed and legislated for by their House of Commons and those who are responsible to it; in short, whether they will keep or lose their own self-government.[†]

Were one to substitute the past tense for the future, one might, in this one prophetic utterance, set out what became the constitutional condition of the United Kingdom and its Parliament in the succeeding forty years.

The Bill to introduce the treaty into law, the European Communities Bill, won a second reading by a majority of eight on 17 February. Its passage was assured on 2 May after approval of a 'guillotine' restricting time, by a majority of eleven. Powell said that debate was 'for or against the continuance of a free House of Commons', since it was considering 'renunciation of the heart of its own sovereignty'[‡] in a Bill

---

† Chester-le-Street, 29 January 1972.
‡ Hansard, 2 May 1972, vol. 836, cols 279, 282.

which, in three respects, has no parallel in centuries of the life of Parliament. It is a Bill which transfers out of this country the right to legislate directly for this country. It is a Bill which transfers out of this country the right to tax the citizens of this country directly. It is a Bill which establishes a superior jurisdiction to the courts of this country over the citizens of this country.[†]

It received royal assent on 17 October. Just two days later, at an EEC summit in Paris, Heath agreed to the intention to 'transform the whole complex of their relations' into a 'European Union' by the end of the 1970s.[‡] He also agreed to 'irreversible' economic and monetary union 'not later than 31 December 1980'.[§]

Wilson's tactics on the 1972 Bill had included a pledge that a Labour government would 'renegotiate' the terms. To this he added, in April 1972, a commitment to a referendum on its outcome. In fact, this signified that, whatever its party conference said, Labour in government would not oppose membership outright in principle. But it did offer the prospect of opening the door that Heath had closed. Although Powell had previously opposed the device of a referendum, so important was the EEC question to him that he inevitably sought to secure a chance for the British people to decide.

On Saturday 23 February 1974, less than a week before a general election, he gave perhaps the second most sensational speech of his life, to a Get Britain Out rally, in the bleakly modernist Bull Ring in Birmingham. It was on 'the long, epic deception' of Europe. He reminded his audience that, having broken his 1970 manifesto promise 'to negotiate; no more, no less', Heath had left out his 1974 manifesto the objective of 'economic and monetary union by 1980' that he agreed in Paris in October 1972. Heath had also failed to honour his undertaking in 1970 that British membership of the EEC would require the 'full-hearted consent of the Parliament and

---

† Hansard, 2 May 1972, vol. 836, col. 277.

‡ Challenged to explain what he meant by 'union', Heath said: 'Our concept of a European Union is the same that this country has always had, which is that in developing institutions one develops them to meet the needs of the organisation concerned.' Hansard, 23 October 1972, vol. 843, col. 796.

§ *Bulletin of the European Communities*, October 1972, no. 10.

people'.[†] Now Wilson had promised a referendum on the EEC. Powell declared starkly:

> The question 'Who governs Britain?', which at the moment is being posed frivolously, if not absurdly, might be taken, in real earnest, as the title of what I have to say. This is the first and last election at which the British people can be sure of the opportunity to decide whether their country is to remain a democratic nation, governed by the will of its own electorate expressed in its own parliament, or whether it will become one province in a new European superstate under institutions which know nothing of the political rights and liberties that we have so long taken for granted.

In planning a transfer of power from Britain's democratic institutions, Heath was

> the first Prime Minister in 300 years who entertained, let alone executed, the intention of depriving Parliament of its sole right to make the laws and impose the taxes of this country … He does not want the British people to decide at the ballot box the most momentous transformation in their history.

But the people could not be so prevented, Powell declared. For there was a 'clear, definite and practicable alternative, namely a fundamental renegotiation directed to regain free access to world food markets and recover or retain the powers of Parliament'. That alternative was now offered to them 'by a political party capable of securing a majority in the House of Commons and sustaining a government'.

He ended with advice to 'that large element of the electorate … which finds it impossible, as I do, to accept that Britain can be embodied in a European superstate without her people's consent openly given, or that any advantage can compensate for accepting

---

† Powell did not accurately quote Heath's words: 'Nor would it be in the interest of the Community that its enlargement should take place except with the full-hearted consent of the parliaments and peoples of the new member countries.' (Paris, 5 May 1970). Those weasel words sought to avoid a UK referendum commitment. Powell distilled the logical conclusion that Britain must be included.

Community membership on terms which deprive this country of its free, self-governing institutions': 'If that for us is the overriding issue – and how it could be less I do not understand – then we have a clear national duty to help to decide it in the only way of which parliamentary representation admits.'

Monday's *Times* editorial condemned Powell's speech as a distraction, calling it 'preposterous' and a 'bogy', having 'no connexion with reality'. 'Mr Powell assumes that economic and monetary union by 1980 means ... a federal economic system. In probability ... when it is achieved [it] will be a more modest affair.'[†]

Later that day, in Shipley, Powell was undeterred by that widely held Establishment view. He advised a vote for Labour even more explicitly. In a ringing conclusion, he cried: 'I was born a Tory, I am a Tory and I shall die a Tory'; but his speech lashed back at the argument of where the true danger and realities lay:

> Once authority has been ceded to an executive untrammelled by parliaments and to a power-hungry bureaucracy, it will not, at the drop of a hat, return effortlessly and instinctively to whence it came, like a carrier pigeon homing to its loft. Those who dragooned the British House of Commons ... to yield up to an external power the right to make the laws, to impose the taxes and to decide the policies of this country are not going to throw it all back again into our laps. It was a usurpation in the first place; an usurpation grows by what it feeds on. Those who imagine that the Community ... will relinquish with an unprotesting sigh its legislative powers, its taxing and spending plans, its ambitions for harmonisation, its Common Agricultural Policy ... are not living in the world of realities.

If the Conservatives won the election the 'question of Britain and the Community will be settled and irreversible, and the full surrender of Britain's separate political existence will be driven ahead without hesitation'. On the other hand, if powers were returned to Britain, then 'of socialism you can have what instalments or reversals you choose from time to time, and you, the British electorate, will remain the arbiters of it.' Powell argued firmly that Labour's

---

† 'False danger and true', Editorial, *The Times*, 25 February 1974, p. 13.

commitment to renegotiation and referendum could be trusted –
more than Heath's 'breath-taking, thoroughgoing ... acrobatics'.
The electorate had a 'real and rational choice', between what was
reversible and what was not. 'I never yet heard that it was any part
of the faith of a Tory to take the institutions and liberties, the laws
and customs, which this country has evolved over centuries, and
merge them with those of eight other nations into a new-made
artificial state.'

For Powell, it was now time for all Conservatives who rejected
the dismantling of the 'British right to govern and to tax ourselves
through Parliament' to stand side by side with those with whom, on
lesser matters, they totally dissented. 'If we fail now, the hour will
not return.'[†]

In 1974 Labour was returned, twice. After the second election,
Powell, against his expectations when he renounced his seat in
February, had returned to the House of Commons. Wilson then
let it be known that it was his wish to stay in the EEC. After some
diplomatic theatricalities the Cabinet voted 16-7 for the 'rene-
gotiated' terms in March 1975. On 5 June 1975 the British people
were invited to vote whether to 'stay in the European Community
(Common Market)'. Until that day the process of 'renegotiation'
and the prospect of a referendum had held open a possibility that
the British people might say 'No'. They said 'Yes', by a margin of
two to one, on a 64.5 per cent turnout. They have never since been
given another chance to speak.

This second crushing defeat in this struggle was one of the bleak-
est facts of Powell's political life. His party had backed a leader he
despised in a project he deplored. Any hope that Labour might save
the day proved a delusion. The British people then followed the
House of Commons in 'giving away' what he had repeatedly said
they never would. He later compared his shame to the appeasement
of the 1930s:

---

† It is true that Powell did not say 'Vote Labour'. The message was 100 per cent
  clear through any rhetorical circumlocution; at one point he erased 'that party'
  in his typescript and wrote in 'the Labour Party'. A heckler famously shouted
  'Judas' – to which Powell replied 'Judas was paid'.

The second period of shame has run to this day from 1972, when the British people witnessed their most precious possessions, national independence and parliamentary freedom, being surrendered by their own House of Commons. It was an act which one of the great parties in the state, with only minority dissent in its ranks, accomplished and defended. It was an act which the British people even though a large minority at the time and eventually a majority disapproved of it, were content, as it seemed, to treat with resigned acquiescence and to regard as no more than one political issue among others of equal importance. I would not have believed, if I had not lived to see it, that this nation could so far forget itself. It is cause for shame.[†]

This chapter concentrates, deliberately, on Powell's earlier speeches on Europe, as there his forecast of what would follow over a generation is the more striking. Yet he did not relent from pressing the argument that Britain could recover what it had lost. He witnessed and exposed, with the same eloquence, the false dawns of the Single European Act, which was accompanied by decisive institutional concessions; Mrs Thatcher's Bruges speech in 1988, the last brief rattle of Tory populism in high places on the European question; and the first news of Mr Major's euro opt-out at Maastricht in 1991.

After the Single European Act was passed, he remarked that it should have become clear to all that it, no more than the 1972 Act, was not just a question of free trade or of 'completing a market'. It was another step in the 'irreversible' process of political harmonisation and unification:

> The deliberate development of the European Economic Community into a political state is now not merely visible, but no longer sedulously concealed. Freedom of trade, intercourse and investment between nations is compatible with diversity of national laws and fiscal systems. The community on the contrary asserts with increasing rigour the doctrine that trade can only be genuinely free between those who live under the same laws, have the same systems and levels of taxation, and use the same currency.

---

† London, 4 June 1983.

The doctrine is false. It equates international trade with the relations between citizens living in a unitary state. Under this doctrine harmonisation becomes the instrument of amalgamation, of the elimination of sovereign states to form a new political unit. Its logical consequence is that within that new unit laws must be made and government carried on by a single central authority.

The doctrine of harmonisation is incompatible, and was always intended to be incompatible, with sovereign British institutions. The writing showed up on the wall already when harmonisation was extended beyond the removal of discriminatory barriers against trade into areas of purely domestic and internal concern. The levels of purity of bathing beaches or drinking water do not need to be harmonised in order that French people may spend holidays in Cleethorpes or English people in Cannes. It is no restraint of trade to be obliged to observe the standards of safety or quality which a state sees fit to insist upon for articles sold within its jurisdiction.

For a long time now the vast and growing volume of European Community legislation which harmonises for harmonisation's sake has been shrugged off with innocent ridicule as a manifestation of rampant bureaucracy rather than of a consistent will to political power. Of late that innocence has begun to be breached.[†]

Powell also developed a penetrating attack on the dimension of the courts. As seen above, he had early identified the European Court of Justice as a potential mechanism for extending the competence of the Community. To this he added the dangers to national self-determination from the 1951 European Convention of Human Rights. Though separate from the EU, it entails similar external jurisdiction:

It is hard for anyone who retains any vestige of national pride or attachment to comprehend the mentality of those who, cheerfully and without any apparent sense of shame, if dissatisfied with the law or the courts of their own country, push off to the continent to seek to have Parliament or the Crown overruled. So far, however, from such persons being shunned or despised, their conduct appears to be

---

† Blackpool, 8 October 1987.

received with at least equanimity, if not approbation … Yet a state whose citizens can plead their case against it in a foreign court has no claim to be a nation.[†]

Powell made the above comments in the early 1980s as the extent of European litigation increased. However, he considered that rights could not be detachable from the society to which a person belonged, where reciprocal rights and obligations intertwined. Enforcement of a universalist approach was by definition coercive:

Since rights and obligations are opposite sides of the same thing they are indissociable from compulsion, namely from the compulsion which a society exercises over its members to fulfil the obligations recognised in that society. No meaning can be attached to a right apart from the possibility, and indeed the intention, of enforcement. This is the reason why all international conventions to recognise human rights, however vague and fatuous they first appear, involve the cession of sovereignty; that is, they imply the transfer to an external authority of the power to secure enforcement of its decrees inside the respective states. What is more, this transfer touches the most central and jealously guarded aspect of sovereignty, namely judicial sovereignty, that by which, as the parliamentary prayer has it, 'kings reign and princes decree justice'.

It is impossible to exaggerate the revolutionary significance of the recognition of a binding judicial tribunal external to the realm …

The signatories of the European Convention, worthy predecessors of the signatories of the Treaty of Brussels, put an end to a period of more than four centuries during which no causes have been carried out of this realm …

The consequences are political as well as judicial; for they strike at the right of the people of this country to live under the laws made by their representatives in Parliament. This ceases to be possible where a document accepted as binding is bindingly interpreted by an external court. In order to arrive at its findings, the European Commission did what no court in this country can do, namely sat in judgment upon the policy and justification of an Act of Parliament … What

---

[†] Grays, 30 October 1981.

is more, and equally incompatible with our conception of parliamentary democracy, the judicial interpretation of the terms of such a document as the Convention is not susceptible to statutory control or modification. In the system to which the European Convention belongs, the judiciary are the legislators, and their powers as such are the more sweeping because of the necessarily wide and general terms in which the so-called human rights are defined ...

It ill befits us to complain when others pick up and use against us our inherent judicial sovereignty which we carelessly or selfrighteously threw away. If we do not like being judged by an external tribunal ... the remedy is in our own hands. If we really believe that the rights we enjoy under our laws compare favourably with those in other societies, then let us tell the world so. If not, let us put our own house in order and not wait for others to do it for us. In either case, let us call off our participation in the dangerous humbug of international conventions of so-called 'human rights'. I don't expect we shall – not yet. But one day, if the long sickness of self-abnegation and denigration is ever over, we shall have to do it.[†]

This is the question now resurrected by the UK's costly humiliation by an unlawful immigrant, Abu Qatada, whom successive Home Secretaries have considered too dangerous to be at liberty, and whom British courts have said may be deported. The European Court of Human Rights, in a constructionist verdict, says otherwise. Will Mr Cameron then ignore, or denounce, this sixty-year-old convention, and uphold the British courts – or continue a strategy of trying to coerce Jordan, a friendly nation, to bow to the expanding requirements of this external tribunal, to which it does not even subscribe and in relation to an offence it denies? Enoch Powell might have observed that we may yet see from this from what metal Cameron is made.

No issue, arguably, was more important to Powell than Europe. This is now a critical juncture in European affairs. Events will crowd in on Cameron, forcing difficult but inescapable choices about the future of the UK that will shape his historical reputation as a national leader. Mrs Merkel's reaction to the Greek people's

† London, 26 February 1977.

plight – namely that the *Einigungswerk* must be intensified and the euro defended by all means – is shared by other eurozone leaders, who have agreed to external coercion of budgetary policies and a redoubled programme of convergence. It vindicates Powell's forecasts of the ultimate override of national policies. Even Mr Osborne has, somewhat perplexingly, implied that the emergence of a major political unit, with a common currency and economic government, covering much of the European continent, is now 'massively in Britain's national interest'.

Cameron, however, has used a veto and opted out, thus far, from the projected programme and new treaty revision. This is far from recovering ground given up. His reward was scorn and derision from the EU lobby and deep scepticism from the opponents of integration, who have seen such spasms from UK governments before, with no long-term reversal of the remorseless logic of the unification process. It is the same place – the 'squeezed middle', it might be called – that has entrapped all British Prime Ministers since Mr Heath, whether enthusiasts or sceptics, as the *Einigungswerk* grinds, glacier on boulder, on the continuing instinct of the British people that they want to be Europeans, but not governed by Europe. Powell's hand-written question of 1968 – 'But what is Europe?' – lies unanswered.

In terms of legislation, regulation, the drive to unification and loss of parliamentary sovereignty, Powell's predictions seem spectacularly prescient, even if not all would share his apocalyptic language and baleful view of the consequences. Yet public opinion has not reacted as he expected. It has not been a major election issue, even if this was only frustrated in 2005 by a dishonest commitment by all pro-EU parties to a referendum on the new EU constitution. How is this, if Powell's main analysis of the continuing course of EU development is correct? Have the British public been sleeping, as he said forty years ago? Or is there is a growing (if sullen) acceptance that being in the EU may be an inescapable reality of an 'interdependent' world?

Certainly, membership of the EU has changed our constitution greatly – the role of Parliament and the courts is no longer sovereign. Many of our laws arise elsewhere. Had this been known in 1975, as Powell had for years foreseen, then the result might have been different; but democratic decisions are made of truths perceived.

European Union

**The Association des Chefs d'Entreprises
Libres, Lyons, 12 February 1971**

It is a principle of British politics, and no doubt of the politics of
other countries – it is certainly a principle to which I subscribe
wholeheartedly – that one does not, when abroad, criticise the policies
of one's own Government nor attack one's political opponents – or
even one's political friends! There are ample opportunities for doing
so at home, and it is at home that one should seek to alter, if necessary,
the external as well as internal policies of one's country. However,
there are exceptions which prove rules; and I believe that the subject
on which I have undertaken to address you is such an exception.

The decision whether or not Britain is to become a member of
the Economic European Community must in a special sense be a
collective decision of Britain and the countries of the Community
together. The area of this debate forms a single arena bounded
only by the frontiers of what would be the enlarged Community if
Britain acceded. Moreover, it is debate in which the people themselves must participate. It cannot be left to be conducted in that
upper air which is inhabited by minsters and governments. This
is because the meaning of this decision is different from all other
external acts of government: a connection is to be formed which is
not intended again to be dissolved but which is to result in all the
peoples of the Community coming to form in effect one electorate.
The debate must therefore anticipate that result in imagination, in
order to determine whether it is a possible result, and, if possible, a
desirable one.

The French public and electorate have the right to attend, as it
were, the British debate, to participate in it, and to hear not merely
what Her Majesty's Government are saying but what the British
people are saying. This is one of those final decisions, to be or not
to be, which are normally entrusted not to governments but, by way

of plebiscite, to whole peoples. The fact that a referendum forms no part of customary British institutions does not alter the nature of this decision. It seems to me therefore wholly right and necessary, not to say urgent, that the British case against, as well as for, accession to the Community should be placed before the peoples of the Community, who are to decide, together with us, what the limits and membership of their community are to be.

Not everyone may agree with me in this; but at least those in Britain who advocate British accession can have no complaint. After all, it is they who wish to see in future the most crucial economic and political questions debated and decided for Britain on the continent of Europe. They actually look forward to an administration and a parliament on the Continent taking counsel for the entire Community. They, of all people, cannot object to the debate on Britain's accession to the Community being conducted on the Continent as well as on the British Isles.

What I have to tell you, because it is fair and necessary that you should know it, is the fact that the greater part of the people of Britain are profoundly opposed to British accession to the Community. I must also tell you what I believe are the principle reasons for the repugnance, which I myself share. But before I do so, I ask to leave to present my credentials.

You, above all people, appreciate the importance of verbal precision, and the dangerous power of words misapplied. Unhappily such misapplication is common in Britain on the topic of the Community. The word 'European' has been appropriated to membership of the Community. Consequently those who advocate British membership have arrogated to themselves the style of 'Europeans' and describe their opponents as being 'against Europe'. As I shall argue, if these labels have to be used at all, they ought to be transposed, and the label 'anti-European' affixed rather to those who wish Britain to accede to the Community than to those who oppose this. It is as a European among Europeans that I claim to speak to you.

Both in the years when I was my party's official spokesman on defence, and also before and since, I have always argued that Britain's commitment to the alliance with her continental neighbours is second only in importance to her commitment to the air and maritime defence of her own islands. In fact, my stress upon the continental commitment of Britain's main forces has got me into frequent troubles with the 'East of Suez' brigade. In particular I am passionately Francophile and have for many years believed and publicly stated that a breach in understanding between France and Britain could have as serious consequences in the future as it has actually twice produced during the present century. The profound differences of social, cultural and political idiom between our nations conceal the identity of our devotion to individual liberty: I would dare to say that there is no third nation in the world which shares with us the same meaning and the same instinctive valuation of personal freedom. The forms under which we respectively seek and maintain it may sometimes be almost mutually incomprehensible; the substance is the same.

The word 'comprehension', and its converse 'incomprehension', which I have just used by implication, have much to do with what is and is not 'European'. From boyhood I have been devoted to the study of Greek and Roman inheritance, which in varying measure is common to all that is Europe, and not only 'Europe' of the six or eight or ten but Europe from the Atlantic to the Urals – and beyond. I also claim that reverent enthusiasm for the history of my own country which commands an equal reverence for the past that has formed everything else which is European. The truest European, in my opinion, is the man who is most humbly conscious of the vast demands which comprehension of even a little part of this Europe imposes upon those who seek it; for the deeper we penetrate the more the marvellous differentiation of human society within this single continent evokes our wonder. The very use of the word 'Europe' in expressions like 'European unity', 'going into Europe', 'Europe's role in the world' is a solecism which grates upon the ear of all true Europeans: only Americans can be excused for using it.

Perhaps the fact that I address you this evening in French is the beginning of my explanation why the British have this preponderant sense that their national destiny cannot be merged in that of the Community. I mean that observation in the most serious manner possible. With equal delight and effort, like those who have climbed a frontier range of mountains, one surmounts the linguistic watershed and looks out, like Winckelman looking from the Alps into Italy, over another land – a different past, and a different future. There is no more ignorant vulgarity than to treat language as an impediment to intercourse, which education, habit, travel, trade abolish and remove. The function of language in the life of nations, as a means both of differentiation and of self-identification, is rooted in the very origins of humanity, and increase of knowledge tends to enhance its significance rather than diminish it. Everything that nationality means is represented and, as it were, symbolised by language, which becomes less and less like a common currency the more one penetrates its inner meaning. When one of our poets write, during the Napoleonic War, 'we must be free or die who speak the tongue that Shakespeare spoke', it was a description of the British nation as precise as it was relevant. I come, then, to you, with my imperfect French, as one equally conscious of his own nationhood and yours.

I have deliberately dived into the debate at the deep end. Eight years ago, when your president pronounced the funeral oration upon Britain's previous negotiation with the Community, the issue was seen and presented on our side of the Channel as, I do not say economic, I say merely commercial: the substitution of one system of preferences and trading arrangements for another. It was viewed in the context of a progressive expansion of trading opportunity which had been taking place: the liberalisation measures in OECD; the negotiation for a Free Trade Area with the Rome Treaty countries; the proposal of a European Free Trade Area; the 'Kennedy round'. Some pedants insisted on actually reading the Treaty of Rome and talking about political unification; but this received scant attention, on the ground that such ideas were typical continental theorising, remote from practical possibility, and in any case destined to be held in check by British pragmatism, once Britain should be 'inside'. All the greater was our astonishment when the president's veto seemed to be concerned with Skybolt and Polaris, Americans and Anglo-Saxons. What on earth had that to do with being inside or outside a customs union or with what had seemed to us the only burning issue – Commonwealth preference? As for myself, I had entered Mr Macmillan's Cabinet only six months before the veto fell; but I am prepared to confess that in those days I used to argue the case, and answer objections, on purely commercial grounds with the same sort of reasoning as no doubt Richard Cobden deployed when negotiating the Anglo-French commercial treaty of 1860. At least in this respect I shared the general mood of the public which was vastly unmoved either by the negotiation or its failure.

Of course we were wrong. Events have proved us wrong. We did not hear or believe or understand what you were saying and doing on the Continent. Only somewhere about two or three years ago, with the emerging possibility what a new negotiation might somehow succeed, did the public wake up, rub its eyes and unstop its ears. What it heard, to be perfectly fair, was very different on both sides of the Channel – but particularly in Britain – from what it had been hearing when it last went to sleep. The case for British accession is now both economic (in the full sense) and political. The economic argument is not so much the classic, Cobdenite case of as large an area as possible for the division of labour – the 'large home market' – but the claim that, if integrated into an economy which was growing at a fast rate, Britain would be dragged, or shocked, or inspired, into growing at a similar rate – anyhow faster than has been its experience recently, or (it might be added) for a hundred years and more.

This economic argument is, however, officially declared to be secondary in importance to the political argument. This claims that Britain can only have 'power' or 'influence' or 'a voice' in the world of the future by being part of what is called 'a united Europe', which will be in the same class as those unitary great powers, Russia and America. Sometimes this 'power' or 'influence' is given a specifically military content, in terms of self-defence against Russia with less, or eventually no, direct American assistance.

What is undeniable about this modern version of the case for British accession is that it is not only compatible with economic and political unification, but positively requires it: the advantages now held out can only be realized *pari passu* with the progress of unification; and some of them, particularly the military advantages, do not accrue at all until unification is completed.

The realization of all this has produced a marked reaction on the part of the British public. Before, during and since the General Election the hostility of the electorate to British entry into the Common Market (we still prefer this name for the Community, in an effort to cling to the concept of a customs union) has been

sharp, unmistakable, growing and already – even on the admission
of protagonists of British accession – preponderant. The prime
motive of the hostility is not 'economic': it is not the fear either
of more intense competition or of higher food prices and consequently higher cost of living, though both of these are voiced. The
motive is political. In a word, it is nationalist. It is repugnance or
incredulity towards the possibility of being politically integrated
with continental Western Europe. In a recent debate in the House
of Commons our Minister of Agriculture said: 'If one were to ask
the average British person whether he would rather have two shillings in his pocket with our present economic sovereignty or four
shillings without it, I have no doubt what answer he would give.'
Neither have I; but it is the opposite answer to that which the
Minister meant. The average British person would reply: 'I don't
believe I shall get four shillings by giving up my sovereignty; but I
wouldn't if I did, because I never shall and I never will.'

Given this widespread resentment, the British Government find
themselves forced to argue against their own case, by representing
steps towards economic and political unification as remote and in
any event capable of being slowed down or vetoed by Britain as a
member of the Community. When at home, Ministers find themselves talking down such documents as the Werner Report and
quoting with approval any statements from their opposite numbers
on the Continent which imply reluctance to hasten the pace of
unification. There are, however, three distinct contradictions in this
attitude. One, as I have noted, is that it involves arguing against
the very grounds on which British accession itself is commended.
Secondly, it involves asserting a British attitude which is highly
suspect at Brussels; it is necessary to stress the constitutional
impossibility of one British parliament binding its successors and
the intention of Britain to act as a brake on unification. Finally, it is
little consolation to those opposed to losing national sovereignty to
be told that it will only happen later on and that sovereignty will be
retained in detail after entry, provided it has been ceded in principle
before entry.

It must be admitted that the news which the British hear
from inside the Community is extremely puzzling to them
and that this assists our politicians in the necessary process of

anaesthetising the British people while they undergo the operation to remove their national sovereignty. One cause of confusion and, as I believe, misunderstanding is the reported, and perhaps real, contrast between the attitude of France and of the other five countries, particularly Germany. The most common rhetorical question among protagonists of British accession, both before and since the resignation of the President de Gaulle, is: what national sovereignty has France lost by being a member of the Community? It is fallacious on one obvious count, that it refers to the past, not to what is at issue, namely the future; but it is dangerous in that it conveys the suggestion, which the British are prone enough anyhow to believe, that the Continentals say one thing (in this case, political unification) and mean another (in this case, the indefinite preservation of national sovereignty and exclusive national interest). It is dangerous on a third count, too. The British are quite human, in preferring others to take the awkward decisions rather than themselves. Having been able to leave to President de Gaulle, while he was there, the brutal business of saying no to British accession, they need little persuasion that, now he is gone, they can still leave it to the French Government to veto any genuine pooling of sovereignty.

The rhetorical question about France is the marker buoy over a submerged British suspicion which is real and sharp, but rarely or never exposed to the air. It starts with puzzlement over the reasons why the members of the Community want (if they do want) Britain to join it; for the natural instinct of those who find that they are 'on to a good thing' has not historically been to share it as soon as possible with as many others as possible. Some people, it is true, find no difficulty in believing (against the evidence) that mankind has recently and drastically altered for the nobler and more altruistic. Others are sufficiently British to believe that everybody secretly admires them and wants to have more nice, honest, brave, reliable, accommodating English in the home team. Most, however, have to cast around for some other explanation, and are not even convinced that this is a simple case of 'the bigger the stronger the richer the better'. After all, British accession means no more than a 25 per cent expansion of the Community, and most Continentals look down, rather than up, at Britain's economic performance in the last twenty years.

The explanation that holds the field is one which occurs very naturally to the British mind: balance of power. Each member of the Community, this explanation runs, hopes that the British will tip the scale – in their own direction, naturally – on a crucial line-up. There are indeed systems of weighted voting and qualified majority; but the addition of one piece in the top class enormously increases the possible permutations. Even more important, in the democratic institutions which the Anglo-Italian declaration of 1969 foresaw, the counting must, broadly speaking, be of heads. Thus, so it is argued, the Low Countries foresee the historic intervention of Britain on their behalf; the French hope for a counterpoise against the Germans; and each of the present three large powers gains a potential ally if the other two 'gang up' against it. The interpretation assumes, it is true, that the elements of the population of the Community remain nationally self-conscious; but even more manifestly it assumes majority power as the pattern towards which the Community is expected by all its members to tend. If the Community was to be no more than a group of nations which co-operated when all were agreed, there would be no point in bringing Britain in.

As so often in politics, a study of matters actually in hand is more revealing and more reliable than the assertions and the protestations of the actors. The negotiations in which Britain is engaged at Brussels relate not to the content of the Treaty of Rome and the rules and nature of the Community – these the United Kingdom openly accepts as not being negotiable – but to the duration and stages of the transition by which the United Kingdom would accomplish her accession. One of the subjects of negotiation is the size of the British quota of the Community's common budget, which will presently accrue automatically from the yield of certain defined taxes in all the member countries. One of these taxes is the value added tax, a percentage of the yield of which is to be paid into the Community revenues, to be applied by the Community centrally. It follows that there would not only have to be a value added tax in Britain but that it would have to be precisely the same tax, with the same exemptions and the same incidence, as in the other countries. Now, at present, Britain has no VAT, and the questions whether this new tax should be introduced, how it should be levied, and what should be its scope, would be matters of debate in the country and in Parliament. The essence of parliamentary democracy lies in the power to debate and impose taxation: it is the vital principle of the British House of Commons, from which all other aspects of its sovereignty ultimately derive. With Britain in the Community, one important element of taxation would be taken automatically, necessarily and permanently out of the hands of the House of Commons. This is something quite different from an undertaking by Britain to subscribe, for instance, so much to the various agencies of the United Nations: no one in consequence takes out of our hands the decision what taxes to levy and how and on whom.

Here, in microcosm, is the logic of that harmonisation which none can deny to be inherent in the nature of the Community. What is true of the value added tax applies, with parity of reasoning, to every other subject of harmonisation. Those matters which sovereign parliaments debate and decide must be debated and decided not by the British House of Commons but in some other place, and by some other body, and debated and decided once for the whole Community. There is no need to resort to theory and speculation to ascertain whether membership of the Community means the loss of national sovereignty: the fact is implicit in the very negotiations themselves as they proceed at Brussels through a mass of seeming detail. The popular instinct in Britain, that this is what it is really all about, is right.

Whether the answer should be yes or no, for accession or against accession, depends on whether the people of Britain will accept the voice of the people of the whole Community as binding upon them – at first in some, then in more and more, and finally in all the essential matters of fiscal, social, economic and political determination. When I say 'accept', I mean accept heartily and willingly, no less than the people of all parts of the United Kingdom today accept as self-evidently binding upon them the fiscal, social, economic and political decisions of Her Majesty's Government and of the British Parliament, resting upon the electorate of the United Kingdom. In brief, can we be, and *will* we be, one electorate, one constituency, one nation, with you and with the rest of the people of the Community? I do not believe that anyone who knows Britain can doubt that the answer to the question is No.

It may be said that neither would the electorate of any of the founder members of the Community answer that question in the affirmative at this moment, and that consequently the fact that the British cannot is irrelevant. Even if this were true of your own countries – and it is no business of mine to judge whether it is or not – I believe there are several reasons why the argument is not valid. In what I am about to say I mean not the slightest deprecation of the institutions or of the national identity of any of the nations of the continent or the tenacity with which that identity has been formed and defended. Nevertheless, it is a fact that the British parliament in its paramount authority occupies a position in relation to the British nation which no other elective assembly in Europe possesses. Take Parliament out of the history of England and that history itself becomes meaningless. Whole lifetimes of study cannot exhaust the reasons why this fact has come to be; but fact it is, so that the British nation could not imagine itself except with and through its parliament. Consequently the sovereignty of our parliament is something other for us from what your assemblies are for you.

What is equally significant, your assemblies, unlike the British parliament, are the creation of deliberate political acts, and mostly of recent political acts. The notion that a new sovereign body can be created is therefore as familiar to you as it is repugnant, not to say unimaginable, to us. That deliberate and recent creation of sovereign assemblies on the Continent is in turn an aspect of the fact that the Continent is familiar, and familiar in the recent past, with the creation of nation states themselves. Four of the six members of the Community came into existence as such no more than a century or a century and half ago – within the memory of two lifetimes. You will not imagine that I am treating with less than profound respect the historical and human background to the *risorgimento,* or to the rise of the modern German state, or to the establishment of the two kingdoms in the Low Countries. I say only, what I believe cannot be contested, that it is far more natural for nations with this kind of experience to imagine and participate in the further creation of new sovereign political entities in Europe than it is for us. An outside observer is not therefore surprised that the French, who of all the six most resemble ourselves in the duration and natural evolution of their national identity, appear to have more difficulty than the other five members in giving an affirmative reply to that question which the British instinctively answer in the negative.

It would be wrong not to add one thing more which contributes to the British response. An essential element in forming a single electorate is the sense that in the last resort all parts of it stand or fall, survive or perish, together. This sense the British do not share with the inhabitants of the continent of Western Europe. Of all the nations of Europe Britain and Russia alone, though for opposite reasons, have this in common: they can be defeated in the decisive land battle and still survive. This characteristic Russia owes to her immensity. Britain owes it to her ditch. The British feel – and I believe that instinct corresponds with sound military reason – that the ditch is as significant in what we call the nuclear age as it proved to be in the air age and had been in the age of the *Grande Armée* of Napoleon or the Spanish infantry of Philip II. The proposition is not one to be developed here; I must content myself with barely stating it. Error or truth, myth or reality, the belief itself is a habit of mind which has helped to form the national identity of the British and cannot be divorced from it. I began by mentioning that I personally had been and still am a fervent advocate of Britain's' military commitment on the Continent. I am not contradicting this when I say that the British commitment on the Continent, psychologically and materially, must always be limited; it can never be total. Yet total commitment is implicit in the merging of sovereignty, in the unification of an electorate.

That assertion brings me to the last thing that I want to say, which is indeed the reason for my speaking at all. It is often urged in Britain that one need not take too seriously the commitment of the Community to political unity, and that because the realisation of the commitment, if it is realised at all, will be gradual, there is no reason against taking into membership of the Community a Britain which is not merely neutral but positively hostile towards political unification. If unification comes, the British will have grown used to it – in the jargon this is disguised as 'the habit of working together'; and if it does not come anyhow, no harm will have been done. I totally dissent. It is not for Britain to gauge the sincerity of the Community's member governments and of the public opinion behind them. It is not for us to judge what you ought to want to do, or what it is possible for you to do. What would be as dishonourable as foolish, would be for Britain and her people to allow the Rome Treaty to be acceded to on their behalf with mental reservations. The enterprise of the Community is on so lofty a plane, the commitment of those who join is so solemn, that we dare not enter upon it, and you on your part dare not accept us into it, unless we can do so *ex amino,* with a genuine and hearty intention that in the fullness of time political as well as economic union shall come out of it. Therefore it is right that you should have no illusions about the true state of mind in Britain and not be misled by that unanimity and show of confidence which all who speak officially are in duty bound to maintain. There is a saying which we have that 'the Queen wants no unwilling subjects'. I cannot believe that you of the Community can want unwilling partners. The question of British accession to the Community was not presented for decision to the British electorate at the General Election last year; and as both major parties professed themselves ready to negotiate and ready to accede provided the terms – which now prove to be purely transitional terms – were satisfactory, there was no means for the feeling of the electorate to express itself. I myself, however, told my electors in my address to them that I would oppose, and do my personal utmost to prevent, British accession; and I am in no doubt that in that at any rate I was expressing the preponderant opinion not only of those who voted for me but of those who voted on other grounds against me, and (what is more) that this would be generally true throughout the country. It seems to me therefore to be part of my duty, so far as I am able, to carry the debate on to the continent of Europe and in one country after another of the Community, commencing, as is most fit and proper, here in France, to leave no one in doubt that those who seek to make the United Kingdom a member of the European Economic Community are not speaking for the people of Britain.

Enoch Powell as a Parliamentarian

Frank Field

When I joined the House in 1979, Enoch Powell was firmly established as one of the greatest political figures in the Commons. Whilst admired he was also feared and herein lay the strength of his parliamentary presence and its weakness.

As a schoolboy I was already aware of Enoch and there were three aspects of his political life that had already impressed themselves on my mind by the time I entered the House. There was first, his protest against the shenanigans that had led to Alec Douglas-Home being installed in No. 10 in place of R. A. Butler. Secondly, there was the undoubted quality of his intellect and his harnessing of this extraordinary set of abilities in the making of a most radical minister. Lastly, there was the issue which will forever be linked to Enoch, that 'Rivers of Blood' speech. How did my impressions change once I had the opportunity to witness Enoch close up within a parliamentary system to which he devoted practically all of his working life?

First, then, his stand against the way the 'magic circle' (as Iain Macleod dubbed it) had moved to put Douglas-Home into No. 10 in preference to Butler. Why did this action so impress me? And why did my admiration for this action by Enoch so long ago grow once I became a Member of Parliament?

Only after coming to the Commons did I become fully aware of Enoch's courage in refusing to serve under Douglas-Home, an act whereby he effectively removed himself from office. True, the courage required to stand apart in this instance was less than it would have been had Enoch stood alone against Macmillan's successful plot, but there was courage nevertheless in his willingness to confront the ruling political gang on his side of the House.

The outside world has some appreciation of what it means to resign in protest at the treatment of a friend or colleague. Voters can relate such an action to their own life. But a resignation in the Commons adds a further dimension to such a drama. The House has its very public side where our activities are presented for good or ill to the public. But what the public are less aware of is how the Commons has its own political culture where MPs are rated by their peers. Most Members share the honourable instinct of wishing to climb the greasy pole of political advancement. Not to make this ascent, either by not wishing to do so, or by failure before reaching senior office, separates out Members in what our House culture deems, at best, to be members of the second eleven.

Enoch's behaviour suggests that this conventional criterion for success meant little to him. As I came to know him, I found his eccentric attitude on this score increasingly attractive. It was impossible not to conclude that, while Enoch fought his corner as ably as any, the struggle, for him, was about achieving long-term objectives, not simply a mastery of the flotsam and jetsam of current events.

Enoch, at the beginning of the Falklands War, questioned the strength of Margaret Thatcher's character. The Prime Minister derived obvious pleasure from being referred to as 'the Iron Lady'. How well, Enoch asked, would the Iron Lady live up to the soubriquet she so obviously relished now that the battle was joined? This challenge, we are told, rattled Downing Street. And yet once the noise of battle had subsided, Enoch wittily complimented her on her conduct. Similarly, in setting the course for enacting fundamental change in British politics, Enoch's own principles were, to paraphrase Thatcher, not for turning.

A second side of Enoch that impressed was his sheer intellectual ability and how this played into politics. Even in the sixth form I was aware of this extraordinary MP who had become a professor of Greek at the age of twenty-five. That his chair was in Sydney rather than Oxford or Cambridge somehow added for me a greater sense of achievement. (I still had much to learn about English snobbery.) But the high intellect that was so obviously on display early in his life, and which served Enoch exceptionally well in the military intelligence post he occupied with such obvious distinction during the war, was a double-edged weapon in the Commons.

By the time I reached the Commons, anyone who sought recognition in the chamber feared Enoch. It was not a fear based simply on how Enoch would marshal his argument. Nor did that fear stem only from his ability to make an opponent's argument appear at best lacking in logic, and at worst just plain idiotic. That was of course part of the fear factor. But this fear operated in an even more fundamental way. Even those who sought to be his allies could not always be sure upon which side Enoch would dispose his affections.

This fault was not wholly Enoch's. Anyone who cared to look at his career would see the line of his thinking and how his disparate speeches and activities combined to explain the whole man. Even so, it must be conceded that Enoch was in part responsible. For here was the downside to his fierce intelligence. When the good fairy stood at the foot of his cot in those far-off days in 1912, many gifts were bestowed on the young son of Albert and Ellen Powell. But that same good fairy was either struck by a spasm of absent-mindedness, or had departed, before she could balance the baby's extraordinary intellectual intelligence with the social skills and clubbiness that would have made his character overwhelmingly attractive for a party leadership role. His lack of emotional intelligence and, given his character, his inability to be other than his own man, ensured that the number of Indians wishing to follow their chief was limited, perhaps too limited, for someone who might otherwise expect to lead his party. Worse still, that intelligence often drove him into dangerous territories where the fatality rate among his friends was particularly high.

There was, however, another, much more positive side to Enoch's intelligence, and it was how he utilised those gifts in government. My early impression, no doubt acquired from the near unanimity of political commentators, was the perceived inability of intellectuals to make much immediate impact on current policies. That conventional observation was utterly confounded by the impact of Enoch's thinking on policies. Enoch was Minister of Health from 1960 until he resigned over what he regarded as Macmillan's 'sheer devilry' in fixing the Tory leadership for Douglas-Home. Enoch's time at Health paralleled my undergraduate years. Even then I was startled that it was he who began the first NHS building programme. Here was the man, who happily presented himself as wrestling with angels, also having the ability to get stuck in and wrestle money from the Treasury, not just for the odd hospital rebuild, but also in getting the Treasury to sign up to a ten-year building programme. No dandified intellectual here: this was a shrewd and effective politician.

Equally important for me, as an MP, was the growing understanding of how a political intellectual could not only initiate a new debate, but also set the contours within which that debate would be conducted. Here Enoch used his position as minister to set in motion the debate on community care that has still to run its course. His starting point was the treatment of the 'criminally ill' as well as the much larger population housed in what are euphemistically called 'long-stay hospitals'. Enoch was determined to seize, if not the advantage, at least the issue of how the community cared for its citizens with mental illness. He asserted that the criminally insane should never be released, but argued that there were new ways of caring for people with mental illness and that taxpayers had to face up to the fact that this more humane approach was one that would cost more, not less, money.

Yet Enoch's stewardship of the Ministry of Health was not without its paradoxes, which continued to fascinate me, largely because so few politicians or commentators made much of it after the 'Rivers of Blood' speech. It was Enoch, after all, who, as Health Minister, had not only sanctioned, but actively supported the NHS strategy of recruiting large numbers of immigrant workers. This brings me, inevitably, to that speech, a speech that changed the trajectory of Enoch's life just as much as it set a course by which so much of British politics would flow.

Enoch came to this issue with a track record of which any MP would be proud. The speech he gave on the Royal Titles Bill in 1953 drew heavily on the changes that the Attlee government made in its 1948 British Nationality Act. Enoch regarded this 1953 speech as the finest he ever gave. I happen to disagree. It was, for me, his contribution against the actions of the British government over the Kenyan Hola Camp scandal that stands out for me as the pinnacle of his oratory. In that latter speech, Enoch insisted that there could not be a standard of conduct that the English maintained as right in this country, while believing a lower one could be appropriate for our conduct elsewhere. This was particularly true, he believed, in Africa, where 'our own high standards in the acceptance of responsibilities' was paramount.

How then to explain that 'Rivers of Blood' speech? I must confess, I still cannot think through clearly what Enoch thought his goal was. I had been, at the age of sixteen, a Young Conservative. During one of the campaigns against apartheid, I organised with a fellow sixth-former, a Young Socialist, our own campaign in Chiswick to boycott South African goods. The word 'campaign' is, I suppose, a grandiose term for what we actually did. We printed leaflets and handed them to shoppers at the local Co-op. For this crime, committed just before Macmillan's great 'Winds of Change' speech in Africa, and with it the resulting realignment of views of many Tory activists to the evils of apartheid, I was shoehorned out of the local association. Nothing so crude, you understand, as an expulsion, but an exclusion just as effective. So I came to the 'Rivers of Blood' speech from a hostile perspective. What was Enoch up to? By citing those Roman texts he knew so well, and in particular the reference to the river Tiber foaming with blood, he must have appreciated its likely impact. If the imagery was applied with the due care Enoch always prided himself on in his use of language, we can only conclude he was describing the fate which he believed awaited his country.

What results did Enoch want from this speech? If it was to awaken the country's political elite to the dangers of sustained large-scale immigration and to debate the consequences, then it must rank as Enoch's greatest failure. At a stroke he made the subject of immigration a no-go area for elected politicians. I only felt safe in trespassing onto this territory once the mass of immigration from eastern European countries reached our shores, when the issue was no longer one of colour.

Why was it then that I never raised 'Rivers of Blood' with Enoch? The simple truth is that I dared not confront Enoch on this issue as I felt that it was not only his biggest, but almost the only major political error he committed. The outcome of that speech is the stuff of which great Greek tragedies are made. Enoch's talents had destined him for a commanding position in British politics. The 'Rivers of Blood' speech gave him a commanding position among voters, as Enoch was expressing their fears. But his political gang, who were, under Heath, only too pleased to strip him of any leadership potential, closed ranks against him. If I am right, this great mistake over the speech must have caused Enoch huge and profound regret and I never wanted to stray uninvited into this national and personal tragedy.

It has been recalled elsewhere how important the House of Commons' lavatories are in the pursuance of politics. It was one such chance encounter that offered Enoch the opportunity to tell Harold Wilson of his intended 1974 general election speech in which he would inform his audience of his intention to vote Labour. It was Wilson's commitment to renegotiate the terms of our EEC membership that prompted Enoch to plan this extraordinary step. The press reported that 1,500 were in that Birmingham hall to hear Enoch make his announcement while a further 7,000 were turned away.

My encounter, and probably the basis of our friendship, took place, not in the 'Aye' Lobby gents', as did his meeting with Wilson, but in another off the Library Corridor. Enoch had been giving a series of lectures at Zion College, then an outstanding library established for the use of London clergy. The lectures were being picketed by groups who billed themselves as radical Christians. I apologised to Enoch for missing the lectures, whereupon he enquired if I would be interested in reading them.

'Of course I would,' I replied.

'They will be on the board within the hour,' was his terse response. The board in the MPs' Lobby is a place where internal post is given. Well within the hour Enoch delivered on his word and the text of the lectures was accompanied by a beautifully handwritten note expressing interest in my response.

I remember that night well. The Commons was involved in one of its intolerable all-night sittings. To me, as a new Member, the events gave me some idea, if not of hell, then of a form of purgatory not that far removed from the torment of the eternal fires. Enoch, of course, saw these parliamentary manoeuvres as a crucial part of the Commons' attempts to control the executive. The long hours of the night and the early morning offered me the opportunity to read those lectures.

They excited me, and I longed to discuss them with their author. But when I went to look for him, he was most unusually not occupying his traditional seat in the Library, nor did I catch him at any of the early morning votes, although the record showed that he'd voted. It was the following day, I believe, that our paths again crossed.

He enquired of my reading. 'You're opening yourself up for a heresy trial,' I replied, for this beautifully written text argued either that Jesus was stoned to death or that the key New Testament figure was John the Baptist. I cannot now remember which. Enoch laughed. 'Could you arrange such a heresy trial, for that would ensure my safe return in South Down?' I failed, I regret to say, to translate our laughter into action and there was no such favourable event.

One other reminiscence tells much about Enoch's reserve and the strength of the common decencies that ran through his veins. My mother and I were walking into Westminster Abbey one Sunday morning. Coming towards the west door, but from a different angle, were Enoch and Pam, his wife. They were a little ahead and Enoch passed through into the abbey without any acknowledgement, let alone breaking those ever-so-stiff face muscles into just a hint of a smile.

I was more than a little miffed. As we were going out it proved more difficult for Enoch to avoid me. 'Why are you ignoring us?' I enquired.

Enoch's eyes fell on me. 'I had no wish to embarrass you by presuming our acquaintance in front of a person to whom I had not been introduced.'

Laughter from my mother and myself greeted this extraordinary statement. 'Enoch!' exclaimed Pam. And with that we entered a taxi and sped towards their home in South Eaton Place. There was much merriment and some drink, with me becoming, as my mother commentated later, a little squiffy.

On our way home, in another taxi, my mother commented what a wonderful morning she had had. 'Meeting Enoch and Pam?' I asked.

'No, you silly boy,' she replied firmly. 'It was going to the abbey for the Holy Mysteries, and then to encounter the mystery of Enoch and his so lovable Pam,' she said in a stunning summary of our morning adventure. Both mysteries endure.

— SPEECH —

Hola Camp, Kenya

House of Commons, 27 July 1959

At 1:15 a.m. on 27 July 1959, Enoch Powell rose to his feet in the House of Commons to deliver an often forgotten but none the less magnificent speech criticising his own government for attempting to cover up the Hola Camp massacre, which had resulted in the deaths of eleven Mau Mau at the hands of British officials. One can argue that the speech ultimately destroys any claim that Powell was a racist; instead it paints him as a defender of racial equality as he powerfully condemned parliamentary colleagues for referring to the eleven Mau Mau as 'sub-human'. Powell recognised that it was wrong for Britain to have different standards at home than abroad, arguing 'we must be consistent with ourselves everywhere'. It would later be described by Denis Healey as 'the greatest parliamentary speech I ever heard' with 'all the moral passion and rhetorical force of Demosthenes'. As Parliament has evolved and oratory has all but died in the Commons its elegance and conviction are unlikely to be matched in today's politics. Enoch's speech reminds us of the sanctity of human life, and his justified moral outrage could well be applied to the conditions of Guantanamo Bay and other detainment facilities around the world today. When future generations look back at past parliamentary speeches, this will surely be viewed as one of the finest pieces of oratory ever delivered on Britain's colonial relationship with Africa.

Many aspersions have been cast and many imputations made by Hon. Members opposite in the course of this debate with which I could not for an instant associate myself. And yet I cannot regret that even at this hour the House is once again considering the affair of Hola Camp. For the further documents relating to the deaths which were issued as a White Paper last week confirm what was already pretty clear from the earlier evidence, that it could be to the credit neither of this House nor of this country that the matter should rest where it now stands.

The affair of Hola Camp was a great administrative disaster, and to that administrative disaster there were three aspects. There was the authorisation of an operation which in its nature was likely to have fatal results; there was the failure to see that that operation, such as it was, was at least carried out with the minimum of risk; and, finally, there was the incident, which it is difficult to find a word to describe, of the water cart communiqué. The new documents show that the responsibility for all three aspects of this administrative disaster goes higher than can be discharged by the premature retirement of the officer in charge of the camp or by the retirement, accelerated by a few weeks, of the Commissioner of Prisons.

The central document in the White Paper of last week, and it has often been referred to in this debate, is the minute of 17 February addressed by the Commissioner of Prisons to the Minister of Defence. That Minute enclosed two other documents, Folios 9 and 10 on the file. Folio 9 was the Cowan Plan as drafted and intended by Cowan and put up by him as a proposal to his senior officers. Folio 10 was the extraordinary message which Sullivan had sent to Cowan on the fourteenth which can hardly be described otherwise than as a *cri de coeur*. It is impossible to read that document without sensing through it the state of mind of the man who wrote it or being aware of the risks which were attendant upon the situation which it reveals.

I will only remind the House of the ominous facts which it disclosed, that the Ministry of Works on the site had asked to be 'disassociated entirely from any such operation' and the request for a senior superintendent, 'with appropriate powers of summary punishment', to 'be present when the policy outlined is implemented'. It was clear evidence, among other things, that the Cowan Plan, Folio 9, was not what Sullivan, vide Folio 10, thought he was expected to implement. Incidentally, therefore, if there is blame for the failure to implement the Cowan Plan accurately, that responsibility must rest on all those who should have become aware, through seeing Folio 10, that Sullivan had misunderstood the Cowan Plan. With these two documents underneath, went this Minute, Folio 11, from the Commissioner of Prisons to the Minister of Defence. The Commissioner of Prisons had not yet taken a decision on the Cowan Plan. Indeed, when he saw it he gave instructions that 'no action should be taken until authority was given' by his office. When he looked at 9 and 10 together, he decided that he, on his responsibility, could not authorise any action to be taken, and submitted it to his Minister, saying – and I am sorry to quote these words again, but they are essential – the plans Mr. Cowan worked out at (9) could be undertaken by us, but it would mean the use of a certain degree of force, in which operation someone might get hurt or even killed. I think this situation should be brought to the notice of the Security Council and a direction given on what policy should be adopted. He then again referred to the action as planned at (9), with the risk of someone getting hurt or killed. Those were not idle words, the reference to someone getting hurt or killed. He said in evidence to the Committee of three that the risk he had in mind that someone might get killed or hurt included 'warder staff as well as detainees'. Since the Commissioner of Prisons knew that in the Cowan Plan the numerical superiority of the warders to the detainees was to be overwhelming, the fact that he regarded the likelihood of being killed as applying to warders as well as to detainees is evidence of the degree of risk and danger which he associated in his mind with the Cowan Plan – the original, correct Cowan Plan, Folio 9. This was apart from the evidence in Folio 10 that things were going wrong, that it would not be that plan which would be put into effect, and that Sullivan had misunderstood.

He considered the responsibility for putting this into effect was not only one that he could not take, but it was one he could not advise his Minister to take alone, without reference to the Security Council.

Incidentally, the action of the Commissioner of Prisons disposes of the notion that the Cowan Plan for Hola was, as has often been said – and I quote the expression in the leading article in the *Daily Telegraph* yesterday – the application of a long-standing and highly successful technique of rehabilitation. The truth is that it was the application of a modification, and a very important modification, of the technique which had elsewhere yielded good results.

When my Right Hon. Friend spoke in the debate on 16 June last, he was careful to put that correctly. He said: 'The proposals were the adaptation of a proved and successful technique to the circumstances of Hola.' [OFFICIAL REPORT, 16 June, 1959; Vol. 460,

c. 280.] They were, in fact, as proposed now in the Cowan Plan, something which represented such a serious departure from anything attempted before, something so dangerous in themselves, that he could not envisage the responsibility to carry them out being taken otherwise than by the Security Council itself.

The Minister of Defence decided that it was not necessary, and the Minister of Defence and the Minister of African Affairs took upon themselves the responsibility for authorising an operation which they had been warned involved the risk of death, in a minute accompanied by a paper which showed to anyone who cared to read it that not even that operation, dangerous as it was, was the one which Sullivan contemplated carrying out.

The Hon. Lady the Member for Blackburn (Mrs. Castle) was a little too kind to the Minister for African Affairs. She overlooked the fact that he as well as the Minister of Defence had all the relevant papers in front of him. Those two men took upon themselves, with their eyes open and with full knowledge, not only the responsibility for the Cowan Plan but the responsibility for allowing the deformed version of it to go forward. It was authorised – now we come to the second phase, the execution – with the indication that it should go forward 'subject to the proviso that' the Commissioner should first ensure that he has a sufficient number of warders at Hola to cope with possible eventualities. So, warned of the danger implicit, aware from the S.O.S. that all was not well, the Ministers responsible, the Ministers who had given the decision, left the matter there and just sent it down the line.

Those two men, who knew that they had authorised – without reference, as advised by the Commissioner of Prisons, to the Security Council – an operation involving the risk of death, learnt on the afternoon of 3 March that on the day on which that operation was carried out ten men had died at Hola Camp; and on 4 March, after – and these are the words of the publicity officer: a good deal of discussion as to whether violence was the cause of the deaths of these men in a meeting presided over by His Excellency the Governor, they were parties to the issue of the water cart communiqué.

Those documents, that evidence, prove to me conclusively that the responsibility here lies not only with Sullivan and Lewis, but at a level above them. It lies with those to whom they actually appealed for help, whom they warned of the danger, from whom they received indeed a decision which transferred responsibility upwards, but no other help or guidance. That responsibility, transcending Sullivan and Lewis, has not been recognised; but it cannot be ignored, it cannot be burked, it will not just evaporate into thin air if we do nothing about it.

I am as certain of this as I am of anything, that my Right Hon. Friend the Secretary of State from the beginning to the end of this affair is without any jot or tittle of blame for what happened in Kenya, that he could not be expected to know, that it could not be within the administrative conventions that these matters should be brought to his attention before or during the execution. When I say my Right Hon. Friend was in this matter utterly and completely blameless, that is of a piece with his administration of his high office generally, which has been the greatest exercise of the office of Colonial Secretary in modern times. It is in the name of that record, it is in the name of his personal blamelessness, that I beg of him to ensure that the responsibility is recognised and carried where it properly belongs, and is seen to belong.

I have heard it suggested that there were circumstances surrounding this affair at Hola Camp which, it is argued, might justify the passing over of this responsibility which might justify one in saying, 'Well, of course, strictly speaking, that is quite correct; but then here there were special circumstances.'

It has been said – and it is a fact – that these eleven men were the lowest of the low; sub-human was the word which one of my Hon. Friends used. So be it. But that cannot be relevant to the acceptance of responsibility for their death. I know that it does not enter into my Right Hon. Friend's mind that it could be relevant, because it would be completely inconsistent with his whole policy of rehabilitation, which is based upon the assumption that whatever the present state of these men, they can be reclaimed. No one who supports the policy of rehabilitation can argue from the character and condition of these men that responsibility for their death should be different from the responsibility for anyone else's death. In general, I would say that it is a fearful doctrine, which must recoil upon the heads of those who pronounce it, to stand in judgement on a fellow human being and to say, 'Because he was such-and-such, therefore the consequences which would otherwise flow from his death shall not flow.'

It is then said that the morale of the Prison Service, the morale of the whole Colonial Service, is above all important and that whatever we do, whatever we urge, whatever we say, should have regard to that morale. 'Amen' say I. But is it for the morale of the Prison Service that those who executed a policy should suffer – whether inadequately or not is another question – and those who authorised it, those to whom they appealed, should be passed over? I cannot believe that that supports the morale of a service.

Going on beyond that, my Hon. Friend the Member for Leicester, South-East (Mr. Peel) reminded the House how proud the Colonial Service is of the integrity of its administration and its record. Nothing could be more damaging to the morale of such a service than that there should be a breath or a blemish left upon it. No, Sir; that argument from the morale of the Prison Service and the Colonial Service stands on its head if what we mean is that therefore the consequences of responsibility should not follow in this case as they would in any other similar case.

Finally it is argued that this is Africa, that things are different there. Of course they are. The question is whether the difference between things there and here is such that the taking of responsibility there and here should be upon different principles. We claim that it is our object – and this is something which unites both sides of the House – to leave representative institutions behind us wherever we give up our rule. I cannot imagine that it is a way to plant representative institutions to be seen to shirk the acceptance and the assignment of responsibility, which is the very essence of responsible Government.

Nor can we ourselves pick and choose where and in what parts of the world we shall use this or that kind of standard. We cannot say, 'We will have African standards in Africa, Asian standards in Asia and perhaps British standards here at home.' We have not that choice to make. We must be consistent with ourselves everywhere. All Government, all influence of man upon man, rests upon opinion. What we can do in Africa, where we still govern and where we no longer govern, depends upon the opinion which is entertained of the way in which this country acts and the way in which Englishmen act. We cannot, we dare not, in Africa of all places, fall below our own highest standards in the acceptance of responsibility.

Royal Titles Bill

House of Commons, 3 March 1953

I assert that the essence of unity, whether it be in a close-knit country or in a loosely-knit federation, is that all the parts recognise that in certain circumstances they would sacrifice themselves to the interests of the whole. It is this instinctive recognition of being parts of a whole, which means that in certain circumstances individual, local, partial interests would he sacrificed to the general interest, that constitutes unity. Unless there is some such instinctive, deliberate determination, there is no unity. There may be alliance, indeed. We may have alliance between two sovereign Powers for the pursuit of common interest for a particular or for an undefined period; but that is not unity. That is not the maintenance or the creation of any such entity as we refer to by the name 'Empire' or 'Commonwealth'.

I deny that there is that element, that minimum basic element, of unity binding India to Her Majesty's dominions. I deny that there is present, in that former part of Her Majesty's dominions which has deliberately cast off allegiance to her, that minimum, basic, instinctive recognition of belonging to a greater whole which involves the ultimate consequence in certain circumstances of self-sacrifice in the interests of the whole.

I therefore say that this formula 'Head of the Commonwealth' and the declaration in which it is inscribed, are essentially a sham. They are essentially something which we have invented to blind ourselves to the reality of the position. Although the changes which will be made in the Royal titles as the result of the Bill are greatly repugnant to me, if they were changes which were demanded by those who in many wars had fought with this country, by nations who maintained an allegiance to the Crown, and who signified a desire to be in the future as we were in the past; if it were our friends who had come to us and said: 'We want this,' I would say: 'Let it go. Let us admit the divisibility of the Crown. Let us sink into anonymity and cancel the word "British" from our titles. If they like the conundrum "Head of the Commonwealth" in the Royal style, let it be there.'

However, the underlying evil of this is that we are doing it for the sake not of our friends but of those who are not our friends. We are doing this for the sake of those to whom the very names 'Britain' and 'British' are repugnant. We are doing this for the sake of those who have deliberately cast off their allegiance to our common Monarchy.

Mr. Nicholson

I appreciate my Hon. Friend's giving way, and I thank him. I beg him to measure his words and to remember the vast sacrifices and the oceans of blood that India has poured out in the past, and to recognise the deep affection and feeling that exist throughout India towards this country.

Mr. Powell

I am obliged to my Hon. Friend. I, who have had the advantage and privilege of serving with the Indian Army in the war, am not likely to be unmindful of it; but it was an army which owed allegiance, an enthusiastic allegiance, which was its very principle of existence and its binding force, to the Crown. That allegiance, for good or for evil, has been cast off, with all that follows.

Now, I am not under any delusion that my words on this occasion can have any practical effect, but, none the less, they are not, perhaps, necessarily in vain. We in this House, whether we are the humblest of the back benchers or my Right Hon. Friend the First Lord of the Treasury himself, are in ourselves, in our individual capacities, quite unimportant. We have a meaning in this place only in so far as in our time and generation we represent great principles, great elements in the national life, great strands in our society and national being.

Sometimes, elements which are essential to the life, growth and existence of Britain seem for a time to be cast into shadow, obscured, and even destroyed. Yet in the past they have remained alive; they have survived; they have come to the surface again, and they have been the means of a new flowering, which no one had suspected. It is because I believe that, in a sense, for a brief moment, I represent and speak for an indispensable element in the British Constitution and in British life that I have spoken. And, I pray, not entirely in vain.

Constitutional Reform

Michael Forsyth

I imagine it has been the common experience of everyone who spent
a great part of a lifetime in politics that at the end he was like some
traveller who, having journeyed on from day to day, finds himself at
last in a strange country, where the landscape is no longer recognisable and the people speak a foreign tongue.
Hatfield House, 12 October 1987

If there is an underlying theme which underpins almost everything that Enoch Powell said on any subject, it is the British
parliament – or more accurately, the British Crown in Parliament,
which, according to Powell, 'brooks no concurrent or superior
authority'.[†] In the final analysis, it was Powell's devotion to this
country's 'unwritten' constitution, and his unflinching defence of
this country's institutions, which meant that he could never be
described solely as a 'libertarian' or as a 'Whig', even though his
economic analysis contained much of both.

If he were alive now he would be shocked by the behaviour and
attitudes of the ruling political elite and would have his work cut
out in defending Parliament from the continuing onslaughts upon
its authority. On the subject of constitutional reform he has proved
to be most right and most wrong in his analysis: right in so far as so
many of the problems and dangers he identified have come to pass
but wrong in his naive belief that the electorate would never permit
the emasculation of Parliament. It is only in the area of European
integration that there are any signs today of the popular revolt he
anticipated, as the EU drives inexorably towards political union
and the destruction of democratic accountability, as he predicted

---

† London, 1 December 1979.

more than forty years ago. Perhaps if he were alive today he would find there is something to fight for. The arguments would be very familiar to him and he might have grounds for confidence that at some moment through the House of Commons, the people might recover what has been surrendered on their behalf.

Unfortunately, this is not the case with the other two constitutional issues which dominate our debate today, namely Scottish independence and House of Lords reform. Here, his voice sounds less topical and relevant. Powell's logic, while so often impeccable, does to some extent rest on premises which do indeed seem 'to belong to a different world' from the one we live in now. Here are a few quotations from his speeches to illustrate the point:

> The Queen we love is our Queen in Parliament.
> Our unique and most precious possession, our Parliament.
> Our whole constitution rests, uniquely in the world, upon what Burke called 'prescription'.[†]
> The same institutions which exert the magnetic force of authority inside a society imply the denial and repudiation of similar magnetic forces from outside.

Of course it is hard to imagine any contemporary politician using such language or even, in some cases, having the slightest notion of what Powell is talking about. In this chapter I would like to explore whether there is still time for a new political generation to embrace the constitutional lessons which Powell's speeches contain, and withstand the latest assaults upon our country's institutions and Parliament.

The best place to begin is the nature of parliamentary democracy itself, because for Powell this is the spring from which everything flows. He was always at pains, when speaking about the House of Commons and British parliamentary institutions, to highlight their essential characteristics – for example, the role of 'prescription', the supremacy of the electorate 'over the House of Commons',[‡] and

---

[†] The meaning of 'prescription' in this sense is of a title or an institution having become legally established or accepted by long usage or the passage of time (*New Oxford Dictionary of English*).

[‡] Nene College Lecture, 1 November 1991.

the fact that the 'Crown, as the enduring and continuous source of all legitimate authority, governs, but it governs only through those who can command a majority in the representative House of Parliament'.[†] Such observations may appear esoteric to anyone other than a constitutional expert, but sometimes Powell managed to pull the various threads together and emphasise their application to modern politics:

> Unlike every other parliament in the world, the parliament of the United Kingdom does not owe its existence to any document or treaty. It has the lawful power to pass, amend or repeal any existing law whatsoever, whether common law or statute law, nor can its decisions be called in question or overturned by any other body. In law it is the nearest thing to omnipotent. Omnicompetent it certainly is: there is nothing which it does not have the legal power to do. In recognition of this supremacy, it has often been called the High Court of Parliament, and Henry VIII ... was apt to declare that 'we are nowhere so high in our estate royal as in this our High Court of Parliament.' He was right. The Crown of England is supreme in all causes temporal and ecclesiastical, but it exercises that supremacy most effectively, surely and incontestably through Parliament.
>
> The assertion which I have just made has not been invalidated by the Act of Parliament which in 1972 subordinated the British parliament to the fiscal, financial and legislative organs of the European Economic Community and the courts of the realm to the European Court ... No treaty binds, or can bind, what Parliament does or can do. Treaties bind governments in international law, but not Parliament ... This omnipotence of Parliament is the reason why parliamentary procedure is so important as to be virtually the equivalent of a constitution. The British people accept and (upon the whole) obey the laws as made by Parliament because and only because Parliament does so proceeding in accordance with precedent ... When a citizen says 'This is the law which Parliament has made, and I must therefore obey it' he does not mean 'made any old how'; he means made strictly in accordance with due procedure. The quickest way to ensure a rebellion would be for any parliament to say 'Let's cut out some of this procedure, and get the job done in double quick time' ...

---

† Lisbon, 7 May 1990.

We are faced in fact with a paradox. The proceedings of Parliament are valid only because they are conducted in accordance with precedent; and yet parliamentary procedure itself is continuously changing and evolving ... There is a really important point at stake here for the understanding of the British and their parliamentary institution: evolutionary change over time is not incompatible with the strongest emotional attachment to precedent. In fact it may even be that attachment to precedent is itself the condition of successful evolution ...

By the theory of the British constitution for the past three centuries and a half, if not longer, the government of the United Kingdom has been exercised in the name of the Crown upon advice tendered by ministers who command a majority in Parliament. In practical terms, because of the predominance of the House of Commons, that means ministers who command a majority in the lower House. In order more effectually to frame that advice and command that majority, ministers are drawn from the membership of one house or the other – nowadays principally from the membership of the House of Commons. It is one of the distinguishing characteristics of British government that the House of Commons is the nursery of ministers and Prime Ministers. They sit in Parliament, and if they are wise they continue to participate in and to enjoy the life of Parliament: it is the life from which they emerged and to which eventually, when their day is done, they will return. Understanding British government is therefore about understanding Parliament and especially about understanding the House of Commons.

The essential work of the House of Commons is talking, but not of course mere talking. It is the sort of structured, specific talking which is called debate and in that small, deliberately overcrowded chamber is a quite peculiar sort of talk. It is more like a conversation, the discourse in relative intimacy between those who know one another and live together; conversation between equals, because all are treated as equals in that chamber, despite the privilege which ministers enjoy of opening and closing debate and the privilege which former ministers possess of being called to speak in preference to others when (as the phrase is) they rise to catch Mr Speaker's eye.

The members of the House of Commons have no fixed places, apart from the traditional separation between the government's supporters and its opponents on the two facing sides of the rectangular house. Members sit cheek by jowl with others; and when called to speak, they speak from wherever they are. There is no podium, no rostrum, no orating place and although there is oratory, and great oratory, it is not the ranting oratory of the demagogue nor prepared speech declaimed from a written script but such oratory as might be heard from a man exhorting or admonishing a group of his companions.

There is another peculiarity of debate in the House of Commons which it is crucially important to understand: it is debate preceding decision, and the decision which it precedes is known in advance, since, unless the government is going to fall that very night, it will have a majority in the voting lobbies. Parliamentary debate is therefore addressed to those who already know how they will vote – it is not to persuade them which way to vote, but to persuade them that in their hearts they ought to know they are wrong, or right, as the case may be. I have experienced many a debate after which the members who voted in the majority lobby were heard saying to one another as they did so: 'You know, this won't do; we're wrong about this.'

Debate in the House of Commons is open ended. The House sits at 2.30 p.m, but it rises at any old hour; and frequently the debates which are best and most characteristic take place after midnight when only connoisseurs are abroad, nobody is in the Press Gallery and precious few, and those by mischance, are in the public gallery. The good old days are long gone by – by which I mean over a century gone by – when the House continued any debate so long as one single member was still rising to speak and disciplined itself by shouting 'Divide, divide' when it was bored to death and wanted to come to a decision in the voting lobbies. Nevertheless the House to this day has no timetable and no unalterable hours – for a single but important reason. If the House had a stopping time as well as a starting time, one of two things, both unacceptable, would happen: either the government would always get its business, or the government would never get its business. Finishing with a vote at a fixed hour means that the government need not debate but only needs to watch the clock. On the other hand, finishing without a vote at a fixed hour would mean that the House continued to talk, which is itself a negation of parliamentary debate because, as the victor of Torres Vedras used to say, 'The Queen's government must be carried on,' and Parliament is there to debate it while it gets carried on.

My affectionate description of the home from which I am forever exiled has set the scene for my central assertion about British government. If it is a democracy, it is not a democracy as others are: it is a democracy because it is government under debate in the House of Commons ... It is debate which holds government to account or, to put the matter less pompously, forces government to make sense – if it can. For hour after hour or, if the subject is legislation, in detailed debate after detailed debate, ministers have to prove, if they can, the truth and the common sense about what they are doing or proposing. In the end, they and the whole House know what to make of it all; and because the House of Commons knows what to make of it all, the people outside also get to know. That is the real restraint upon what government can do. That is the inner meaning – I almost said 'the private meaning' – of British democracy; for it is distinctively a parliamentary democracy ... Government upon advice is the secret which has enabled the British to retain intact through so many vicissitudes the monarchy which remains the focus of national loyalty as well as the dynamo by which the machinery of the state is driven.[†]

This speech was delivered three years after Powell ceased to be a Member of Parliament. I was reminded, by the reference in it to Members of Parliament being equal and having no fixed place, of my first encounter with Enoch in 1983 as a newly elected Conservative MP. Like all new boys I had no desk and was forced to perch in the library in order to deal with my constituency correspondence. As I worked away at a table towards the back of the room I was interrupted by the most infernal racket as books were slammed on the table accompanied by deep sighs of irritation. I looked up to discover to my surprise that the culprit was Enoch Powell. As he retreated I asked a colleague if he was always so noisy. 'No,' he replied. 'It's just that you are sitting in his seat!' Horrified, I leapt up and chased after him. I apologised for occupying his place and pleaded ignorance in my defence. Powell immediately chastised me: 'My boy, there are no special seats for anyone in this

† Paper delivered 8 May 1990, Oporto.

parliament. We are all equals here and must be treated as such.' He paused and then said with a smile: 'But I should be greatly obliged if you do not sit there again.'

Powell himself describes his reflections on Parliament as an 'affectionate description', and he can be excused for doing so. If his first wish was that he should have been killed in the war, his second was that he should have died a member of the House of Commons. He was disappointed in both and there is a sense, therefore, that the rest of his life after 1987 was spent in 'exile'. But of greater significance is that this description, which today appears so idealistic and 'belonging to a different world', would have been shared by virtually every Member of Parliament up until the decision to join the Common Market in 1972.

The enactment of the European Communities Act of 1972 was a watershed. It would not be true to say that all that has followed since was consequent upon Britain joining the European Union. No doubt, there would have been pressure for many of the changes anyway. But the House of Commons would have had more self-confidence to question and challenge these changes had it remained 'sovereign' in the way Powell understood.

Many of the attributes of Parliament which Powell took for granted or upheld as unique have been swept away in a tide of so-called modernisation. There is no doubt that the new hours of business in the House of Commons and the guillotining of all Bills (despite a manifesto promise by the Conservatives to end that practice) have removed the crucial weapon of time from both the official opposition and every backbench Member of Parliament. The increasing interference from the centre by political parties in the selection process in constituencies and the vendetta against outside interests has undermined the independence of MPs and helped to create a new class of professional politicians. The result has been a shift of power away from Parliament to the executive, a process magnified by the appointment of excessive numbers of MPs to payroll positions as junior ministers and PPSs. Vast tracts of legislation now reach the House of Lords which have not even been discussed by a House of Commons which no longer seems capable of doing its job.

Powell's emphasis on the physical layout of the Commons chamber is important. One can imagine how foreign it must be to some ears to be told that 'the essential work of the House of Commons is talking.' This is certainly anathema to the modern breed of MP whose ambition is to become a minister as soon as possible in order to take executive action. But if the House of Commons were ever to succumb to adopting the physical layout of the Scottish or European Parliaments – if the adversarial benches were to be removed, if there were to be a podium for speakers, if voting could take place electronically without any need for the MP to be present or to mix with his fellow MPs – then it would not be long before Parliament forgot entirely the oratory 'as might be heard from a man exhorting or admonishing a group of his companions'.

The fact that the House of Commons has voluntarily renounced so many of the powers and procedures described by Powell above presented him during his lifetime with a mounting dilemma. The House of Commons had behaved in a way which he believed to be inconceivable. And while it is true, as Powell pointed out, that the legislation which a Parliament had been persuaded to pass could be repealed by that same or future parliaments, there is little denying that the authority of the current House of Commons is a pale shadow of the Parliament which Powell first joined as an MP in 1950, or even of the one he left in 1987.

I empathise with this sense of regret. A few years after I left the House of Commons in 1997 a taxi driver, who recognised me, asked as we drove past Barry's magnificent building if I missed it. I replied by stealing some lines from my friend Eric Forth MP. I said the place I missed no longer exists. My puzzled driver fell silent, no doubt concluding I had lost my marbles.

Powell explained how this came about by identifying three epoch-breaking events which 'quite suddenly, after the Second World War, 400 years on from the Henrician declaration of independence', caused the beginning of what he considered a collapse of authority. As Powell said: 'At first what was happening was scarcely noticed; but after a generation the cumulative revolution that has occurred is indisputable and imposing. What for four centuries was literally unthinkable has already become commonplace.'[†]

† A paper read to the Carlisle Club, Peterhouse, Cambridge, 24 May 1980.

Powell listed these events as follows. First, Parliament agreed in 1946 that, from that moment, any change in the law which was necessary to comply with a mandatory resolution of the United Nations could take place through an Order in Council. Powell maintained that allowing such potentially large changes in the law to take effect with virtually no parliamentary process or control whatever – other than having to be 'laid' before Parliament – should never have been approved. Then, in 1951, 'Parliament provided, by ratifying the European Convention on Human Rights without debate, that both the Crown itself and any of its subjects within the realm, corporate or personal, could be arraigned and judged before an external court, which could give orders accordingly.' Finally, in 1972 'the Crown in Parliament made a comprehensive surrender to an external power of all the aspects of sovereignty, domestic and foreign, from the right to conclude treaties to the right to tax, from the right to make laws to the right to judge causes.' Powell continued: '"Authority", it is said, "deserts a dying king". It certainly deserts an abdicating king.'[†]

Ironically, one of the few battles which Powell won to maintain the supremacy of the House of Commons has resurrected itself in today's proposals to replace the House of Lords with an elected second chamber. Powell believed he had seen off this threat when, in 1968, he and Michael Foot demonstrated that any attempt to strengthen the House of Lords must in turn lead to a diminution of the powers of the House of Commons. But, as Powell pointed out on more than one occasion, 'it is a sad truth of humanity that each generation has to make the same mistakes as its fathers and learn the same lessons equally painfully.'[‡] The House of Lords had a special place in Powell's heart, and he is the author of an authoritative and highly scholarly history of the institution. But as a politician, his main objection to reform was based on the unshakable belief that it was impossible to increase the democratic legitimacy of the House of Lords without posing a mortal threat to the House of Commons.

[†] A paper read to the Carlisle Club, Peterhouse, Cambridge, 24 May 1980.
[‡] Ibid.

Powell argued that the House of Lords 'is an integral part of Parliament simply because that is how Parliament evolved, and its powers, like those of the House of Commons, derive not from a theory but from precedent'.[†] True, the House of Lords underwent radical change in the twentieth century. It lost all control over fiscal matters in 1911, and under the same Act lost its co-equal power to reject Bills originating in the House of Commons, retaining only the power to delay for a period of years. In 1958, the Crown was given the right to create new peers which were not hereditary but for one lifetime only; and in 1963, hereditary peers were given the right to renounce their peerages for their own lifetime and so become eligible for election to the House of Commons. But however much Powell deplored these changes (with the possible exception of those in 1911), they did not in his view destroy the essence of the institution. He would not have been able to have said the same had he lived a little longer. Powell was not alive to witness in 1999 the abolition of the right of 600 hereditary peers to belong to the House of Lords, leaving ninety-two hereditaries to remain there until long-term reform is completed. But it is not hard to deduce what he would have thought. His most important objection to a 'democratic' second chamber was the threat it posed to the first:

> There can be no elective second chamber in the legislature of a unitary state. Wherever elective second chambers exist, they exist in federal states, where one chamber represents the component parts as such, and the other chamber represents the whole population, as such. The classic case is the United States. The proposition is axiomatic, because it is self-evident that there cannot be two alternative equally valid representations of the same electorate. If one is more valid than the other, they cannot co-exist: for where a more valid representation exists, there is no justification for paying attention to a less valid representation.
>
> A few simple theorems are sufficient. Suppose, in a unitary state like the UK, one chamber is elected by a simple majority (like the House of Commons) and the other chamber by some variety of

---

† Oporto, 8 May 1990.

proportional representation. Which is then to prevail? The simple majority chamber says: 'We represent the people and cannot be gainsaid.' The proportional representation chamber says: 'No, it is we who represent the people: you are only a caricature and distortion.' One chamber must destroy the other, and no constitutional device or convention will avert that. One could not, for example, say that some issues should be decided by an inaccurately representative body and others by an accurately representative body. In any case, the new-fangled body would claim, with invincible logic, that unless their form of representation was superior, it would not have been created.

Again, suppose that one chamber is elected all at once, and the other – whether or not upon the same electoral method – at different dates or piecemeal. The more recent representation of the public must prevail over the less recent, since otherwise one would have to argue that the electorate is always wrong now but was right previously, which leads inexorably to the conclusion that the electorate is always wrong, which, as Browning observes in another connection, 'may not be'. All this in a unitary state. Of course in a federal state, where the units are represented and entrenched as such, no logical difficulty arises over their representation being constituted upon a different time-scale from the representation of the population as a whole.

It follows that all attempts to 'reform' – as the phrase is – the House of Lords on a representative basis are foredoomed as inherently impracticable. Any alternatives to election resolve themselves into some form of nomination; and needless to say, an infinite number of nominators – ranging from the Prime Minister to the district councils or the General Synod of the Church of England or a combination of some or all of them – is available. They all fall down not so much upon the evident risk that such a body becomes the 'poodle' of a party or a person as upon the obsolescent or obsolete membership in which they result – incurring, in even acuter form, those absurdities of staggered election which we have just looked at. If one wants a body nominated by past political power, one has got it already in a House of Lords produced by 500 years of political history. These were in fact the reasons why the reform of the Upper House put forward in 1968–69 by both front benches was shipwrecked by gales of mirth upon the hidden reefs of absurdity and had to be ignominiously withdrawn by its authors.[†]

Powell believed that any reform of the composition of the House of Lords was doomed to failure. His view was that 'the justification of the House of Lords is its essential difference from the House of Commons and even – if it is permissible to be jocular – its indefensibility.'[‡] There are some who might concur with many of Powell's onslaughts against reforming the composition of the House of the Lords while still maintaining that the current situation is indefensible and unsustainable. Such people argue that too much attention has been given to the composition of the House, and not enough to its powers and what it is there to do. They imply that if only the House of Lords could be prevented from seriously delaying or obstructing the will of the House of Commons there would be less concern over how it was elected or appointed. In short, they would argue that a revising chamber with specified powers would avoid many of the current anxieties over its lack of democratic legitimacy. Powell was aware of this argument, but dismissed it:

> I am not therefore going to waste your time with a debating society argument about a revising chamber, because if 'revision' means anything more than correcting misprints and tidying up drafts – which it does not need a House of Parliament to do – there has to be the power to resist and to prevail, which we have seen is not available.[§]

There is no escaping the fact that Powell would have much preferred the abolition of the House of Lords to any plans to replace it with something different. But this does not mean that he believed there were no practical advantages to be had from having the upper house. As he put it: 'The House of Lords is a political convenience for all governments, which would be lost if it could be reformed or if it were to be abolished. Its irrationality gives it that precise combination of selective and limited effectiveness with ultimate impotence

---

† Leicester, 16 May 1980.
‡ 8 May 1990.
§ Leicester, 16 May 1980.

which is indispensable.'† On another occasion, he elaborated in
more detail on exactly how this 'convenience' worked in practice:

Nothing is more handy for those engaged in political management,
otherwise known as the art of governing, than a goodly reservoir of
patronage, a pocketful of baubles by the description of which the
wheels of government can be greased. Thanks to the English virtue
of snobbery, we enjoy in this country the blessings, unknown across
the Atlantic, of inexpensive patronage. Of that patronage there is no
source more convenient or plentiful than is afforded by a prescriptive
upper house of the legislature. When knighthoods for long, laborious
and obedient service in the lower house have been devalued in one
of the main political parties and are eschewed on principle in the
other, the attraction which a peerage offers of honourable retirement
or honorific dismissal is precious indeed. Wherever else the abolition
of hereditary privilege is favoured, there is one quarter which can be
relied upon to defend it. That is the whips' offices, upon whom falls,
in government and in opposition equally, the duty of securing attend-
ance and organising support whenever the respective leaderships
stand in need of it. For a prescriptive second chamber of Parliament
patronage is a recommendation not to be despised or overlooked.

A second legislative chamber has other charms. Governments in
being and governments in waiting have an invincible propensity to
overload themselves with commitments to legislate, and to legislate
upon novel and complex subjects. From this propensity flow two
pressing requirements. One is an unslakable thirst for legislative
time. Take no notice of contemporary noises – they emanate from
all newly elected parliaments – which call for government business to be timetabled so as to economise the available time. That
is a stampede which comes to a speedy halt as soon as the newly
arrived innocents discover that armed with a timetable (including a
limited working day), government always gets its way or else never
gets its way – neither of which outcomes is manifestly acceptable.
Parliamentary debate, by definition and necessity, is open-ended
debate. There is therefore no easy device for extracting more legislative time from the pint pot of a parliamentary session; and in this

† Leicester, 16 May 1980.

predicament there presents itself to those who govern or aspire to government the delightful relief of being able to initiate and process legislation in an alternative chamber to the House of Commons, a chamber moreover which the deteriorating physical condition of its members and the absence of party rancour produced by the extinction of political ambition predisposes to eschew pertinacious and wearying opposition ...

Pressure to legislate produces further inconveniences for governments. In their haste and eagerness they are liable, whether legislating against killer dogs or upon other like subjects which currently cause excitement, to lay before the House of Commons proposals which presently turn out to be nonsensical or impracticable. If there has ever existed a minister who enjoyed admitting that he had introduced an absurd or unworkable Bill, I am sorry to say that I fail to recall him. This being so, a second legislative chamber enables the blemishes, if possible, to be removed with the minimum of publicity and embarrassment.

The second legislative chamber might even come in handy for defeating government legislation ... Governments, particularly governments of a radical or reforming tendency, can come into office committed to legislation which either they do not really want or which they presently discover to be undesirable. What to do? Thank heaven if there stands ready a murderer whom they can disavow or over whom they have no visible means of control. And what could fit that specification better than an independent legislative chamber?

Since the days of the old Liberal Party we have been accustomed to hear much about the House of Lords being the poodle of Conservative administrations, so much that we have overlooked the more interesting fact that the House of Lords is the patent incinerator of a radical government. To serve this purpose, however, it must be possible to heap upon it all the familiar terms of abuse: non-elected, undemocratic, obsolete; it needs to be. A 'don't-blame-us-for-what-it-does-we-are-going-to-reform-or-abolish-it-only-we-have-not-got-time-just-at-the-moment' legislative chamber is just the job. The horrid secret is that the vested interest in an allegedly indefensible second chamber is the vested interest of the Labour Party, whom alone it enables Cronos-like to destroy its own unwelcome offspring. If anybody has wondered how the House of

Lords survived so many radical administrations which came and
went and came and went, let him wonder no more.[†]

I must confess that, having been a member of the House of Lords
now for thirteen years, I could not adopt quite such a utilitarian,
even cynical, justification for its existence. Of course it is true that
the House of Lords provides any government with an alternative
place to start and amend legislation. No doubt, it provides a useful
way of exercising patronage. But despite the almost total removal
of the hereditary peers, and despite the ever-growing number of
appointed peers by the government of the day, the current House
of Lords still manages to retain some of the best qualities of the
old House of Commons. We do more than simply 'revise': we can
cause any government to rethink seriously its legislative intent; as
members we still retain a spirit of independence and experience
denied our counterparts in the House of Commons; and we are still
able to deploy the weapon of 'time' although the executive are now
beginning to attempt to undermine that. Even the small hereditary
element provides a long-stop to what otherwise would be a totally
appointed House. Hence, I wouldn't agree with Powell if he were
to argue today that it would be better if the current House of Lords
was abolished, or didn't exist in its present form.

But Powell was surely right in warning that there is a limit to how
much further the House of Lords can be reformed without preferring its abolition, and the question today is whether the House of
Lords can survive the reforming zeal of a coalition government.
Depressingly, it is unlikely that today's ministers would understand,
let alone agree with, Powell's contention that something which
is theoretically 'indefensible', but which works in practice, should
remain in existence. Indeed, the greater probability is that they will
dismiss such arguments without even a moment's thought on the
grounds that they belong 'to a different world' from the one they live
in. But this merely serves to emphasise the constitutional illiteracy and
institutional blindness of many members of the new political class.
They do not confront, they simply ignore the arguments expressed by
their predecessors – Powell and Foot among them – which are still

---

[†] University College, Oxford, 20 September 1992.

valid today. Powell's faith in the House of Commons to resist such innovations was shown to be unrealistic and fanciful; but that does not mean that the arguments he deployed have been confounded.

And the same is true concerning Powell's arguments on devolution, and how this relates to today's debate on Scottish independence and 'devo-max'. Yet again, for a brief moment, Powell might have thought he had helped to quash the argument when, in 1979, the referendum in Scotland failed to achieve the required majority for establishing the Scottish Assembly under the 1978 Scotland Act. In January 1976, he had described 'devolution' as a manifestation of 'loss of pride, hope and faith in the United Kingdom which is destroying the union'.[†] But it was not long before the issue resurrected itself in a different form and in a way which Powell had long associated with the House of Lords, namely that 'there can be no elective second chamber in the legislature of a unitary state.' His argument was that 'parliamentary devolution within a state must be applied to all parts or to none; in other words, it implies a federal state, and is impractical in a unitary state.'[‡]

For some advocates of devolution, this wouldn't necessarily be a bad thing. But the constitutional implications are enormous, which is why for constitutionalists like Powell, Scottish independence would be infinitely preferable to further legislative devolution. It is not only because Powell had a special place for England since 'England alone found the way to transmute its feudal assembly into a matchless instrument of free government, which the rest of the world vainly aspire to imitate.'[§] More importantly, as has been discovered so often in the past, the West Lothian question is incapable of being answered satisfactorily. Lord Irvine of Lairg, the former Lord Chancellor, mentor to Tony Blair and advocate of devolution, famously opined that the best answer to the question was not to ask it.

> The devolution debate will be based upon a proposition no less objectively false than to assert that two and two make five. It is the proposition that it is possible to establish one or more local parliaments within the

---

† Brighton, 6 January 1976.
‡ Leicester, 16 May 1980.
§ St George's Dinner of the Honourable Artillery Company, 21 April 1988.

unitary parliamentary state known as the United Kingdom ... The simplest way to prove that two and two make four ... is to consider how the electorate of the regions endowed with their local parliaments would be represented in the parliament of the unitary state.

There are four possible answers, and every one of them is incompatible with the continued existence of the unitary state. One possible answer is that these electorates would not be represented at all. This is clearly ruled out unless all political power is to be transferred to the new assemblies, in which case the state itself has been dissolved; for as long as the parliament of the whole state exercises any powers at all, the inhabitants of every part of it must plainly be represented there. The second possible answer is that the inhabitants of the regions would continue to be represented fully in the parliament of the unitary state. This is indeed the promise which has been officially made, even before the impending debate commences, to the would-be electorates of legislative assemblies in Scotland and Wales. But it is clearly unsustainable; and the fact of being official does not make it any less unsustainable. If the Members of Parliament from these regions could participate in legislating upon subjects for which they were not responsible to their constituents and upon which the representatives of their constituents were legislating in their own assemblies, that would be intolerable; for their participation could not merely be decisive on the legislation on those subjects, it could even decide the political complexion of the majority in the parliament and consequently the complexion of the overall government – and that, perhaps, after an election which had turned largely upon the very subjects on which the local assemblies were autonomous.

This, of course, is precisely the situation which the United Kingdom faces at the moment. It is entirely possible that a Scottish referendum in favour of independence could be followed by a general election in which the overall result is determined by Scottish MPs – MPs who represent that part of the nation which has just declared itself independent! The prescience of Powell's analysis can hardly be exaggerated. He continued:

But there is no half-way house or compromise either: for consider now the third and fourth possible answers. The third is that the electorates of the regions in question would be less than fully represented in the parliament of the whole state. But reduced representation does not solve the problem of irresponsible participation in other people's business. In addition it is illogical, because the fact that, say, half the subjects of government have been transferred is no reason for half as many members voting on all subjects, both transferred and non-transferred. This leads to the last despairing suggestion, possibility number four, that the representatives from the regions having their own assemblies should speak and vote upon non-transferred subjects only. Even this, however, will not do; for, apart from the abomination of creating first-class members and second-class members of the same parliament, no line of demarcation can be drawn in a unitary state between one set of subjects and another – for example, between social subjects and economic subjects, or between domestic subjects and external subjects. As Members of Parliament know very well and are never allowed to forget, a debate on defence is also a debate on education. The pursuit of this line of thought leads, in fact, to entrenched separation of functions between the overall parliament and the subordinate parliaments – in a word, to changing the unitary state into a federal state.†

Here again, Powell's mistake – if it be a mistake – was his disbelief that the consequences of creating a Scottish Parliament and Welsh Assembly in 1998 would be tolerated by the House of Commons. In this he was wrong; but his predictions of the actual consequences have been vindicated. Scottish and Welsh MPs are allowed to vote upon issues only affecting England. The composition of the United Kingdom government could theoretically be decided by the number of Scottish MPs. To the extent that it is voluntary, the 'abomination' of first- and second-class members of Parliament now exists. All of this was to be expected. All that Powell did *not* expect was that Parliament would agree to live with the proposition which he described as 'objectively false'.

Neither would he be surprised that legislative devolution has failed to satisfy the appetite for more. It is for this reason that while Powell would have much preferred the union to have been maintained, there is little doubt that, having reached this point, Powell

---

† City Conservative Forum, 12 November 1975.

would favour outright independence to any further attempts to extend legislative devolution. He would regard both England and Scotland as impoverished should the Union break up; but from an English standpoint he would see this as a preferable outcome to devolving even more powers to an executive parliament in Scotland. However much he might have regretted it, he never denied the possibility that Scotland could prefer to be independent – especially once the House of Commons had surrendered so many of its powers to the European Union – and he would not have supported resistance to this demand if democratically expressed.

In exactly the same way that he entered politics to protect the Empire but was the first to acknowledge that it had passed away, he would have come to terms with the dissolution of the United Kingdom, especially if this were the only way of preserving the authority of the House of Commons. And for avoidance of doubt, this does not mean that he would have supported an English parliament in a federal structure. The state might be smaller, but the authority of the House of Commons within that smaller state would have remained intact if Powell were here to argue his case, and win the argument, today.

When one takes the European Union, the reform of the House of Lords and legislative devolution together, it becomes clear that Powell was fighting a rear-guard action on the constitution throughout his entire parliamentary career. The final area where, unfortunately, his warnings were not heeded concerns the judiciary, and the primacy of British over foreign courts. This impinged upon the issue of 'human rights', as Powell sought to explain:

> 'Rights' concern what may be claimed by an individual as against the rest of the members of the society to which he belongs and is accorded to him by them. They imply, moreover, that such claims are enforceable by or through the authority which the particular society collectively acknowledges. 'Rights' in isolation from any particular society and 'rights' which are not enforceable in a particular society elude the grasp of my mind.[†]

---

† Cardiff, 2 December 1988.

In other words, Powell was second to none in acknowledging the importance of a citizen's 'rights', especially as guardians against injustice and the abuse of power: but he believed equally strongly that it was Parliament's and the judiciary's job to offer this protection.

The problem is that this is another area where Parliament has forfeited yet another constitutional principle which Powell held dear – that no person should be tried by an external court for a crime committed within the jurisdiction of the United Kingdom. Powell was adamantly opposed to 'the mistaken notion of something envisaged as an international offence, whereby crimes committed in one jurisdiction would become triable and punishable in another'.[†] He was especially concerned that crimes relating to terrorism or drugs would be used as an excuse to break with the British judicial inheritance:

> We obey our laws because we feel them to be *our* laws; we submit to be governed by our institutions because we feel them to be *our* institutions. They are identified with us, intuitively and emotionally, because we are, we think, part and parcel of them and they of us ...
>
> It is true that evidence to support or rebut an accusation is most reliably to be found where the alleged offence was committed: justice belongs at the location of offence. But that logic does not get to the heart of jurisdiction. A court is acknowledged, a judge is acknowledged, the verdict of a jury is acknowledged, because the person judged is judged by his own. In the old phrase, he has 'put himself upon the country'. That is why there is so close an affinity between jurisdiction and allegiance, the term which denotes the natural and spontaneous impulse to obey. It was an unhappy hour when in 1948 we allowed our citizenship to be severed from our allegiance; and we have been made to suffer severely for the mistake. The voice of the tempter is now being raised to persuade us to divorce justice from jurisdiction, and jurisdiction from allegiance. That way lies the substitution of force for affection, and the breaking of the invisible bond that holds human society together.[‡]

---

† Orpington, 17 November 1989.
‡ Orpington, 17 November 1989.

I return to my original question as to whether the constitutional changes have gone so far as to be incapable of reversal. On one level, Powell's description of the House of Commons may strike today's generation as hopelessly romantic and sentimental. His arguments rest upon assumptions concerning honour, convention and tradition, which today find little echo in the hearts of today's 'establishment'. And this is not just true of politics. One sees the same in the City of London, in business and in the media. Nobody can be trusted to regulate themselves, not least the House of Commons.

But for Powell, the House of Commons was unique. The sovereignty of Parliament was not for Powell an abstract concept. It was the practical realisation of the right of this country to be governed by its own laws, in its own courts. Powell's obsession was to demonstrate how even a piecemeal constitutional reform, seemingly attractive in itself, could destroy the whole edifice upon which this country's liberties are based if the changes were not of an evolutionary character. Powell's fundamental error was to assume that the House of Commons would uphold its sacred duty.

Perhaps he was more a victim of 'wishful thinking' than a miscalculation of substance. Powell was not blind to the possibility that he was on the losing side of the argument. He himself concluded in 1990 that he had 'been living the life of an Ishmael in British politics since 1972'. Seen from today's perspective, it is not so much as if a new political generation has knowingly and deliberately broken with all the constitutional principles and assumptions upon which Powell based his thinking. It is not that constitutional changes have proved him incorrect. On the contrary, most of his predictions on devolution, Europe and parliamentary reform have been vindicated. He was right to identify the consequences of the decisions which he opposed. But what he couldn't face up to was the possibility that the House of Commons wouldn't care – that it would all be given up, and that only a small minority, often dismissed as a 'weird' or 'eccentric' minority, would persist in their warnings and objections.

My question was whether Powell's defence of the constitution is 'not merely not accomplished, but seems to belong to a different world from the one he lives in'. I think Enoch Powell answered it himself in a speech in Portugal in 1990. Let us hope he is right.

Like all human institutions, it [the state] too is mortal. An observer watching the behaviour and listening to the language of British politicians since 1972, behaviour which, to put it at the very lowest, has been indulgently treated by the public and the electorate, would have been reasonably entitled to conclude that the British had become disenchanted with the unique form of government which continues to distinguish them from their continental contemporaries and had resolved to abandon parliamentary self-government under an unwritten constitution in order to be embraced by a single state – and that a unitary, not a federal state – comprising western Europe, the Iberian peninsula and Greece and live forever under treaties interpreted by the European Court. I am not the person best qualified to advise you whether that judgement would be premature, because my own obstinate refusal to countenance the abandonment of parliamentary self-government by the United Kingdom has resulted in my living the life of an Ishmael in British politics since 1972.

I will therefore do no more than leave you with some cautionary words of a general character. Nations do tend to behave remarkably like themselves and to revert to past habits even after appearing to have departed from them for sometimes lengthy periods. The most reliable indication of a nation's future behaviour is its history. It would be an exaggeration no doubt, but a venial exaggeration, to say that the history of Britain is the history of British parliamentary self-government.[†]

---

† Lisbon, 7 May 1990.

The Role of Government and the State of the Economy

Simon Heffer

When Milton Friedman won the Nobel Prize in Economics in 1976 Enoch Powell observed, only half in jest, that he should have had half of it. Powell felt, with some reason, that he had put monetarism into practice twenty or so years before Friedman expounded his theory, and in one of the world's leading economies. In 1957, when Powell was Financial Secretary to the Treasury – then the deputy position to the Chancellor of the Exchequer – he had worked out that inflation was caused by expanding the money supply at a rate faster than that of inflation and growth combined. Sadly for him, the Prime Minister of the day, Harold Macmillan, did not agree with him, and he and his two fellow Treasury ministers – Peter Thorneycroft, the Chancellor, and Nigel Birch, the Economic Secretary – all resigned when, in January 1958, Macmillan persuaded the Cabinet to refuse to endorse a Treasury policy of spending cuts at a time when higher inflation was threatened.

Macmillan had taken the lead in refusing to agree to a further cut of £50 million in public spending, and had carried a largely cowardly and economically illiterate Cabinet with him by raising political fears about the effect of cuts on certain vulnerable groups in the electorate. He was also supported by Sir Roger Makins, the Permanent Secretary to the Treasury, whose appointment he had secured while Chancellor of the Exchequer, even though Makins was a lifelong diplomat with no feeling for, or interest in, economics. Macmillan had also been egged on by his unofficial economic adviser, Roy Harrod, an Oxford don who subsequently wrote a hagiographical biography of his hero, John Maynard Keynes. Macmillan too was an instinctive Keynesian – believing in a creed of expansionist and inflationary economics diametrically opposed to Powell's austere philosophy – and in Harrod he found explicit support for his prejudices, beefed up by Harrod's undoubted intellect. Harrod told him that no one had believed the Powell view of economics 'since 1908'. This was an exaggeration, but one that the style-obsessed Macmillan found it easy to swallow. It was always easier for Macmillan to go with the cautious option rather than the radical, particularly if the former course of action helped avoid a confrontation.

The part of Powell's political life in which he devoted a great deal of time, thought and energy to economic questions falls into four unequal sections. First, there is the Treasury episode of 1957–8, mentioned above. Then there is his economic thought on the back benches or in opposition between 1958 and 1960, and from 1963 onwards, mostly expressed in the Friday night and Saturday lunchtime speeches he would deliver to Conservative associations and businessmen's groups, but also in set-piece speeches in the House of Commons. This campaigning phase of his economic policy subdivides into three parts. When on the back benches, before his return to office as Minister of Health, Powell was circumspect in what he said and did, not least because he wished to return to office. His interventions were limited, but he did give further proof of his ability to think originally when he published *Saving in a Free Society* in 1960. That work was produced in collaboration with the Institute of Economic Affairs, which had been founded only three years earlier and had already struck out in the anti-statist, low-spending direction disparaged by Harrod and supposedly extinct for half a century.

The second subdivision runs from 1963 to 1970. For the first year he was a backbencher and, in the run-up to the 1964 election, he argued for lower taxes and spending and a retreat by the state from what had become its expanded function in the post-war period. Between 1964 and 1968, when he served as a member of the shadow Cabinet, he concentrated on attacking what he saw as the heretical policies of the Wilson government, notably the incomes policy they designed to curb inflation. This was difficult for the Conservative Party, because Powell was attacking a policy they believed in – or claimed to believe in. Ted Heath, leader after 1965, strongly supported an incomes policy. Since Powell believed that only controlling the supply of money could control inflation, he argued that incomes policies were irrelevant and damaging. His refusal to follow Heath's line on this was one of the things that contributed to Heath's determination to sack him after the so-called 'Rivers of Blood' speech in April 1968. The climax of this phase of Powell's economic thought came in his 'Morecambe Budget', outlined at the Lancashire coastal resort in October 1968. He delivered it a few miles from the site of the Conservative Party conference, and on the night before Heath was about to make his leader's speech, which Powell successfully and comprehensively overshadowed.

The third and final subdivision runs from 1970 to 1974, and was concerned with Powell's critique of Heath's statist and social-ist economic policies. When Wilson called the election for June 1970 the Conservative Party opposed him on an essentially free-market manifesto, cobbled together at a meeting early in 1970 at the Selsdon Park Hotel in Surrey. This introduced the party's brief 'Selsdon man' phase. Powell was dismayed, even distraught, when Heath won the election against the odds. When Heath, in the face of economic adversity, decided to reverse his previous free-market precepts and use interventionist tactics (including a ludicrously bureaucratic incomes policy) to try to rev the economy up, Powell went for him, relentlessly and ultimately (for Heath) fatally, over a period of nearly two years. His vindication was very public, and contributed to Heath's defeat in 1974. The points he proved were taken on board by the Thatcher administration, and formed the bedrock of the economic policy after 1979, and until the mistaken shadowing of the Deutschmark after 1987.

I shall examine the course of Powell's economic policy in detail. First, it is worth considering where he acquired his ideas from. He had read Adam Smith and imbibed some of them from there. He also claimed simply to have thought about the nature of profound economic questions, notably the true cause of inflation, and used his powers of logic to arrive at his 'monetarist' policy. But although, as he often put it, 'born a Tory', his Toryism was about his social outlook and his essentially conservative regard for institutions. In all other respects he was an economic liberal. He would have been with Cobden and Bright against the Corn Laws, and with Gladstone in trying to reduce and abolish income tax. Bright was for some years

MP for Birmingham, where Powell was born and grew up, and Powell also admired the commercial championship exercised by Joe Chamberlain, though he did not endorse Chamberlain's later protectionist ideas. Powell's instinctive economics was an extension of his upbringing and his native instincts, and a practical policy fitted to a city that had been the workshop of the world. Had Powell become Chancellor, it is likely the closest historical parallel with him would have been Gladstone.

Powell was appointed to the Treasury when Macmillan became Prime Minister in January 1957. Each of the three ministers in the team he joined had distinctive talents. Peter Thorneycroft, as Chancellor, was a consummate politician, untroubled in large part by ideas or intellectual analysis. Nigel Birch, the Economic Secretary, had made a fortune before the war as a stockbroker and brought enormous practical experience of finance, and a head even harder than Powell's. Powell was the intellectual motor of the department, and presented an awesome challenge to Keynesian-schooled civil servants who had driven policy in the same direction for decades. In the aftermath of Suez the economy was under attack, and sterling in trouble. In September 1957, to counteract a mounting crisis, Thorneycroft raised the Bank rate by 2 percentage points from 5 to 7 per cent. The policing had been driven by Powell, who saw it as necessary to choke off excessive demand, which was causing inflation. It deeply unsettled the rest of the Cabinet, who had hoped the Suez debacle would be consequence free for the electorate. The effect of higher interest rates on businesses and homeowners was not something the Conservative Party wished to have to be associated with.

Inflation remained a serious problem even after the rise in the Bank rate. In a proposed, but deleted, introductory paragraph to a speech delivered in Newcastle on 29 November 1957, Powell spoke of the 'present phase' of the inflation Britain was experiencing as having been 'marked by special attention to the supply of money'. We can only conjecture why Powell crossed this paragraph out: perhaps he considered it too technical for his audience. Perhaps the rhetoric was considered by Thorneycroft to have been provocative, given Macmillan's firm view that the supply of money was an irrelevant consideration. It does, however, prove exactly what his thinking was at the time of the great debate in government about public spending, and it shows what ideas were current in the debate within the Treasury, and how Powell was influencing the other two ministers.

Powell then, however, made the same point more obliquely. 'There are three main classes of Exchequer commitment: current expenditure, investment financed by the Exchequer, and maturing debt. Unless all three are met – if not more than met – by taxation or by non-inflationary borrowing – inflation is promoted.' He also made it clear, in Gladstonian fashion, that he wanted taxation reduced, something that was 'the Government's declared intention'. He said that since there was a limit to the debt that could be sold, savings had to be made in either investment or expenditure, or quite probably both.

He felt that there was a chronic failure (and he felt this throughout his career) on the part of politicians to find all the savings and spending reductions that were possible: too many MPs liked to see their respective client groups looked after, or bribed with taxpayers' money. He pointed out that it was his job, as Financial Secretary, to look for such savings. He knew he was up against 'the great organs of public opinion' that were 'agitating' for more public expenditure. He wished to challenge and scrutinise every additional demand for public spending, as well as scrutinising those already being met. This would, over the next few weeks, be the point of contention between his department and the rest of the Cabinet, and he would be deaf to the appeals made to the Treasury to guarantee certain areas of spending – deaf to the point where the three ministers had to resign.

For Powell the management of the economy was a moral issue. The government not only set the rates of taxation that deprived people of part of their earnings. It also managed the economy generally, and the nature of its macroeconomic management would affect the value of the currency. A currency dwindling in power because of the ravages of inflation, and depreciating on the foreign exchanges because of both inflation and growing debt, had been weakened by a negligent government. This weakening was a betrayal of the public, and as a minister with some direct power over the issue Powell was determined to have no part of it. His two colleagues agreed with him, and they all went together in an act Macmillan glibly dismissed as 'a little local difficulty'. As a backbench MP in later years, or as an opposition spokesman, he would never let up on reminding those who controlled the supply of money that the debauching of the currency was down to them, and it was in their power to stop it.

For the two and a half years he was out of office between his resignation in January 1958 and his appointment as Minister of Health in July 1960 he behaved in the circumspect, and indeed circumscribed, way that people who wish to return to government must. His economic comments were scarce, and limited to philosophies already expressed during his time at the Treasury. He was coaxed out of this silence by his work on *Saving in a Free Society* for the Institute of Economic Affairs, published as he returned to office. It is a work of such technical abstruseness that it was hardly likely to excite the attentions of Macmillan, his whips, or his unintellectual Chancellor, Selwyn Lloyd. While Minister of Health – the job he did until resigning over the leadership change in October 1963 – he was bound by collective responsibility and did not advance an economic policy in public. Once freed from those shackles, he developed his policy widely.

Its starting point was always the supply of money, and how it affected the fundamentals of prosperity within the economy. He never stopped emphasising that the control of the supply of money was the responsibility of the government, and therefore was always subject to the execution of a political decision. In Powell's economic world view, the political alternatives were those of securing long-term benefit by following a policy of rectitude, or short-term gain by using money to bribe voters on certain issues.

New economic issues, beyond simply controlling the supply of money, came on to Powell's agenda once he was out of office in 1963, put there largely by the rhetoric of the Labour opposition, but also because of the sympathy some in the Conservative government had for Keynesian or socialist methods. Powell railed against the notion of economic planning, particularly the idea of five-year plans on the Soviet model. He had, for his time, a far more elevated and sophisticated view of market economics than most other politicians. Planning would, he argued consistently, be futile because it could not allow for the vagaries of human nature. It was pointless asking any company what it expected to be producing five years hence, because that depended upon the demand for its goods. And demand depended on the economic circumstances, and the will, of individuals; but in 1960s politics, run by technocrats like Heath and cynics like Wilson, individualism counted for very little, and markets, it was believed, could be 'planned'.

The other new target for Powell in the 1960s was the prices and income policy. This had been tried under the Conservative administration, including when Powell had been a member of it, and he had bitten his lip. Once the policy began to be pursued by a government of which he was neither a member nor a supporter he could say what he liked about it, and he did not hold back. The very idea that inflation would be reduced because the government ordered employers not to pay their staff more than a certain percentage in pay increases was absurd to Powell: he knew that inflation would only be reduced when the government stopped telling the Bank of England to increase the supply of money by a measure that was inflationary. Equally, he went against the grain of the Conservative union-bashing of the 1960s by saying that trade unions did not cause inflation by demanding large pay increases.

In October 1963, barely a week after he had left office, he used a speech in the constituency of the former Prime Minister, Harold Macmillan, to outline his vision of Toryism. Its message was, funda-mentally, 'trust the people'. The section on economics addressed the question of the supremacy of individual wishes in a free society, and is a clear statement of the Powell credo.

> The collective wisdom and the collective will of the nation resides not in any little Whitehall clique but in the whole mass of the people – in the producers, listening to the voice of the customer at home and abroad; in the savers and investors, using their eyes and their brains to lay out their resources to best advantage; in the consumers themselves, expressing through all the complex nervous system of the market their wishes, their needs, their expectations. In short, the true national plan is being made all the time by the very people and institutions which the intellectual arrogance of the socialist affects to despise.

Two months later, in an address to his own constituency party in Wolverhampton, he said: 'We have to ask our countrymen, quite simply, if they wish the future of their economy, their society, their country to be shaped by themselves or by the state.'

From this seed grew the whole liberal economic critique not just of Labour policies over the following seven years, but also of the supposedly Conservative economic policy that Heath followed – in, it seemed to Powell, emulation of the socialist ideal – from 1970 to 1974. Powell had seen the administration of which he had been a member, in 1961–2, introduce a capital gains tax (which he abhorred as a tax on risk and also as the second taxation of income, given that income had often been used for investment purposes); a national economic planning authority, which he regarded as self-evidently useless; an incomes policy, which he considered pointless; and regional planning, which he regarded as a damaging intervention in the market. He regarded all these things as having had a negative impact on investment and therefore on national growth and prosperity. But he had seen a Conservative government do these destructive things, and was determined to warn the party against making such intellectual and ideological mistakes in its economic policy again.

Yet Powell found himself heavily criticised, in 1964, when he ventured the opinion that the Conservative Party was a capitalist party. He said it was the system 'to which we owe our economic progress and our material well-being'. He could not understand the distaste with which some people who regarded themselves as Conservatives viewed capitalism.

Here is a nation who lives by capitalism; which by means of capitalism has achieved standards for its people exceeded only in one other country, the capitalist United States; which depends for its existence on satisfying the demands of customers throughout the world in competition with all and sundry. Here is a party engaged in a life-and-death struggle with political opponents who are pledged and dedicated to socialism and whose every policy is aimed at eliminating the processes of capitalism from our economy and our society. Yet the same nation and the same party will stop their ears and turn the other way if they hear mention of the very word 'capitalism'; and even the various synonyms or euphemisms – 'market economy', 'free

economy', 'competitive private enterprise' etc. – all share to a greater
or less degree in the same denigration.

Powell struggled to understand why capitalism should be a concept
to cause embarrassment, or even be used as a term of abuse. He
pondered that it might be because there was something nineteenth
century about the term – this was the era when attempts were
being made to demolish St Pancras station, and the Victorians
were deeply unfashionable whereas the command economy and
centralised planning were in some way 'modern'. He referred those
who felt difficult about the concept to look at West Germany,
then the economic miracle of the western world, and whose
successes had been entirely down to its having 'steadfastly and
almost pedantically held to capitalist principles' for the preceding
fifteen years.

While he regarded union pay demands as irrelevant to inflation,
he regarded the absence of individualism in collective bargaining as
a fraud on the people who paid subscriptions to trade unions:

> Millions of trades unions members want to believe that their
> subscriptions, their solidarity, their doughty leaders wring an annual
> rise in real wages from the flinty employers. They do not wish to
> know that similar or larger rises are being obtained silently and
> effortlessly by millions of other employees who have no unions
> and no collective bargaining. Their own employers could not long
> pay them either more or less than the marginal value of their services
> in the market.

The Wilson government set up a Department of Economic Affairs,
with the improbable figure of George Brown in charge of it,
precisely to carry out the intention of the economic plan of which
Powell was so contemptuous. History would prove Powell right:
all efforts at economic planning came to nothing. When Brown's
department sent questionnaires to businesses asking why they were
raising prices, Powell was outraged: he told entrepreneurs that the
only feasible response they could make to Brown was 'Mind your
own business'. He said that 'the behaviour of the government would
be intolerable even if what these gentlemen were saying about prices

were economic sense. As it is they are talking economic nonsense.'
Powell understood that a decision to raise prices was an effect of
the operation of the laws of supply and demand. It frustrated and
angered him that Labour seemed not to. All other attempts to
tell businesses to order their affairs according to what the government thought feasible or desirable, as opposed to what the market
ordained, he regarded as profoundly fatuous and dishonest.

The Wilson years saw considerable rises in public spending – 9 per
cent, or 5 per cent in real terms, in 1965–6. Powell branded this inflationary, and branded as ludicrous the assertion by the Chancellor,
Jim Callaghan, that national income would grow at such a rate
that the rise in public spending could be afforded. Powell knew
it would not – he was right – and that such incontinent spending would undermine the soundness of the economy. He was right
about that too, and Labour's policy of letting the country live far
beyond its means had as one of its consequences the devaluation of
September 1967.

Once Powell was dismissed from Heath's shadow Cabinet in the
spring of 1968, and seeing that there was no way back so long as Heath
was leader, he could, and did, take the gloves off in dealing with
economic policy. No longer bound by the prejudices and doctrines
of Heath's attachment to Keynesianism, Powell decided to outline
a comprehensive economic policy that would, he believed, enhance
the prosperity of the country. He advanced an alternative Budget,
with tax and spending policies radically different to those offered by
the incumbent Wilson administration, and to those contemplated
by Heath. He chose to set out his programme at Morecambe in
Lancashire, on the last evening of the Conservative Party conference, just a few hours before and few miles up the road from where
Heath would be making his leader's speech at Blackpool.

A week before Morecambe, and by way of an overture, Powell
spoke at Berkhamsted in Hertfordshire of the abolition of food
subsidies in the 1950s – subsidies that would return under the
Labour government in the 1970s – and how once this had been
done no one would have thought of bringing them back come the
next election. It had been considered impossible to get rid of them
because they were a means of 'vote-buying'. He invited the country to consider that other forms of vote-buying, using excessively

high rates of taxation to fund them, were unacceptable and wasteful. He declared his opposition to the principle of nationalisation, something the rest of the Conservative Party now seemed to be resigned to He harked back to the party's 1947 Industrial Charter, which warned how the state's purchase of industry would lead to totalitarianism. Where, he asked, was the movement for denationalisation? Investment crises when funds had to be raised to keep these industries going had caused the net borrowing requirement to rise and fuelled inflation in 1957, 1961 and 1965.

At Morecambe Powell followed on from this and set out a programme of radical ideas to take the economy out of its consensual, post-war stagnation. He attacked the 'it can't be done' mentality, and told his audience that with the requisite boldness economic salvation was at hand. The nationalised industries were costing £1 billion a year and losing another £180 million on top of that: yet no one believed private enterprise could step in. Similarly, the public had become resigned to a high burden of taxation and didn't believe it was possible to reduce it. He promised to reduce income tax from 8/3 to 4/3 in the pound (41.25% to 21.25%), and to abolish capital gains tax and selective employment tax. He criticised the separation of taxation and spending in the parliamentary process, and reminded people that the two were linked, and had to be regarded as linked.

Powell had to suggest savings of £2.9 billion to make his tax cuts. He proposed to do this by abolishing the grants given under regional policy, on the grounds that it was not the role of government to decide where investment should go. This accounted for nearly a quarter of the total savings. He intended to abolish what we would now call quangos, especially those advising the government on industrial policy. Agricultural subsidies would go on the grounds that they were no more justified than subsidies to industry would be. He promised to abolish housing subsidies, on the grounds that they caused more squalor than they cleared up, and that rent controls were the real barriers to decent housing provision. Private enterprise would regain the duty of housing people, which would save the Treasury £450 million a year.

The real gains were to be made from the nationalised industries. Money for investment in these industries would come from the capital markets and not from the Treasury. Leaving aside the coal mines and the railways 'for the moment' – he fully intended to privatise, or as he then put it 'denationalise', them too – he said that by selling off everything else and transferring their liabilities to the private sector would save £1 billion. The reductions in the size of the state would also entail a reduction in bureaucracy and the public payroll, saving more money. Borrowing would fall and so would the cost of servicing it. Powell was sufficiently political to point out that he had not cut the social services – a term he used to embrace both education and healthcare as well as social security – and that the cuts in housing would not affect anyone's social security benefits, which would be used to pay for the private provision they would receive instead.

He had a subsidiary ideological point, which explicitly set out the rationale of his economic policy. 'We set government free to perform what we regard as its proper tasks. There are services today, services which only government can provide, that are scandalously undernourished.' He had in mind particularly the police and the prison services: in later life, when a Conservative government privatised aspects of penal services, Powell was outraged, saying that it was highly improper for these to be provided by anyone other than the state.

Powell's economic thought never had a higher profile than during the Heath government. The moment Heath became an apostate from the Selsdon manifesto, Powell went for him: not purely because he had betrayed undertakings given to the electorate in order to persuade them to vote Conservative, but because of what he regarded as the damaging fatuity of Heath's arguments, ideas and policies. There had been tensions during Powell's time as an opposition spokesman under Heath, notably over Heath's refusal to challenge Wilson over economic planning and, most of all, over the belief in the efficacy of an incomes policy. As Heath gradually resorted to more and more socialist measures during his premiership, so Powell raised the volume of his attacks on him.

It was not merely the incomes policy that aggrieved him. Heath also decided to bail out Rolls-Royce, an act of nationalisation that Powell regarded as a defiance of market realities and a wicked waste of public money. But it was the measures that Heath chose to take once economic crisis overtook the country in the autumn of 1972 that really angered him.

Before the oil crisis that struck the final nails into the coffin of the Heath government, the administration had been expanding the money supply in order to try to keep unemployment below a million. Powell predicted inflation and, to Heath's embarrassment and annoyance, his adversary was proved right. Powell might also have predicted the measures that Heath, in the autumn of 1972, chose to take to correct the problem: a prices and incomes policy.

This was no simple demand that no one's earnings, or no retail price, should increase by more than a certain percentage. The policy was infinitely more complicated than that, and it was to be presented to the public in several phases. The bureaucracy of the plan was as bemusing as the logic behind it. When Heath announced it to the Commons on 6 November 1972 Powell, in one of his most famous interventions, asked him:

Does my Right Hon. Friend not know that it is fatal for any government or party or person to seek to govern in direct opposition to the principles on which they were entrusted with the right to govern? In introducing a compulsory control of wages and prices, in contravention of the deepest commitments of this party, has my Right Hon. Friend taken leave of his senses?

Heath's reply was simply that 'the present government were returned to power to take action in the national interest when they were required to do so'.

The following day the Commons had a full-dress debate on the question, and Powell took the opportunity not merely to twist the knife into Heath a little further, but also to expound his own economic philosophy. In doing so he gave a preview of what, within a decade, would become the prevailing policy of the next Conservative administration, under Margaret Thatcher. Powell was determined to paint Heath as a leftist, not least in his determination to seek to control prices as well as incomes. 'Since prices are one of the great levers of the economy, it is an essential part of logical and consistent socialism to control them.' In pointing out the fallacy of a prices and incomes policy, he referred to four occasions in previous years when one had been implemented. His speech merits quoting at length, for it is the finest exposition of his economic belief:

> Those four policies were all adopted for the same purpose – the endeavour to stem inflation; and they all arose from a simple analysis, indeed a simplistic analysis, of the cause of inflation. They were all based upon the assumption that inflation occurs – that is, that prices in general rise – because people raise their prices and because people raise their wages; because trade unions demand, and employers concede, excessive increases in wages. That is the assumption which lies behind this present prices and incomes policy – the Bill and whatever is to follow – and the similar policies which have preceded to.
>
> Of course, if it were true – if that assumption were well founded – these policies would flow from it logically. But then we should all long ago have lived happily ever after. If prices in general rise because people put up individual prices, one need only tell them to stop it, and if, when they are told to stop it they refuse, then force them to stop it. If the assumption were well founded, so far from a counter-inflationary Bill under that or any other name, being a *rara avis* – a rarity and an exception – it would be just as natural and normal as laws against burglary or murder; for if this general evil were caused by individuals or groups deliberately doing what they have it in their power to refrain from doing – namely, increasing a price or a wage unduly – it would be a natural maxim of state to prevent them. The law of prices and incomes would be a normal part of the system of law.
>
> However, the assumption is not merely a simplistic assumption; it is a ludicrous one, which cannot be matched with reality or with experience. The desire of people to get the maximum price for the goods or services which they have to offer, the desire of workers, individually or in combination, to negotiate the maximum wage and remuneration that they can obtain from their employers, is not something new, something which has been escalating at a breathtaking rate. It is part of human nature – a constant, if ever there was a constant. The monopoly power of the trade unions, of which we hear so much – and there are senses in which there is a quasi-monopoly

power in some trade unions and in some circumstances – is not new. It would be a bold man who would argue that the monopoly power of the trade unions has increased – I do not refer back 50 or 100 years, although I think I could do so – in the last five or ten years in the ratio in which inflation has increased during the same period. Whatever may be the monopoly power of the unions, whatever the natural greed and folly of individuals, these are constants, and cannot explain the phenomenon that confronts us, which is not a constant, which not merely fluctuates but in recent experience increases alarmingly.

If we are to explain that, we must find something which is not a constant, something which also changes, both rapidly and on a great scale. There is no secret about what that is. In order for all prices to rise – in other words, in order for the value of money to fall – it is necessary, it is elementary, that the supply of money, whatever precisely is meant by that, or whatever precise measurement is applied to it, should be increasing relative to the supply of goods and services; and since the supply of goods and services, however unsatisfactory we might find its growth, is certainly not diminishing, we are clearly confronted with the effective consequences of a growth in the money supply. Indeed, in a modern economy, long-term inflation – that which we have experienced in the past and of which we are experiencing an acute phase at the moment – can be explained or accounted for only in terms of the rate of increase of the money supply.

There was a time not so long ago when that proposition, which the House has accepted at any rate without violent tumult, was regarded as a way-out, esoteric theory. I have even heard it treated as if it were a personal possession or patent of my own. That time has passed. There was a remarkable passage – not the first of such passages, but the most remarkable of them – in the speech of my Right Hon. Friend the Chancellor of the Exchequer this afternoon. A major assertion of the importance of money supply also came today from my Right Hon. Friend the Member for Thirsk & Malton [Sir Robin Turton]. But I think that the most significant recent assertion of money supply as the condition *sine qua non* of inflation was made last week at Luxembourg by the Finance Ministers of the Six.

They were addressing themselves to 'measures to tackle the problem of inflation'. The House might care to recollect that there was nothing about prices and incomes policy, statutory or voluntary, in the conclusions they arrived at. They agreed on three points. They agreed first on a target: they would aim provisionally at 4 per cent inflation only. Then they said how this was to be achieved. They decided that increases in the supply of money should be cut back by the end of 1974 to the same level as the real growth in gross national product after allowance, of course, for whatever degree of inflation, in consistency with their target, they were prepared to admit.

They therefore agreed to identify the congruence of the rate of increase of the money supply with the rate of increase of the real gross national product as the prescription for stable money values. The Finance Ministers of the Six said, in effect, 'If you want to diminish inflation or eliminate it, you have to bring back the rate of growth of the money supply towards, and eventually to coincide with, the rate of real growth of the national product.'

They then went on to put their finger upon the cause of undue increase in the supply of money. They agreed – we were not among the Six for this purpose – that increases in budgetary spending should not exceed growth in the gross national product. In other words, they agreed that the cause of excessive increase in the money supply is excessive reliance by governments on inflationary financing of their expenditure.

There they stated, in classic form – I am not above going for wisdom to anywhere I can find it, even to Luxembourg – the proposition that in a modern economy long-term continuing inflation is the result of excessive increases in the money supply produced by inflationary financing of government expenditure.

That morning *The Times*, a pro-Heath paper, had anticipated what Powell would say in criticism of Heath, and had attacked him in a leading article. Powell continued his speech with his response to that article:

At this point, however, the spectre of unemployment raises its head. A challenge was issued to me this morning in a leading article in *The Times*: 'We can see no evidence that inflation can be controlled simply through the money supply without abandoning full employment as an objective. Nor is Mr Powell prepared to state the price in unemployment he would have to accept.' Once again, it will be noted, 'money supply' and 'Enoch Powell' are treated as almost interchangeable expressions. To that challenge, issued to me and to the increasing throng who also believe that unless money supply is controlled inflation cannot be controlled, I shall respond in their name. The connection between the control of inflation and unemployment is that if a substantial level of inflation is in operation and that level is reduced, then to that extent it is inevitable that transitionally unemployment should result. I say again: it is inevitable that controlling inflation, in the sense of reducing or eliminating it, causes transitional unemployment.

Powell believed the economy would be restructured, and that there would be new areas of activity that would soak up the surplus labour. That was not a risk Heath was prepared to take. Thatcher did take it in the 1980s, when she pursued Powellite policies, leading to the closure of many old, heavy industrial units and the displacement of the workforce first to the dole queue, and then in many cases into new areas of employment. Powell added:

> It is the rate at which inflation is reduced and the fact of its being reduced which is the relevant connection with unemployment. It is mere falsification to pretend that it can be reduced by one means with no effect upon employment, whereas if it is reduced by another means – given the same rate and given the same publicity – employment will be affected. We are engaged in deceiving ourselves if we imagine that prices and incomes policy or anything else will slow down and eliminate inflation without consequences for unemployment. It is spoof if a freeze, a statutory policy, a counter-inflationary Bill is presented as though it could bridge that gap and resolve that contradiction.

After the oil price crisis of 1973 Heath tried to protest that Britain was put at the mercy of events, in particular at the mercy of an oil-producing cartel that had chosen to quadruple the price of its product. Powell conceded that the terms of trade had changed, and in a very significant way, but he did not concede that the change should have been fatal. This was the year when the supply of money rose by 30 per cent: in 1975, as a consequence, inflation would peak at 26.9 per cent. Powell's logic dictated that if instead of expanding the supply of money to cope with the rise in the price of oil the government had left things as they were, the prices of other goods would have fallen as demand for them dropped off because of the shortage of money with which to buy them, given the inelasticity of the demand for oil. So the problems the country found itself in at the end of 1973 were of its own making.

These problems included, as well as rampant inflation, huge pay demands by the trade unions that could not possibly be contained within Heath's prices and incomes policy. A wave of strikes went across the country. Coal was running short, there were energy strikes, and a three-day week had been instigated. Powell was categorical in his belief of where the blame for these economic disasters lay:

All these purely external forces are not such as in themselves to have proved disastrous or incapable of being met with our customary resilience and the resources which adversity brings into play. The wounds from which this country is bleeding today have not been inflicted by an external enemy. They are self-inflicted wounds; they are what we have done to ourselves.

Domestic inflation, the fall in value of our own money, proceeding at what would until recently have seemed the impossible rate of 10 per cent per annum and upwards, has in the first place produced a fall in the exchange value of sterling which has done us far more damage than any mere alteration in the real terms of trade. In case anyone, within or without the House, should be tempted to reach for the flattering unction of pointing to other countries and saying 'They too have such and such a percentage rate of inflation', we ought to remember that the exchange rates of those countries' currencies rise while ours falls. In addition, our domestic inflation is the reason for the catastrophic trade deficits, antecedent altogether to the oil crisis, which everyone recognises are a signal set at danger, past which it is absolutely impossible for any government or any country to drive.

These are the consequences of the internal behaviour of the value of our own money. It is our inflation in this country which has imposed these penalties upon us. Yet even they are not the most serious results of our inflation. Its most dangerous poisoned fruit has been the clash and head-on confrontation, which lies at the heart of the announcement made last Thursday by my Right Hon. Friend, between the state and great masses of workers engaged in the energy industries, speaking through their unions. It is that clash, the direct result of our cumulative domestic inflation of the last few years, which has brought the House and the country to the pass which we are debating this afternoon.

The collapse of the Heath government and its defeat in February 1974, followed by the catastrophe for the Labour government in 1976 that led to the intervention of the International Monetary Fund, were vindications of Powell's economic theories. The ultimate vindication, however, came with the advent of the Conservative government under Margaret Thatcher in May 1979. Monetarism was now the order of the day. Income tax was cut and the burden of taxation shifted to consumption taxes. The pressure was on to reduce public spending. In her second term, the process of privatisation – as denationalisation was now called – transformed the industrial economy. The Powellite message had not gone direct to Thatcher, though she would much later concede that it had influenced her more than she admitted. She had cited Keith Joseph as her economic guru. However, Joseph had imbibed these theories both from Powell direct and from the Institute of Economic Affairs, which had been Powell's think tank of choice. The twenty-one years between 1958 and 1979 had been a grim episode in British economic history: but Powell could at least console himself that, however difficult the struggle had been, his arguments had been proved to be right in the end. As the principal economic architect of Thatcherism, his position as one of the prime intellectual influences in British politics in the twentieth century is secured.

The Role of Government and the State of the Economy

Conservative Rally and Mass Meeting at the Alhambra Theatre, Morecambe, 11 October 1968

The trouble with this nation is that we have been brainwashed for years into believing that 'it can't be done'. Britain has become the 'Mr Can't' of the modern world. There are too many who are glad to sit around her, like Job's comforters, explaining why no great change is possible and that therefore she had better like it or lump it. We moan and mope about our nationalised industries, which put nearly £1 billion a year on to the borrowing requirement of the Exchequer and lose another £180 million a year on top of that; but as soon as anyone suggests that if you don't like them, you had better set about getting shot of them and calling in private enterprise and the capital market to do the job, a whole chorus starts up to tell you not to think of such a thing. They don't even say 'How wonderful it would be if that were possible! There must be some way or other to surmount the obstacles. Let's try and find it.' They seem not merely reconciled to the impossibility, but positively delighted about it.

The same applies to taxation. We have got into a frame of mind in which we are resigned to carrying approximately the same load of taxation until Kingdom Come, and think ourselves mighty lucky if it gets no heavier. So we spend our time debating whether it wouldn't be a bit more comfortable if we shifted a little of the load from one shoulder to the other. Why, only yesterday the Conservative Party conference chose to debate not reduction of taxation – oh dear, no; nothing so wild and irresponsible as that – but taking a bit of taxation off some people and putting it on to other people. Mind, you can hardly blame the public if they regard the tax burden as a whole as being something no more to be altered than the English weather or the other dispensations of providence. After all, during, the thirteen years of Conservative administration they watched the proportion of public expenditure to national income move downwards until 1958 and then move back up again till it was at the same level when Labour came back in 1964 as when Labour went out in 1951. It begins to look as if there were some law of nature behind it all and that one might as well try to eliminate gravitation as reduce taxation. The same chorus make their appearance, like the chorus of old men in a Greek tragedy, to sing to you the dirge of fate and tell you that every other nation is taxed just as much, or nearly as much, and so you had better keep a stiff upper lip, and shut up about it.

This is the perfect breeding ground for socialism. When the population are reduced to a condition of apathy and of disbelieving that it could ever be very different, the virus – I had to get that word in! – attacks them. The Tempter whispers in their ear: 'Why struggle? In any case you can't escape. State socialism has all the inevitability of gradualness. So why don't you be sensible? Relax and enjoy it!'

Maybe we shall. I don't know. What I do know is that we don't have to. We are still free to choose. We are free, if we wish, to choose a dramatic retrenchment in the claims of public expenditure and a drastic reduction in taxation. I have come here tonight to prove it to you. I intend before we leave this hall to reduce income tax and surtax by half; for the centrepiece of my budget is 4/- off the income tax, or income tax at the standard rate of 4/3 in the pound, with broadly corresponding reductions at the lower rates. In addition to this I shall indulge myself by abolishing my pet aversion, the capital gains tax. Nor have I forgotten the Party's pledge to abolish SET, and I shall carry that out too, not merely by abolishing the selectivity – which I believe is strictly the letter of our undertaking – but by abolishing the whole blessed thing. Of course we all have our preferences. There is no more delightful sport than devising reductions of taxation - except perhaps devising increases. It would be possible to distribute the same relief differently, and place the emphasis instead on the reduction of indirect taxation or spread it evenly over direct and indirect. Obviously an infinite range of permutations and combinations is possible; but I'm going to stick to my 4/3 income tax, for two reasons. It makes the point in a good clear fashion, and once accepted, you can commute it as you please. Also, though there are several indirect taxes beside SET which I heartily detest, I confess to preferring a good solid attack on direct taxation. I believe in 'letting the dog see the rabbit', and there's no better way than letting him see a good large chunk of his income.

Like all Chancellors of the Exchequer I have some preliminary remarks to make before I come to my specific proposals. The first is that this is not only the first time the budget has been opened in Morecambe – and surely Morecambe is a good place to open a budget - but it is the first time in more than a hundred years that a budget showing at the same time proposals on both sides – expenditure as well as revenue – (which is what surely a budget ought to be) has been opened at all. We have got so used to discussing taxation and expenditure separately in our parliamentary procedure, that we have almost forgotten there is any connection between them at all. Foreigners attending our Budget Day ritual often leave completely nonplussed: they expected a statement of expenditure and revenue, and heard instead a lecture on economics, combined with some proposals on taxation – usually more and new taxation.

The second preliminary is this. I am taking as my starting point the figures of the present financial year 1968/69 as estimated by Roy Jenkins in March. If I can show that it is possible, and how it would be possible, to achieve the result I aim at on the basis of this year's figures, then that proof will hold good, even though we may not get our opportunity for a year or two yet and even though the result (I must emphasize) would have to be achieved over several years. In that sense we are looking at several budgets telescoped into one. The reason why I can claim this with confidence is because the rest of government expenditure, other than those items on which I propose to operate, would be planned to keep, as a whole, within the rate of increase of the national income from year to year, and that rate of increase would be estimated for this purpose not (as hitherto) as high as possible, but as low as possible. There should therefore, on that ground alone, be further modest room for reductions of taxation which fall outside tonight's major effort.

My third preliminary is a request to you to hold on to your seats and grit your teeth while I deal with expenditure. All government expenditure is popular with somebody, and large government expenditure is popular with large numbers of people. There will be few items in my package which will not make somebody wince. Please remember all the time that the choice is yours; but if you are going to get big results, you must take big decisions. Painless it cannot be, nor can it be done in a hole and corner without anybody noticing. No doubt there are alternatives – of course there are – to my particular proposals tonight, which would produce the same financial result. I can only say that you would certainly like them as little, and probably much less. So here we go.

In order to halve income tax and surtax I must find £2,325 million. Another £45 million will be sufficient to extinguish capital gains tax, though the true net yield of the tax is of course far less, when one takes into account the cost of collecting it in terms of public and private bureaucracy and frustration. To this £2,370 million I must add the net yield of SET from private firms and from public corporations, namely £485 million. I have therefore to reduce my budgetary requirements by the grand total of £2,855 million.

I intend to eliminate, in principle, payments which are directed towards making firms and people take different commercial decisions from those they would otherwise take; in other words, payments which are designed to ensure that effort and capital are put to less profitable use than they would otherwise be. (Note, I am taking no credit, nevertheless, for any increased buoyancy of the revenue that, would result from this at any given rate of tax.) I propose accordingly to abolish all investment grants, saving £360 million, and all assistance to development areas saving a further £250 million, making £610 million in all. This is not the occasion to argue the case exhaustively. I will just say this: there is no ground for supposing that the state knows best either how much investment there should be or what forms it should take. If these are not decisions best taken through price, profit and the capital market, then there is little or no case for capitalism at all, and we had better go and join the Labour Party. Likewise there is no ground for spending money to immortalise a distribution of industry and population which reflects the economic factors and forces of the past. I intend, on the same broad grounds, to send the Industrial Re-organisation Corporation packing, as well as the Prices and Incomes Board, and all the brood of big and little Neddies. This will yield me some chicken-feed to the extent of £42 million, to which, again on the same grounds, the demise of the Shipping Industry Board will add another £12 million. I shall collect £10 million from the Ministry of Technology – part on account of the incipient expenditure under the Industrial Expansion Bill, on which the Party has laid its curse in parliament, and part by disposing of the National Research and Development Corporation. There is a further £10 million from the Land Commission, which we are pledged to abolish.

I now come to the large item of agriculture. It is the Party's policy to take the part of state agricultural expenditure which represents price guarantees out of the budget, by transferring it to a tariff or levy system. This, our latest policy statement estimates, will be worth £250 million to the Budget, which I assume to be after allowance for whatever compensating adjustments would be necessary in social benefits to meet any consequent price increases. However, the same arguments which apply against distortion of manpower and resource in industry generally apply with particular force to the agricultural industry, and I do not know how production grants in all their various forms can be justified in agriculture any more than, for instance, in engineering. I intend therefore to claim the production grants and subsidies as well; at a net figure of £125 million out of motivation and its results. The view, which I myself share and have publicly stated for years, that it does more harm than good to the recipient as well as to the donor, is no longer the perquisite of an academic minority in their ivory towers but is widely and increasingly propounded on both sides of the Atlantic. Even tied aid only represents goods which we manufacture and services we provide simply in order to give them away. If only a fraction of the same effort were devoted – and who doubts that most, if not all, of it would be? – to purposes for which there was a return and a market, it would yield a corresponding addition to our national income. I propose to abolish it, and save thereby £205 million per annum.

I now come to housing. Housing subsidies are running at £160 million a year from the Exchequer. But the provision of subsidised housing puts much more than that on to the budget. Of the annual capital expenditure of local authorities met by borrowing, about three-quarters is attributable to housing.

There is, of course, no way of identifying by destination any specific part of the £500 million borrowed by local authorities which falls on the budget. But if the same ratio is applied to this figure as applies to total borrowing, £375 million of the borrowing on the budget would be attributable to housing. I shall not trouble you at length by arguing once again, that the prime cause of shortage and squalor in housing is the double evil of rent restriction and subsidy. You have only to reduce the price of anything below the point at which current supply and demand balance to create shortage in the present and repress production in the future. These classic consequences we have enjoyed and continue to enjoy in housing: while every other element of the standard of living has streaked ahead, housing for millions has obstinately lagged behind. It is the paradox and the parable of the slum with the television set inside and the motor car outside. If there were not a penny of budgetary saving to be had, it would still be imperative as speedily as possible to let all rents find the level at which supply and demand balance. As this happened, it would be no more necessary for public authorities to contract for the production of houses than for the production of food, clothing and automobiles. The restoration of sanity in housing will therefore relieve the budget of the relevant capital cost. It will also eliminate subsidy; but here of course I must make an offset for increased social security payments, and for this purpose I shall write off half the amount saved in subsidy.

Accordingly, I allow £450 million for the net gain of returning to private enterprise the function of housing people, as well as feeding them, clothing them, amusing them, and all the rest. There will be a further £25 million consequential from the disappearance of the Housing Corporation and the Scottish Special Housing Association. I am now up to £1,740 million, and turn my attention to the nationalised industries.

There are two magnitudes here. There are the running losses which are carried on votes, and there are the capital sums, which, because these industries are in national ownership, are raised through the budget and not on the capital market. The principal item under the first head is the £150 million which falls on the vote of the Ministry of Transport, plus the special payments of £20 million which fall on the Ministry of Power. Under the second, or capital, head the total in the budget of last March was £921 million, though it is worth remembering that in the previous year this particular estimate had been overspent by a little detail of one-third or £300 million. Of this total no less than £804 million is accounted for by three industries: gas, electricity and the Post Office (almost exclusively telecommunications), in that order. A further £100 million is put in for the steel industry, which we are pledged anyhow to denationalise, and a further £49 million for the Airways Corporations, bringing the total to £953 million. From this however I will deduct the appropriate fraction of Mr Jenkins' expected underspending of £120 million (which is very generous of me considering last year's overspending). There are then are only a few small bits and pieces left, and even of these the Transport Holding Company, at £10 million, has itself actually asked to go to the market on its own credit. So we need not quarrel with our friends and colleagues over selling off the coal-mines and the railways at knock-down prices, because there is only £70 million in it anyhow.

So, while leaving the mines and railways nationalised just for the moment – to show how unacademic and down to earth we can be – simply by eliminating losses and transferring the great profit-makers to private management, we have relieved the budget of no less than £1,020 million, bringing my total to date to £2,760 million, or only £95 million short of my objective. In fact I have more than done the trick already. The Conservative Opposition has repeatedly pointed to the growth in bureaucracy caused by the interventionist policies of socialism – an increase of nearly 60,000 in five years, which if costed at £2,000 per head per annum represents nearly £120 million. We are in any case committed, as condemning this increase, to eliminate the greater part of it, and the massive reduction of bureaucratic interference and management and of particularly inquisitorial forms of taxation which has yielded us our major savings will greatly help to achieve that saving and bring us comfortably to our target figure.

In fact, we have done much better than relieve the budget of £2,855 billion. The relief that these measures would produce is greater even than the tax reductions which I set out to achieve. It is important to understand why. For many years past now, the government of this country has no longer been able to borrow from the public, taking one year with another. The difference between estimated expenditure and the estimated yield of taxation is customarily called the 'net borrowing requirement'. But that is now no more than a bitter euphemism. The sum is not in fact obtained by borrowing from the public, because, after years of inflation and rising interest rates and crushing taxation, the public not surprisingly won't lend to the government any longer. So one of two things happens to this deficit. When there is run on the pound the Bank of England has to take in a lot of sterling from foreigners who want to get rid of it, and this sterling can be lent to the government to help meet the deficit; but obviously that little lark can't go on for very long. Therefore there is no alternative to the government but to manufacture the extra money, thus sending prices up and pushing the pound further down. This is the reason why Chancellor Jenkins this year had to impose that savage extra taxation in order to cut down his 'net borrowing requirement'. He would have loved to have gone on printing like his predecessors, but our creditors would not let him. This is why the total expenditure and borrowing of the government today, whether on current or capital account, has to go straight onto the budget.

This position however would be transformed by the huge relief to the budget and to taxation which we have achieved. Consequently the government would once again be able to borrow for its own capital expenditure, for which borrowing is sound and respectable – for instance, for new hospitals, new public buildings, new barracks, new trunk roads. To the extent that the government could genuinely and properly borrow more in a year than the 1968/69 figure of £358 million, there would therefore be a further relief in taxation.

I point this out, because it illustrates how, when once you turn decisively in the right direction again, all kinds of factors which were previously hostile to you begin to work in your favour. I would also emphasize that there are dozens and dozens of smaller but still, in total, substantial pickings throughout the length and breadth of government expenditure with which I have not troubled you tonight. However the great point I want to stress is this. The removal of that colossal sum of £2,855 million from the budget was achieved solely by allowing the system of private enterprise to work, or restoring it where it had been eliminated. We have not needed to cut government expenditure where that is not usurping or distorting commercial operations which can be performed better and more efficiently by the market and the private enterprise system.

You will notice that I have not needed to take one penny from the social services. Where the housing subsidies perform a social security function, they should and would be replaced by other social payments, and we have made allowance for this. Education, health, the whole system of social security benefits – from these I have not proposed to take, I repeat, a single penny. Let no one say there is anything here about 'cutting the social services'.

I am not saying that I do not believe expenditure on these services calls for no attention. Quite the contrary. I believe that we shall have to direct our mind quite radically to the prospective future shape and rate of growth of those services. It is in that context, the context of the future, that the Conservative Party's declaration against increases in social benefit being distributed indiscriminately without regard to need will yield its results. It is in that context that the priorities in our expanding educational expenditure can be altered so as, for example, to give relatively more to primary education. It is in that context that the gradual growth or regrowth of private provision for medical care and schooling will be accommodated. What I want you to see is that by calling back and implementing the economic principles in which we believe, we are not thereby limiting the power and opportunity of government to do whatever we want government to do for us. On the contrary we set government free to perform what we regard as its proper tasks.

There are services today, services which only government can provide, that are scandalously undernourished. I do not repent of having said, six or seven years ago, that the police and prison services are the most seriously neglected of all our social services, and I say so as one who has consistently supported what is wrongly called the 'left-wing' line on punishment, crime and penal reform. How can we handle crime and disorder humanely but firmly if we provide inadequate resources for detection, for control, and for management of the convicted? The state in Britain today is in desperate danger of neglecting and starving its own unique and essential business in order to thrust its arms up to the sockets into business which does not need it and fares better without.

What I have shown tonight is that, solely by removing from government economic decisions and management which it has usurped, this nation, if it so wills, can be relieved of half its current burden of direct taxation and another half billion pounds into the bargain. The material words are 'if it wills'. Of course, it is not easy; the easy things have always been done before you get there. Of course, it demands an intensive effort, spread over the lifetime of a parliament, and the criticism and abandonment of institutions and attitudes, some of which we have ourselves defended and even initiated. Of course, it means that big vested interests, bureaucratic and sectional, must be confronted, and confronted openly and directly. All I say is: there is a choice, the choice is open, and it is yours. Let no one cheat you out of your right to take part in that choice, to make your voice heard on one side or the other, by telling you that there is no choice at all and the thing is impossible. We are surrounded all day long by the great throng of those who lecture us on what we cannot do, until in the end John Bull is replaced as the national type by Mr Can't.

By all means, if you prefer it, go staggering along with your present growing load of taxation, with your present diminishing voice in the disposal of the national income which you create. The process slowed down a little at first when the Conservatives were in, and it has speeded up again since the socialists came in; but the caravan still moves unmistakeably onward and upward. If that is your pleasure and your decision, by all means go along with it. But let it never be said that you took no decision at all because you thought that there was none to take. Only that is impossible which you have not the will to do.

The Language of Enoch Powell

Roger Scruton

To those who remember the man himself, the speeches of Enoch Powell are all but inseparable from the tone of voice with which he delivered them. The level diction, the incantatory rhythms, the impression of being led by the argument as though by a voice speaking from elsewhere – all this gave a visionary character, even to the most plain and prosaic words. Reading the speeches, however, one has quite a different impression. They are of two kinds: one offering rigorous analysis, the other suggestive invocation. And in neither case do Powell's words correspond to the popular image of the man, as a fiery rhetorician, summoning his countrymen with 'ancestral voices prophesying war'. On the contrary; his prose is characterised by a sober, level-headed vision of the human condition, expressed with absolute clarity, and with the unambiguous syntax that his classical studies had implanted. Occasionally you find an idiom from the Bible or the Book of Common Prayer. There are classical allusions – though fewer than you might expect. Most of all, the speeches are characterised by an economy of presentation, a way of going immediately and convincingly to the point, and leaving all arguments to the contrary in shreds.

This is particularly evident in Powell's analytical style. In the time of Margaret Thatcher's leadership the Conservative Party made quite a fuss about the free market, and the need to get the state off our backs, using rhetoric derived largely from the Institute of Economic Affairs and the Centre for Policy Studies. But what was said then, however true and necessary, was not said with anything like the philosophical acumen of Powell, in his speeches from the later 1950s and early 1960s.

Powell was faced with the reality of socialist government, and determined to tell the truth about it. He had understood, as I think no other English politician of the time had understood, the real heart of the anti-socialist argument, as it had been developed by the Austrian economists and delivered to an outraged intellectual establishment at the London School of Economics by Friedrich Hayek. He knew that the planned economy could never offer a solution to the crises that gave rise to it, since it would always destroy the information needed for success. The argument, which had been presented in all its armour of technicalities by the Austrians, is given by Powell with a directness and simplicity that ought to have disarmed all opposition, and which did not do so largely because of the vested interests that kept the Labour Party in business. There has been no more trenchant critic of socialist planning than Powell, and he is able to round off his devastating critique of Harold Wilson's National Plan, which had purported to control the production of coal, the import of fuel and the number of jobs retained in the mining industry, and of course had failed dismally to do any of those things, with unanswerable words:

> Well, they were wrong, dead wrong, and they admit it. So what do they do? Do they conclude that the planning lark is not what it was cracked up to be and that it would be most unwise to fix figures for this, and figures for that, in 1970 and then try to make them come true? Not a bit of it. They plunge right in again as if nothing had happened. Your socialist planner contrives to be the repentant sinner and the Proud Pharisee at one and the same moment. With one breath he confesses his past sins and transgressions and proclaims unhesitatingly that he will live in uninterrupted holiness and right-eousness the rest of his days.[†]

Time and again in his speeches of the Labour years Enoch Powell outlines the way in which planning has not worked, the way in which it will not work, and the theory that says that it cannot work. His defence of the market is not phrased as a defence of business against government, but as a defence of the people against the bureaucrats. The contrast, he insists, is between 'a free economy

---

† Enoch Powell, *Freedom and Reality*, ed. John Wood (London: Batsford, 1969), p. 53.

which trusts the people and the controlled economy which trusts only the people in Whitehall'.[†] And unlike many defenders of the free market, he saw that the natural instinct of the businessman is to collaborate with the status quo, even if the status quo means regulation by people who wish to seize and squander the profits. The Labour Party had created, as he put it,

> a New Model Army of the gentlemen who know best ... the practical men of experience, the businessmen, the industrialists – the sort of people whom the average Briton views sometimes with a grudging envy, but certainly never with amusement or levity ... The assertion that they know best is made with a confidence and absence of dissent which the old-style 'gentleman in Whitehall' never enjoyed, even in the heyday of his authority. The nation is in some danger of hastening to applaud and to obey the commands which issue from their lips – or rather which appear to issue from their lips. I say 'appear to issue'; for though the hands are the toilworn hands of Esau, the voice is really the voice of Jacob. It is like the priest at the shrine of the ancient oracle, who climbed up inside the image of the god and spoke through its mouth. In this case, the voice is the voice of Socialism.[‡]

That powerful résumé of the corruption of business and enterprise under Labour government achieves its purpose partly by direct argument, and partly by allusion. It invokes the Old Testament story and ancient religion in order to suggest another, more distant, longer-term view of things. The new form of bureaucratic government is seen for what it is – just as much a usurpation of the natural order of British society as Cromwell's New Model Army. What should be settled by free exchange and voluntary association is now settled by commands and conscription. And Powell's audience would be led spontaneously to see not merely that the Labour government was misleading them, but that legitimate order was being usurped by factional interests.

---

† John Wood (ed.), *A Nation Not Afraid: The Thinking of Enoch Powell* (London: Batsford, 1965), p. 4.

‡ Powell, *Freedom and Reality*, pp. 80–81.

The style, however, depends on an educated audience. Powell assumes a knowledge of English history, of the Bible, even of the institutions of religion in the classical world. Making such assumptions, at a time when the Labour Party was actively pursuing its most important project, which was to destroy the 'elitist' education that had produced people like Powell, was dangerous. It was to prove Powell's downfall when, alluding to the Cumaean Sybil in Book VI of the *Aeneid*, he imagined that his hearers would remember their Virgil, see the moral of the story and move on. In fact, those who garbled the quotation and imagined that Powell had referred to 'rivers of blood' promptly set out to destroy the man who had dared to allude to their own hidden fears. As Powell was to discover, rhetoric and allusion are dangerous, and never more dangerous than in the minds of those who do not understand them, but whose self-deceptions they reveal.

But to return to Powell's analytical style. The most impressive thing about it, in my mind, is the concreteness with which Powell conveys the abstract theorems of economics – a virtue which he shares with Adam Smith and which was lost in the course of twentieth-century economic theory, when an academic discipline arose in order to pretend that there was an expert science that could amend and replace the findings of common sense. For Powell economics was to be explained in practical terms. His criticism of the new bureaucracy continues thus:

> Now, I yield to no one in my admiration for businessmen and industrialists ... We who believe in private enterprise, and the competitive capitalist society, believe that the businessman and the industrialist, when they are at their job, even if they are not always right, are right more often than anyone else would be – far more often.
>
> The mistake arises when we take two or more businessmen or industrialists, put them together on a committee, set them to manage or advise on other people's business or industries, and then expect that they will be twice as good at it collectively as each of them is separately at his own job. The expectation is vain. At the very moment when we took them, so to speak, from the plough or the forge, at the very moment when we cut the umbilical cord of self-interest which attached them to the nourishing forces of

profit and competition, they became different beings ... It is the presence of self-interest, the fear of failure and the hope of success, which endows the businessman and the industrialist, acting and reacting with others similarly situated, with his significance to the community, with the probability that upon the whole his business judgements will be overwhelmingly superior to those arrived at by other means.[†]

Those paragraphs contain all that Powell's hearers needed of Adam Smith's argument for the invisible hand, and they are unanswerable in any terms available to the Labour Party establishment of his day. In his speeches, delivered in town halls and colleges, to local Conservative parties and chambers of commerce, to schools and dining clubs, Enoch Powell patiently demolished the claim that socialism provided social justice for the nation, rather than advancement for special interests at the nation's expense. The sad thing is that it all had to be said again, far less beautifully and with an alienating shrillness, in the days of Margaret Thatcher, when Enoch Powell's career had been ended, and his thunder stolen by people who threw it more carelessly than he did.

It is not for his analytical speeches that Powell is now chiefly known, but for his invocation of our country, at a time of rapid social and demographic change. Unlike many later defenders of the free market, Powell was not a liberal individualist. He did not believe that collectives are no greater than the sum of their members, and institutions merely creatures of convenience, with no claims of their own. 'Society', he wrote, 'is much more than a collection of individuals acting together, even through the complex and subtle mechanisms of the free economy for material advantage. It has an existence of its own; it thinks and feels; it looks inward, as a community, to its own members; it looks outward, as a nation, into a world populated by other societies, like or unlike itself.'

It was in his invocations of this thinking, feeling collective that Powell made his distinctive contribution to British politics. Whether or not he was right in all that he believed about our nation and its condition today is a matter that I leave to other contributors to

---

† Powell, *Freedom and Reality*, p. 81.

this volume. The point that I wish to emphasise is that through his language he placed this thing as squarely before the consciousness of his listeners as Shakespeare had done in his history plays, and invited them to recognise that he was talking not about an abstraction, but about their own destiny, which is but the microcosm of the larger destiny on which they depended.

Whether his listeners would actually recognise the thing that he described was less important to Powell than finding the right words to invoke it. Thus he expressed his point not in the language of German metaphysics, even though it was Fichte and Hegel who introduced the idea of the nation as Powell understood it, but in the language of the specific and inimitable history of Britain. Or rather, not the history of Britain, but that of England, as the moral core of our nationality, around which the fiction of Britain had been built. 'The Englishman,' Powell wrote, 'instinctively treats loyalty as by its nature unconditional, because he has – so to speak – nowhere else to go: the Crown and the institutions described collectively as those "set in authority under it" are his peculiar possession, they are his own history, his own nationhood, and he can only defy them and divest himself of them at the cost of denying himself.'†

Political allegiance so described partakes of mystery. And Powell's language does not shirk mystery but calmly embraces it: 'A Bill becomes a law because certain words of Norman French are pronounced in specific circumstances: the same words in other circumstances and synonymous words in the same circumstances would not make law.'‡ Powell goes on to explain this mystery in terms of another:

A morsel of bread confers immortality because it is eaten in particular circumstances and in no other circumstances. True, the circumstances can be modified and redefined; but the essence will be lost unless that modification and redefinition is itself authoritative and institutionally validated – by a Royal Assent Act or by the

† Speech to the Carlyle Club, Peterhouse, Cambridge, 24 May 1980.
‡ Ibid.

due exercise of acknowledged functions by the institutions of the Church itself.[†]

Powell is making clear that words can have a sacramental function, in which they *create* the powers that they describe. This is pre-eminently true of the words used at the altar, when bread and wine are refashioned as the body and blood of the Redeemer. But it is true too, Powell implies, of the words used to invoke the nation and our duty towards it. Often Powell's audiences felt that he was speaking liturgically, when he touched on the subject of England. And they were right. In elucidating the idea of sovereignty, Powell invokes 'the Crown in council, the Crown in Parliament and the Crown in judgement', blessing the existing institutions with names that repeat their magic without explaining it. When, in his famous St George's Day speech, he allows himself the use of purple prose (something that he rarely did, and which was by no means required by his message), it is in order to emphasise the mystery of England, the 'real presence' in the heart of politics of that inexplicable thing called the Crown, the very thing over which Shakespeare puzzled in his history plays. Invoking the ancestral faces that look at us 'from brass and stone, from line and effigy' in our village churches, Powell addresses them with the question that clearly dominated his thinking throughout his political career: 'Tell us what it is that binds us together; show us the clue that leads through a thousand years; whisper to us the secret of this charmed life of England, that we in our time may know how to hold it fast.' And after a Balfour-like rhapsody, he moves to his point:

> One thing above all they assuredly would not forget, Lancastrian or Yorkist, squire or lord, priest or layman; they would point to the kingship of England, and its emblems everywhere visible ... Symbol, yet source of power; person of flesh and blood, yet incarnation of an idea; the kingship would have seemed to them, as it seems to us, to embrace and express the qualities that are peculiarly England's.

---

† Ibid.

The style of that passage arises from the desire, of which Powell himself may not have been entirely conscious, to find a political language which would have a sacramental force. The scarcely veiled reference to the Eucharist, the use of anastrophe ('emblems everywhere visible'), the personification of institutions (kingship) and nations (England) – all this builds upon the use of language that we know from religious ritual. And like the liturgy its authority comes from being repeated, not explained. Such indeed is the only authority, according to Powell, that the Englishman will admit: "'Because it has come to be so" is the only, but to him sufficient, answer which the Englishman gives for his institutions and the authority which is immanent in them.'[†]

By embodying this conception of legitimacy within his style, Powell removed it from discussion. His pronouncements concerning authority, obedience and legitimacy were as though spoken by some god-like voice, decrees issued by history with the force of law, conferring authority on our institutions by their own verbal magic. You see this clearly in a speech given at the Wessex Hotel in Bournemouth on 30 August 1980. Here are some of Powell's arresting words, evoking the mystery of Parliament and its inexplicable offices, in order to sound the death-knell of England:

> The Parliament of the United Kingdom of Great Britain and Northern Ireland came to an end in 1972, when the Lords Commissioners prorogued it in the Queen's name on 26 October. A few days later, on 31 October, with all the customary historic pageantry the Queen came to Westminster to open a new session. But it was a different assembly to which she came, though it was called by the same name. It was an assembly unknown to the history of England, whether under the title of Parliament or any other. It was an assembly which was duty bound to register the decrees, to promulgate the laws and to endorse the policies of an authority outside the realm, an authority not English, an authority not British.

Beginning in that way Powell establishes without argument, but by direct invocation of the central mysteries of his political faith, that

---

[†] Address to the Leicester Junior Chamber, 16 May 1980.

our joining the European Community (as it then was) had created a crisis of legitimacy. If legitimacy lies concealed within institutions, and summarised not by reasons but by the power of their sacred names, then fundamental changes to those institutions can never be legitimate. To put it another way: to describe political processes in sacramental language is to rule out all changes which are not adjustments. And although Powell was wrong in one respect – since our national politics continued and our institutions changed without entirely losing their legitimacy – he was right in another, namely that this transformation amounted to a disenchantment of England, and a loss of those magical formulae on which our pride, allegiance and law-abidingness had hitherto depended. To the demoralised nation that we have become, Powell's language seems fraught and quaint. But we look around ourselves in vain for the alternative, recognising that no politician today has the ability to renew through his words the enchantment that has for centuries attached us to our country, and made it so natural to us to make the sacrifices required for its survival.

Enoch Powell and the Nation State

Andrew Roberts

Central to Enoch Powell's political thought, regarding both foreign policy and domestic policy, was the concept of the nation state. His ideas regarding the continuing relevance of nationhood, and especially the hold it exercises over the imagination, identity and actions of much of mankind – not just Britain – drove him in many areas of his life and career, and animated what from 1965 was already beginning to be called 'Powellism'.

Powell saw the world as being made up of discrete nation states, and his views generally echoed those of George Canning, who at the time of the break-up of the Holy Alliance of eastern European autocracies in the 1820s said: 'Every nation for itself, and God for us all!' While he accepted the need for nation states to join alliances – such as NATO – and to sign treaties over trade, he did not believe that these need compromise their essential sovereignty, the ability to self-govern that constitutes the defining characteristic of the nation state.

Powell's principal opposition to British entry into the Common Market was based on his hostility to Britain's losing her sovereign independence, and thus effectively ending her long history as a nation state, which he dated back to the reign of Henry VIII, and specifically the English Reformation. For although the Treaty of Westphalia that ended the Thirty Years War in 1648 is generally seen as the start of the era of the nation state – it brought several of them into being, apart from anything else – some nation states had already been in existence for centuries. Powell believed that England could trace her career as a nation state to the early Tudors, when Henry VIII proclaimed 'this realm of England is an empire'. The aspects most commonly associated with a nation state – the ability to raise taxes, the self-identification of the populace with

the state, centralised command over the armed forces and so on –
were all present in England in the late Middle Ages, by when the
loss of significant territories in France also concentrated the minds
of the ruling elite on the British Isles.

In France much the same process was taking place under
the stronger Valois kings, such as Henri II, and in Spain after the
expulsion of the Moors by Ferdinand and Isabella in the 1490s.
The roughly contemporaneous consolidation of the nation state in
England, France, Spain and Portugal – all four of which went on to
found large colonial empires – meant that although Germany and
Italy were still mere geographical expressions into the nineteenth
century, there was a powerful and successful model for other poli-
ties to adopt as soon as they were able. Thus when the Dutch finally
shrugged off Austrian rule in the mid-sixteenth century, they swiftly
appropriated the attributes of the modern European nation state,
including having a large colonial empire. Indeed until the twentieth
century no nation state, once it had enjoyed the multifarious political advantages inherent in being one, voluntarily gave it up, except
perhaps for Spain for a few short inglorious months in 1808.

There is every reason to believe that had it not been for the catas-
trophes of the two world wars of the twentieth century the nation
state would have continued to provide the essential building blocks
upon which the whole global political system was based. Even the
great polyglot empires of the pre-1914 era such as the Ottoman,
Russian and Austro-Hungarian empires behaved to all intents and
purposes like nation states in the international arena. Yet because
the First and Second World Wars were widely blamed on hyper-
nationalism, which was in turn seen as inherent to the Westphalian
system, it was the concept of the nation state itself that seemed
vicious, outdated and prone to generating conflict. Yet the true
villain of 1914 and of 1939, as Enoch Powell knew and tirelessly
pointed out, was not the nation state *per se*, but the specific nation
state that was ruled first by Kaiser Wilhelm II and then by Adolf
Hitler. As Powell once wrote of a *non sequitur* which Bentley once
attributed to Boyle: 'Because Milo could carry an ox, therefore he
could carry a brace of elephants!' Because Wilhelm II and Hitler
ruled nation states that went to war, it did not follow that nationalism causes war.

Of course Powell never for a moment contradicted the idea that hyper-nationalism could in certain circumstances lead to war. 'Conflicts don't take place between races,' he told his *Frontier* interviewer, Richard Cohen, in February 1973; 'they take place between social organisations. They may be tribes, or nations, which are in turn terms of some difficulty of definition, but at least are social or political terms, not biological terms. Certainly, the term "nation" is a political term; it is between nations that war takes place. War is a political event.' Yet not for a moment did Powell believe that were there no such thing as nationalism, the result would be universal peace and planetary brotherly love. All that would happen is that war would exist between the tribes or whichever smaller social organisms took the place of the nation. Recent work done by the Harvard psychologist Stephen Pinker and others strongly suggests that such conflicts can be even more bloody than state-on-state ones.

Enoch Powell appreciated how the founding principle of the EEC, therefore, was based on a fundamental misconception arising from faulty historical analysis. Nationalism does not lead inevitably to war, indeed no two democratic nation states have ever fought each other, yet the founding fathers of the EEC – Jean Monnet, Robert Schuman, René Pleven, Maurice Couve de Murville, Paul-Henri Spaak and the rest – at least affected to believe that it did. With the United States – another nation that became success-ful almost as soon as it attained nation-statehood – in the 1950s engaged in a Manichean global struggle against Soviet and Chinese Communism, the impetus for European union was strengthened. Somewhat hypocritically, the American State Department – which enthusiastically signed up for the European project thinking it the economic counterpart to NATO – spent five decades promoting closer European integration, and thus decrying the nation state for Europeans, while zealously defending its privileges for the United States itself (and never spotting the anti-American impulse behind much of the European founding fathers' thinking).

For Enoch Powell, the nation state was thus a shibboleth, a totem, an arrangement that had so proven its value and efficacy for the British people over so many centuries that it needed to be preserved at all costs. In a January 1972 Commons debate on the

Common Market, Powell stressed that it wasn't culture, religion or race that were fundamentally at issue, but the nation state, and he was at pains to define nationhood as 'the thing for which men, if necessary, fight and if necessary, die, and to preserve which men think no sacrifice too great'. He was doubtless thinking of the Second World War, in which he had fought, but it has proved true right up to the present day: no one is willing to fight and die for the European Union, rather than his own individual nation state.

For Powell the course of English, and subsequently British, history proved that Britain was not part of Europe, and that she was thus doing something profoundly unnatural in subsuming her nation state into a wider political and economic entity of Europe. His words in that debate in the House of Commons are so central to his thought that they bear repetition at length, not least also because they are as true today as they were forty years ago.

> The whole development and nature of our national identity and consciousness has not been merely separate from that of the other nations of the continent of Europe, but actually antithetical; and, with the centuries, so far from growing together, our institutions and outlook have rather grown apart from those of our neighbours on the continent. In our history, both recent and earlier, the principal events which have placed their stamp upon our consciousness of who we are, were the very moments in which we have been alone, confronting a Europe which was lost or hostile. That is the picture; that is the folk memory by which our nation has been formed.

Far from being Little Englanders, therefore, Powell argued that opponents of Common Market entry were actually those who believed Britain should set 'her face towards the oceans and the continents of the world'.

The concept of the nation state is a prism through which much of Powellite doctrine – not just his opposition to EEC entry – can usefully be viewed. He disliked America because of its support for European unification; he supported the Falklands War because the Falklanders were Britons to whom the nation state owed protection; he was a monarchist in part because the sovereign personifies the sovereignty of the nation state; he denounced Hola Camp because it besmirched the honour of the British nation state; he became ambivalent or even hostile towards first the British Empire after the Suez Crisis and then the Commonwealth because they seemed to compromise the nation state; whenever the United Nations moved from being a mere collection of nation states to a supranational body trying to take on the characteristics of a nation state, its actions inevitably drew his excoriating ire. Domestically, the union with Ulster had to be defended as Northern Ireland had comprised an integral part of the nation state since the sixteenth-century Plantations.

Powell's sense of nationhood was well developed even by the time he left to take up his professorship at Sydney University, and he read in the newspapers of the appeasement policy adopted by Neville Chamberlain's Tory-dominated National Government, which he thought dishonourable. Volunteering to fight for the British nation in October 1939 – or as he described it, to 'put on the King's coat' – he later described as both being one of the happiest days of his life and, absurdly overmodestly, 'perhaps the only important thing I ever did'. The contents of this book disprove the latter.

Powell's Anglicanism after he found religious belief in 1949 was closely bound up with its nation state antecedents and the established nature of the Church of England, something that it used to value in his time. Simon Heffer's biography *Like the Roman: The Life of Enoch Powell* (1998), which, along with Powell's own *Reflections of a Statesman: The Writings and Speeches of Enoch Powell* (1991), forms the *Ur-text* of Powell studies, states that Powell's 'spirituality is partly that of a creed of nationalism, and that the Church of England's value to one of his intellectual disposition is that it is a national church'. Powell's repeated equation of the start of the English nation state to the Henrician Reformation of the 1530s made it clear that his religious belief went hand in hand with his political philosophy. It was a brand of Toryism that looked back with approbation to the now long-dead days when the Anglican Church really was the Tory Party at prayer. 'The existence and welfare of the nation depend upon an opinion or faith shared by its members,' wrote Powell; 'for the nation is neither the product of reason of deliberate human creation, nor does it correspond to any objective reality ... this supernatural character, if it may be so described, of the most important of human relationships is exemplified and inculcated by the Church, in which men join in order to make assertion and to pursue ends which are frankly, even defiantly, supernatural.' He concluded that this 'community of nation and church ... lies at the heart of Toryism'.

Powell was the paladin of the nation state; he never backed away from defending it from its large and growing number of post-war enemies. After the humiliation of the British Empire during the Suez Crisis of 1956, Powell was eager to offer another, equally romantic story to the British people, one more suited to their long-term future interests and one that harked back even further than imperialism in the story of England. He promised a lyrical, indeed sublime, way forward for a bemused, resentful people conscious of having lost their place in History's sun after several centuries. The salvation he offered lay in the resilience of the nation state. In his seminal speech to the City of London branch of the Royal Society of St George on St George's Eve, 1961, Powell summoned a vision of the post-imperial nation state that provided a way for Britons to see the Suez debacle and the end of their empire in a longer, even perhaps a hopeful perspective.

After reminding his listeners of Herodotus's tale of the Athenians finding the sacred olive tree, symbol of their country, somehow still alive in the ruins of their city after Xerxes's invasion, Powell said: 'So we today at the heart of a vanished empire, amid the fragments of demolished glory, seem to find like one of her own oak trees, standing and growing, the sap still rising from her ancient roots to meet the Spring, England and herself.' Considering that France was even then reacting to her imperial collapse by torturing Algerians, toppling governments and attempting to assassinate President Charles de Gaulle, it was a splendid message of hope for Britons. What turned Powell into a pessimist twenty years on was the reaction of so much of the rest of the British establishment, which concluded from the Suez debacle that Britain's future lay in subsuming her sovereignty into the Common Market.

In a debate in the House of Commons on 25 February 1970, the Labour MP George Brown said: 'The outfit which I was envisaging would be a democratic European Parliament controlling all the nation states in Europe.' Earlier in that debate, Powell had asked what would have happened if in 1940, Britain had been part of a political and military unit with a single political government and a single command, a unit much larger in relation to the United Kingdom than the alliance of France and Britain was. I ask: does anyone suppose that the force which saved this country and saved liberty would not have been thrown into the lost battle by that political unit and swallowed up in defeat? That is what is meant by political unity.

When MPs cried 'No', Powell retorted: 'Honourable Members will not face it.' When they shouted 'It is not true', Hansard records him adding:

Honourable Members have to come to face the difference between political unity, which means what is says, and alliance. This is the acid test of whether we identify ourselves with the electorate of the rest of western Europe, so that we regard ourselves as part of that whole just as surely as Coventry and Bristol regarded themselves as part of the United Kingdom in 1940.

When Captain Walter Elliot, Tory MP for Carshalton and a pre-war appeaser, rose to interrupt him, Powell said:

I have almost finished. This is my last word. I do not believe that that is the outlook of the people of the country. I do not believe that they so regard themselves now or will so regard themselves in the foreseeable future. That is why I believe that, whatever we say in this House, whatever white papers we publish, whatever negotiations we enter into, when the reality is comprehended it will be rejected by the people of Britain.

Of course in this he was proved wrong.

On 27 June 1971 Powell was asked about the nation state in a BBC1 interview by Marc Ullman, who argued that

the whole question of sovereignty is now very different from what it used to be in the early fifties. At that time there were a lot of people on the Continent who were anxious to destroy the nation states, because they thought that the nation states were responsible for two world wars in a single generation. Nowadays there is no prospect, I think it's fair to say, of war between western European countries. Therefore the question is not really to destroy or not to destroy the nation states. The question is for the member countries in Europe to do together what they cannot do alone.

Of course Powell immediately went on the offensive, utterly repudiating Ullman's premise, and saying:

> The official case, the official advocacy for British membership, is very much concerned with the prevention of future European conflict. Both Sir Alec Home and Mr Heath have repeatedly emphasised that in their view the supreme reason for the Community itself and for British membership is that, to use their own words, it would prevent future civil war in Europe. I myself think that this is a misconception, this expression. But never mind. The point is that in this country the avoidance of conflict in Western Europe and perhaps the avoidance of conflict in Europe is presented as perhaps the greatest of all the reasons for a community which is intended to grow into a political entity of its own. So you may have got past this stage in France or on the Continent, but here it is in the very centre of the argument.

The reason that Powell did not like the concept of a European civil war, as both the Great War and the Second World War have been described by sloppy thinkers, is that it presupposes that there was a European nation in the first place.

The concept of the national economy being the economy of the nation state, and not part of some higher or lesser organism, was rammed home by Powell in a speech at the Painters' Hall in London on 13 July 1971, when he said:

> The British economy is the economy of a nation state. We could, indeed, talk about the economy of Somerset or Siberia or South America; there is nothing absurd or impracticable in taking either a continent or an arbitrary piece of territory and describing or studying the economic activities carried on by those who live in it any more than in describing and studying its geology or its climate. But when we talk about the economy of Britain, we choose to do so not because

Britain is an economic region or a geographical entity, but because it is the home of a nation state. We take as our starting point the existence of the nation occupying that territory, and we proceed from there to consider the economic behaviour and experience of its inhabitants. In doing so, we are not considering their economic behaviour and experience as individuals or as an arbitrary sample of humanity; we do so because the sum of their behaviour and experience makes up the life of the nation in its economic aspect. It is, as it were, the economic portrait of its physiognomy. There is something else too: we do this because we assume that, Britain being a nation state, political power can, and probably will, be used to alter its economic life.

This he warned his audience to guard against as the clouds of the European Economic Community started to gather over the British economy, and the Conservative Prime Minister, Ted Heath, made ever clearer his desire to enter the Common Market in the lifetime of that parliament, come what may.

Speaking to the Lyons Club of Brussels in the Palace Hotel there on 24 January 1972, Powell expounded his view about the history of British sovereignty in more detail than ever before or since, at least outside his tremendously learned works on the history of Parliament, and so also deserves quotation *in extenso*:

The relevant fact about the history of the British Isles and above all of England is its separateness in the political sense from the history of continental Europe. The English have never belonged and have always known that they did not belong to it. The assertion contains no element of paradox. The Angevin Empire contradicts it as little as the English claim to the throne of France; neither the possession of Gascony nor the inheritance of Hanover made Edward I or George III anything but English sovereigns. Then Henry VIII declared that 'this realm of England, is an empire (*imperium*) of itself'; he was making not a new claim but a very old one, but he was making it at a very significant point of time. He meant – as Edward I had meant, when he said the same over 200 years earlier – that there is an *imperium* on the Continent, but that England is another *imperium* outside its orbit and is endowed with the plenitude of its own sovereignty. The moment at which Henry VIII repeated this assertion was that of what is misleadingly called 'the Reformation' – misleadingly, because it was, and is, essentially a political and not a religious event. The whole subsequent history of Britain and the political character of the British people have taken their colour and trace their unique quality from that moment and that assertion. It was the final decision that no authority, no law, no court outside the realm would be recognised within the realm. When Cardinal Wolsey fell, the last attempt had failed to bring or keep the English nation within the ambit of any external jurisdiction or political power: since then no law has been made for England outside England, and no taxation has been levied in England by or for an authority outside England – or at least not until the proposition that Britain should accede to the Common Market. Remote from one another as the two men may seem in all appearance, Mr Heath is not only the successor, but the immediate successor, of Wolsey, in this sense, that he has been the first statesman for over 400 years to propose to reverse the decision of Tudor England to complete its independence.

With that superbly dry and ironic sense of humour for which he was famed, Enoch Powell then added: 'Cardinal Wolsey escaped the scaffold, though only narrowly. It is naturally my personal hope that Mr Heath will do so too, and by a much more generous margin.' For all that we might legitimately doubt Powell's sentiments in the last sentence – or at least not share them – his historical argument is irreproachable. History mattered deeply to Powell; how could it not as an historian of note himself? British exceptionalism was a straightforward historical fact for him, and it seemed quite extraordinary to him that other Britons could seek to play it down, still less ignore it altogether.

After entering the EEC, sometimes with Commons majorities as low as eight, the Heath government hit massive economic turbulence, much of it self-inflicted. Speaking on 24 April 1973 about the government's counter-inflationary policy and its approach to floating the pound, Powell told Staffordshire National Farmers Union:

During the months in which Britain's entry into the Community was being decided by paper-thin margins, Parliament and people

were repeatedly informed that no significant parliamentary sovereignty or political independence would be lost, since on any matter
where they felt strongly that our national interest was involved, we
could use what came loosely to be called 'the veto'. Well, here is
national interest, so strong that the government has taken statutory
powers in breach of its election promises and maintains a floating
pound in defiance of its international undertakings. Let us see what
our 'veto' amounts to.

Powell was right; the vetoes were so watered down over the
following decades, and on those rare occasions when they were
exercised by Britain – principally by Margaret Thatcher in getting
down Britain's budgetary contributions, but also in December 2011
by David Cameron – there were shouts of fury that Britain was
'isolating' herself in Europe, holding up the European 'project', and
so on. Powell predicted all of this, as well as so much else.

The way in which the House of Commons 'took possession of
me', as Enoch Powell put it, was closely related to his view of the
nation state, for although he was always quick to point out that it
was with the Queen in Parliament that British sovereignty ultimately resided, rather than merely Parliament itself, he felt a deep
love for the House of Commons, its traditions, history and powers.
'It was the incarnation of a nation to me,' he told one interviewer,
and the defence of its position in the national life became what
he freely admitted became 'an obsession'. He was deeply conscious
after 1973 that he was fighting a losing battle; the surprising thing is
that he wasn't even more pessimistic.

There were moments of optimism, such as when on 24 June 1973,
in a debate against Roy Jenkins on Radio 4 moderated by Robin
Day, the question again came up of Britain's emergency flotation of
the pound sterling, of which Powell said:

Well, it's arguable that it shouldn't [float]. But at least it was able to
do so. It was able to take its own line in the face, if you like, arguably
of international agreements. And certainly contrary to the wishes
and predisposition of its prospective partners in the EEC, and
indeed we can't indefinitely go along in the EEC without reversing
that decision. Now there is, after all, in the present a concrete case

where despite all the influences of the outside world, this nation state still had the power – and most people are glad that it had the power – to take its own decisions.

Humour of the most quintessentially English type was never far from Powell's speeches, and it forms much of their delight. On 13 July 1973, in a speech to the Barrow & Dalton Conservative Association in Barrow-in-Furness, he replied to a speech that had been made in Paris by the British Ambassador to France, Sir Christopher (later Lord) Soames, who had said: 'The enlarged Community is something qualitatively different from the nation states of which it is composed; it is not simply a new Roman Empire, nor a greater Britain, nor a France writ large, but something else and unprecedented.' Powell's reply was 'He can say that again', for 'not even the Roman Empire, in its extreme bureaucratic arteriosclerosis, attempted to fix the grades of beer and milk in Britain.'

Of course Powell's decision to break with the Conservative Party – though never with its grass-roots activists – in February 1974 was intimately bound up with his views on the nation state, for, as he told South Kensington Young Conservatives on 30 September 1976, when answering the perennial question of why he had advised people to vote for a party that offered a referendum on membership of the EEC (which turned out to be Labour):

Through the mouth of its leader in the highest office under the Crown, the Conservative Party declared that the nation state as exemplified by an independent and self-governing United Kingdom was obsolete. Thereby for me the Conservative Party ceased to be the Conservative Party which I thought I knew and to whose causes my political life had been devoted. It became an incomprehensible stranger to me, though apparently the incomprehension was mutual, because despite all that I said and did the party seemed unaware that anything had happened. I remember that in June 1973, in a radio programme widely reported and commented on, I declared that I would live my life out, if I must, in a socialist Britain if that was the price of Britain not losing its political independence.

Such was Powell's commitment to the nation state.

It was in 1976, in Douglas Evans and Richard Body's book *Freedom and Stability in the World Economy*, that Powell demolished many of the myths regarding statehood and nationalism that had been put about by the pro-European lobby in the referendum campaign the previous year. He started off by admitting that as the word 'sovereignty' had 'an old-fashioned, imperialistic sort of sound' it would be better to use words like 'independent' or 'self-governing' instead. He set out to point out that 'independence is not the same as omnipotence', and that even the USA and USSR had to act within certain guidelines, and have 'intercourse and co-operation' with others, yet no one doubted that they were self-governing. So why could Britain not enter defensive and trade organisations without being expected to give up its sovereignty? To those who argued that signing treaties meant signing away independence, Powell pointed out that 'a man who has made a contract to deliver a sack of coals is still a freeman and not a slave.' A tariff union in itself does not lessen sovereignty, whereas a nation that permanently relinquished its right to another authority to take decisions over trade clearly had. He then tore into the idea that because the world was becoming more interdependent economically, that should in any way lessen nations' political independence and rights of self-government. 'A visitor from Mars,' he wrote, 'presented with all the data he might request about the population of Europe, Asia, North America or South America, except their political boundaries, would not be able to tell you whether each of these continents contained one self-governing people, or ten, or fifty.'

The concept of the nation state infused Enoch Powell's stance on Britain's relations with Ulster, for, as he told a public meeting in the Orange Hall at Ballynahinch on 8 October 1974:

> Of the two propositions – that Ulster ought to remain part of the United Kingdom and that Ulster ought to become part of an all-Ireland state – there is only one that can be endowed with certitude, only one that can stand. I state this as an indisputable fact, whether or not it is to some a disagreeable fact. It simply is not within the range of political reality that a democratic nation state could sever off a part of itself where the majority of the inhabitants manifest repeatedly, under all manner of testing and despite all manner of

pressure, their determination to remain part of the state and ask no more than to be treated as the other parts are treated.

Some of Powell's most Churchillian rhetoric came when he combined the issues of the EEC and Ulster within the context of the threat to the nation state, as when on 10 December 1976 he addressed the annual general meeting of the Mourne Unionist Association, and told them:

> The very basis of the case of those who voted for British membership, and who now say they intend to vote for a directly elected European parliament which will override and overshadow our national parliament, is that the United Kingdom is obsolete as a nation state, and that we are too small and too weak any longer to expect to be able to govern ourselves and decide our own policies. Now, there are periods in our history, through one of which we seem to be living, when the inhabitants of the greater part of Britain fall into a kind of lethargic slumber, in which they become oblivious of what they are and have been and lose all sense of pride, honour and self-respect; periods, in short, in which they forget what it is to be a nation. But Ulster never forgets what a nation is or what it is to belong to a nation. We never forget because we never can forget. It is ever before us, written often in letters of blood and fire. To tear the people of Ulster from the nation of which they are part is the one end and purpose of all the terror and carnage and destruction that has filled these last seven years. It is about nothing else. We, therefore, if anyone, can remind our fellow subjects what it is to be a nation – and what it means to cease to be a nation.

Similarly, Powell's stance on New Commonwealth immigration needs to be viewed through his concept of the nation state, right from the early days of his opposition to the 1948 British Nationality Bill through to the end of his life. Powell feared that post-war governments' willingness to redefine British citizenship by reference to what he called 'Crown subjecthood', which they then failed to follow through logically when India became a republic in 1948, again when Pakistan became one in 1956 and when several West Indian colonies achieved independence in the 1960s, confused the nation state with an amorphous new concept of New Commonwealth citizenship, which at that time had no rational basis in law or history. As Powell told Nottingham University Conservative Association on 17 February 1984:

> The paradoxical unlimited right of entry into the United Kingdom came to be equated with the free movement of persons inside a nation state, and apprehension of the eventual consequences of mass immigration into Britain was classified under the categories of 'racial discrimination' and 'racism', which were diffused around the world from the focus of debate in America.

The decision of the 1948 Act effectively to take the right of people to enter the United Kingdom out of the hands of the British government ran directly counter to Powell's conception of the nation state.

Since it was over the immigration question that Powell's eminently well-justified hopes of a successful career in Cabinet government were ended forever, it can be argued that his views on the rights of the nation state were central to the most spectacular non-scandal-related fall of any British politician of the post-war period. 'There is nothing in Christian ethics which enables us,' he told an interviewer in February 1973, 'having recognised the existence of nations, to decide what policy a particular nation should follow in admitting or not admitting those who do not belong to it, or in distinguishing among those external to it between some as belonging and others as not belonging. These are concepts of which Christianity knows nothing.' Over immigration, therefore, as with so much else in Powellite thought, it all came down to the nation state and its rights and duties.

Yet Europe was always the most important place where Enoch Powell's fundamentalist view on the nation state clashed with those of the Heathites and Tory wets. Speaking to Swansea East Conservative Association on 17 June 1977, he said:

> The other reassuring misinterpretation of days gone by was to represent the Community as essentially only a large free market orientated towards wider trade but devoid of serious political pretensions. This also has not survived the experience of real life, which proved ever more clearly as time passed that the Heathite

view of Europe as superseding the obsolete nation state was the *true* philosophy and dynamic of the Community.

Later in that same speech he said of the promoters of British entry into the EEC:

> I can still only half believe that I was myself an unwilling witness to my country's abnegation of its own national independence ... I am not to know whether it is destined that my fellow countrymen will be contented with the status of a European province now, will accept that henceforward this nation is unworthy or incapable of being an independent sovereign state like Iceland or Zambia.

Even the 1976 fishery disputes with Iceland were pressed into service to support Powell's beliefs regarding the nation state's continuing relevance to Britain. At a press conference to mark the first anniversary of the EEC referendum, held at the Waldorf Hotel in London on 3 June 1976, Powell said of what was called the 'Cod War' that

> Britain's humiliation is evidence that the day of the nation state, even the small nation state, even the tiny nation state, is not over. On the contrary, the nation state can impose its will within its own environment more effectively today than fifty or a hundred years ago. Britain, however, has been defeated and humiliated not so much by Iceland as by the fact that she herself has lost sovereignty over her own seas by membership of the EEC. By depriving her of any right over her own waters except such as her EEC partners may graciously be pleased unanimously to concede, this has made her powerless to exert the unrivalled bargaining power which a 200-mile economic zone round the United Kingdom would otherwise have given us.

Britain's control of 60 per cent of EEC waters and 85 per cent of its fish in 1972 ought to have kept her as a fisheries superpower, but successive defeats over the years massacred the British fishing industry.

The issue of devolution of power to what he called 'anti-parliaments' in Wales and Scotland was for Powell a symptom of the demise of the nation state. In a particularly pessimistic speech, delivered to Bromley Chamber of Commerce on 9 July 1976, he said:

It is the nation that is dying, it is dying politically – or rather, perhaps, it is committing suicide politically – and the mark of death upon it is that it has lost the will to live. Wherever one looks, near or far, in small or great, one sees the same morphology: the nation is abdicating. Two thirds of the voters confirmed at a referendum the embodiment of this country in the EEC, which its principal advocates openly recommended on the ground that this country was no longer capable of being a nation state and that, indeed, for such countries as this the day of the nation state was over. It is too easy to pretend that the electorate 'knew not what they did'. The fact remains that to be a nation self-governed and self-taxed, living under its own laws and accepting no external authority, meant nothing to the majority of them. What their fathers and their remote ancestors had lived and died for they waved aside with less than a perfunctory sigh. The mirror-image of external abdication is internal abdication. As we no longer believe in the independence of the nation, we no longer believe in the unity of the nation.

Powell was an honest enough politician to state, as he did to the Federation of Sussex Industries at Crawley on 31 May 1978, that although he did not believe that the EEC would bring prosperity, even if it was somehow magically guaranteed to do so he would still oppose it, because some things are more important than material wealth. As he put it:

A person would be guilty of no contradiction who said: 'I believe that everyone in this island would be better off in twenty years' time if it is part of the EEC than if Britain is a nation state; but I wish Britain to be a nation state.' This is an expression of preference which countless times in history men have felt and acted upon: it is entirely rational to say: 'I prefer belonging to a nation state to having two cars and a washing-up machine twenty years sooner, or even to having two cars and a washing-up machine at all.' Men have joyfully accepted severer deprivations, not to say sacrifices, for the sake of preserving a collective entity whose exclusive claim to their loyalty and self-identification they acknowledged.

Elsewhere in that speech he described the nation state as 'the most emphatic form of political society'. The great honesty in admitting that, for all the important commercial, economic and fiscal aspects militating against European integration, the one that ultimately mattered was visceral – stemming from the heart more than the head (let alone the wallet) – is part of what made Powellism such an extraordinary political phenomenon.

This most cerebral of political thinkers was thus ultimately driven by his gut instincts, of which a fierce patriotism was – along with his religious faith – the strongest. And the patriotism stemmed not from some chauvinistic belief in superiority, but from his historical knowledge of the uniqueness of Britain's world role, which in itself could only have been given expression through the concept of the sovereignty of the nation state. In another speech that same month he addressed this concept of uniqueness, arguing:

> Though the nature of the British nation is, like that of others, historically unique, the world around us abounds with nation states, small and large, in full enjoyment of undivided conscience and self-consciousness. The nation state, contrary to many predictions, is neither obsolete nor obsolescent, it is neither a dodo nor a coelacanth. What obstacles there are to recovery and health are subjective; they are psychological; as such, they import the imprisoning circularity whereby we cannot recover our undivided allegiance unless we believe we can or, in other words, unless somehow it is still there, all the time, to be reasserted, re-enjoyed and re-exploited.

As an elder statesman, Powell continued to hammer home the fact that, as he put it in a debate against Edward Heath at the Cambridge Union two days before the May 1979 general election: 'The question of a nation or no nation is the most important and fundamental question that people can ask themselves.' Yet when Heath stated that sovereignty was 'not an issue', a majority of undergraduates supported him. Undeterred, Powell shortly afterwards told the free-market Cobden Club:

> The EEC differs radically from all the rest because its component parts, by virtue of membership, cease progressively to be nation states, which, while having no social relationship with one another,

can still determine their own commercial, economic and fiscal policies. The internal free trade of the EEC ... closely approximates to
what prevails within a single state; its external policy has nothing
to do with promoting free trade but is directed to procuring, either
unilaterally or reciprocally, what are regarded as the interests of the
Community viewed as a single entity.

Speaking in Eastbourne Town Hall on 2 September 1983, Powell
unerringly put his finger on another aspect of the European
project, pointing out: 'There is no limit to the progressive extension
of the exercise by the EEC of the political powers ceded to it by
the nation states.'

Powell confronted head on the question of whether France had
lost her essential national sovereignty by joining the EEC, in a way
that he claimed Britain had. Speaking to the Institute of Directors
of Jersey on 17 January 1981, he started with an unexpected sub-
clause: 'I have never ceased to pay tribute to Edward Heath,' before
going on to say, 'the principal architect, if not the "onlie begetter"
of Britain's membership of the EEC, for having openly and plainly
rested his advocacy of it on the proposition that Britain ought to
cease, if it had not ceased already, to be a nation state ... Those
content to view things upon the surface, however, are often heard to
object: "But what about France and the other members? Have they
too decided no longer to be nations?" I will answer the question. At
least so far as it relates to France, No; and that is why the French
fulfil the obligations of membership only so far as they judge them,
taken separately, to coincide with their own interests. The behaviour
of France is a standing proof not of some moral obliquity on the
part of the French but of the correctness of my analysis. As to
the other states, some fall into the French category and behave or
will behave in the same way, while others no longer do identify
themselves as nations or, like West Germany, regard the Community
as a necessary stage on the way to re-establishing that identity.'

When we look at the cause of the nation state today, we see its
foes as strong as ever, despite the on-going economic and financial
catastrophe that is the eurozone. The anti-Westphalians argue
that the problems of global warming, of international terrorism,
of nuclear accidents, of tsunamis and other extraordinary natural

disasters, of rogue states and of global economic meltdown cross so many borders so easily today that they are simply not conducive to solutions based on the sovereignty of nation states. Indeed many argue that in some cases the very existence of the nation state itself, rather than regional and global multinational bodies and groupings, makes the problems worse by increasing intransigence and parochialism, and that only a world government can solve the planet's problems equitably. They argue that the day of the nation state, which might have made sense in the days of slower communications and immature markets, is now done.

They are wrong, and will continue to be so for as long as people continue instinctively to feel that their first loyalty and love belongs to their nation state before any wider bodies, up to and including Mother Earth. We badly need another Enoch Powell to articulate the role of the nation state in the twenty-first century, but until such a paragon appears, we can return to the canon of his writings and speeches to remind us why the nation state still does and should matter.

In a broadcast on Disraelian political thought on BBC Radio on 19 April 1981, the centenary of Disraeli's death, Powell argued that in books such as *Coningsby* and *Sybil* 'lie perhaps the one political mission to which the kaleidoscopic and enigmatical character Benjamin Disraeli genuinely felt himself called: to teach the English their nationhood', adding that modern politicians 'will recognise the nation as the be-all and end-all of politics, and yet seek in vain for a tenable definition of it'. As well as Disraeli, but very few Tory thinkers since, Enoch Powell himself had a mission 'to teach the English their nationhood', as well as a genius for defining it.

Nationhood

St George's Day Society, 22 April 1961

Once or twice at most in a lifetime a man ought to be allowed, as you have done me the honour to allow me tonight, to propose this toast. Introspection for a nation, as for an individual, is an unhealthy attitude unless it be sparingly practised; but from time to time an Englishman among other Englishmen may without harm, and even with advantage, seek to express in spoken words just cause to praise his country.

There was a saying, not heard today so often as formerly, 'What do they know of England who only England know?' It is a saying which dates. It has a period aroma, like Kipling's Recessional or the state rooms at Osborne. The period is that which the historian Sir John Seely, in a now almost forgotten but once immensely popular book, called *The Expansion of England*. In that incredible phase, which came upon the English unawares, as all true greatness comes unawares upon a nation, the power and influence of England expanded with the force and speed of an explosion. The strange and brief conjuncture of cheap and invincible seapower with industrial potential brought the islands and the continents under the influence, I almost said under the spell of England; and it was the Englishman who carried with him to the Rockies or the Northwest frontier, to the Australian deserts or the African lakes, 'the thoughts by England given', who seemed to himself and to a great part of his countrymen at home to be the typical Englishman with the truest perspective of England.

That phase is ended, so plainly ended that even the generation born at its zenith, for whom the realization is hardest, no longer deceive themselves as to the fact. That power and that glory have vanished, as surely, if not as tracelessly, as the Imperial fleet from the waters of Spithead; in the eye of history, no doubt as inevitably as 'Nineveh and Tyre', as Rome and Spain.

And yet England is not as Nineveh and Tyre, nor as Rome, nor as Spain. Herodotus relates how Athenians, returning to their city after it had been sacked and burnt by Xerxes and the Persian army, were astonished to find, alive and flourishing in the midst of the blackened ruins, the sacred olive tree, the native symbol of their country. So we today at the heart of a vanished Empire, amid the fragments of demolished glory, seem to find like one of her own oak trees, standing and growing, the sap still rising from her ancient roots to meet the Spring, England and herself.

Perhaps after all we know most of England 'who only England know'.

There was this deep, this providential difference between our Empire and those others, that the nationhood of the Mother country remained unaltered through it all, almost unconscious of the strange fantastic structure built around her – in modern parlance, 'uninvolved'. The citizenship of Rome dissolved into the citizenship of the whole ancient world; Spain learnt to live on the treasure of the Americas; the Hapsburgs and the Hohenzollerns extended their policy with their power. But England, which took as an axiom that the American Colonies could not be represented in parliament and had to confess that even Ireland was not to be assimilated, underwent no organic change as the mistress of a World Empire. So the continuity of her existence was unbroken when the looser connections which linked her with distant continents and strange races fell away.

Thus our generation is like one which comes home again from years of distant wandering. We discover affinities with earlier generations of English, generations before the 'expansion of England', who felt no country but this to be their own. We look upon the traces which they left with a new curiosity, the curiosity of finding ourselves once more akin with the old English. Backward travels our gaze beyond the grenadiers and the philosophers of the eighteenth century, beyond the pikemen and the preachers of the seventeenth, back through the brash adventurous days of the first Elizabeth and the hard materialism of the Tudors, and there at last we find them, or seem to find them, in many a village church, beneath the tall tracery of a perpendicular east window and the coffered ceiling of the chantry chapel. From brass and stone, from line and effigy, their eyes look out at us, and we gaze into them, as if we would win some answer from their inscrutable silence.

'Tell us what it is that binds us together; show us the clue that leads through a thousand years; whisper to us the secret of this charmed life of England, that we in our time may know how to hold it fast.'

What would they say? They would speak to us in our own English tongue, the tongue made for telling truth in, tuned already to songs that haunt the hearer like the sadness of spring. They would tell us of that marvellous land, so sweetly mixed of opposites in climate that all the seasons of the year appear there in their greatest perfection; of the fields amid which they built their halls, their cottages, their churches, and where the same blackthorn showered its petals upon them as upon us; they would tell us, surely, of the rivers, the hills, and of the island coasts of England. They would tell us too of a palace near the great city which the Romans built at a ford of the River Thames, a palace with many chambers and one lofty hall, with angel faces carved on the hammer frames, to which men resorted out of all England to speak on behalf of their fellows, a thing called 'Parliament', and from that hall went out men with fur trimmed gowns and strange caps on their heads, to judge the same judgments, and dispense the same justice, to all people of England.

One thing above all they assuredly would not forget, Lancastrian or Yorkist, squire or lord, priest or layman; they would point to the kingship of England, and its emblems everywhere visible. The immemorial arms, gules, three leopards or, though quartered of late with France, azure, three *fleurs de lis argent*; and older still, the crown itself and that sceptred awe, in which Saint Edward the Englishman still seemed to sit in his own chair to claim the allegiance of all the English. Symbol, yet source of power; person of flesh and blood, yet incarnation of an idea; the kingship would have seemed to them, as it seems to us, to embrace and express the qualities that are peculiarly England's.

The unity of England, effortless and unconstrained, which accepts the unlimited supremacy of crown in Parliament so naturally as not to be aware of it; the homogeneity of England, so profound and embracing that the counties and the regions make it a hobby to discover their differences and assert their peculiarities. The continuity of England, which has brought this unity and homogeneity about by the slow alchemy of centuries.

For the unbroken life of the English nation over a thousand years and more is a phenomenon unique in history, the product of a specific set of circumstances like those which in biology are supposed to start by chance a new line of evolution. Institutions which elsewhere are recent and artificial creations appear in England almost as works of nature, spontaneous and unquestioned. The deepest instinct of the Englishman – how the word 'instinct' keeps forcing itself in again and again! – is for continuity; he never acts more freely nor innovates more boldly than when he is most conscious of conserving or even of reacting.

From this continuous life of an united people in its island home spring, as from the soil of England, all that is peculiar in the gifts and the achievement of the English nation, its laws, its literature, its freedom, its self-discipline. All its impact on the outer world, in earlier colonies, in later pax Britannica, in government and law giving, in commerce and in thought, has flowed from impulses generated here. And this continuous and continuing life of England is symbolised and expressed, as by nothing else, by the English kingship. English it is, for all the leeks and thistles and shamrocks, the Stuarts and the Hanoverians, for all the titles grafted upon it here and elsewhere, 'her other realms and territories', Headships of Commonwealths, and what not. The stock that received all these grafts is English, the sap that rises through it to the extremities rises from roots in English earth, the earth of England's history.

We in our day ought well to guard, as highly to honour, the parent stem of England, and its royal talisman; for we know not what branches yet that wonderful tree will have the power to put forth. The danger is not always violence and force: them we have withstood before and can again. The peril can also be indifference and humbug, which might squander the accumulated wealth of tradition and devalue our sacred symbolism to achieve some cheap compromise or some evanescent purpose.

These are not thoughts for every day, nor words for every company; but on St George's Eve, in the Society of St George, may we not fitly think and speak them, to renew and strengthen in ourselves the resolves and the loyalties which English reserve keeps otherwise and best in silence?

Immigration

Tom Bower

Just before 2.30 p.m. on Saturday 20 April 1968, Enoch Powell arrived at a small hall in Birmingham to address the annual general meeting of the West Midlands Area Conservative Political Centre. About eighty-five people had gathered to hear the speech of the party's shadow Secretary of State for Defence. Surprisingly for such an apparently insignificant event, there were a number of newspaper journalists and a camera crew sent by ITV television news to record his speech. Powell was pleased that his advance publicity had worked. Shortly before, he had told an acquaintance about his intention to make a speech 'that would go up like a rocket and would stay up'.† In the event, he surpassed his expectations. The speech he made that afternoon – carefully crafted and dramatically delivered – arguably had more impact on British politics than any rival British politician's speech since 1945.

Powell's theme was immigration. Principally, he was warning Britain that the numbers of Asians and Caribbeans annually arriving in Britain was excessive. At least 50,000 dependants were arriving every year and, according to Powell, their cumulative numbers were disturbing the indigenous Briton's tolerance by placing a burden on the country's schools, hospitals and housing. If left unchecked, he believed, British democracy would be endangered and the growing ghettos of non-whites in the cities would spark widespread violence similar to the recent race riots across the United States.

Within hours of completing his speech, Powell was condemned by Members of Parliament of all the parties in Westminster as an opportunist outrageously playing the race card, not least to topple Edward Heath, the Conservative Party leader. He did receive

---

† Robert Shepherd, *Enoch Powell* (Pimlico, 1997), p. 345.

sympathy from the handful of right-wing Conservative MPs, and across Britain opinion polls reported that up to 80 per cent of the population supported his demand for curbs or even an outright ban on immigration.

The nation was instantly divided about his speech: was Powell a racist or a deluded imperialist? Once the heightened emotions began to recede in the early 1970s, the more profound question was whether Powell's intemperate phrases had permanently prevented Westminster rationally discussing immigration. Thirty years later, when Labour came to power, did Powell's legacy mute any protests as the government removed many controls which allowed about 250,000 immigrants annually to enter Britain? Within the thirteen years of Labour's government, at least three million immigrants had legally settled in Britain and probably another million lived illegally in the country. As a result, by 2011 official statistics disclosed that 40 per cent of London's population was officially non-white. The empirical evidence suggested that the ethnic population was above 50 per cent. Andrew Green of Migrationwatch accused the Labour government of changing the face of Britain forever without either public discussion or the electorate's approval. The question is whether Labour's politicians could have successfully stifled debate if Powell's 1968 speech had not been cast as 'racist'. Did Powell's oratory make immigration a taboo subject by silencing even reasoned opponents of immigration and multiculturalism who feared being tarnished as racists?

Powell's speech in Birmingham was not the first time he had spoken about race and immigration. Twenty-two years earlier, in 1946, he had written a paper about India for the Conservative Party. Influenced by his wartime service in the sub-continent, he opposed allowing Indians to migrate to Britain. The Indians, he wrote, were so unlike the British that they would resist integrating. The values of the Indians, he suspected, unlike the Caribbean immigrants, were incompatible with British principles. Indians lacked, he argued, 'a collective sentiment of belonging' to a single political homogeneity of the nation, which was essential for self-government and democracy. India's communal violence in 1947 confirmed his argument. Britain's democracy, he later wrote, would be threatened if unintegrated groups of immigrants, especially from India, focused on their own sectarian and political interests rather than Britain's, were empowered to influence Britain's politics.[†]

In 1954, he embraced the logical conclusion about Britain's relationship with its colonies. Having assumed that immigrants would form their own political parties rather than join the mainstream if allowed to settle in Britain, he argued that the English would reject being ruled by an immigrant minority holding the balance of power. Accordingly, he abandoned imperialism and the imperial legacy promoted by his Tory predecessors which gave the immigrants the legal status enter Britain, and embraced English nationalism.

His arguments were crystallised by a bus drivers' protest in West Bromwich in February 1955. With the drivers' support, the council had sacked a Sikh driver for wearing a beard and turban, a breach of the council's regulations. Powell sympathised with the drivers, explaining: 'Any readily visible differences between human beings inevitably result in political frictions.' While slight difference should be ignored, said Powell, if the visual differences were 'distinctive' then 'the workings of institutions such as ours cannot fail to be endangered.' He supported the drivers, who had 'apprehended the dangers for the country of any appreciable coloured population being domiciled here'.[‡]

On 9 April, to Powell's outrage, the council capitulated and reinstated the Sikh. A minority of foreigners, he asserted, had imposed their values on English local government in protection of their identity. The council's surrender, he believed, was profoundly undemocratic and threatened Britain's homogeneity. Thereafter, for the following nine years, no one recorded Powell saying anything about the subject.

Immigration resurfaced as a public topic during the 1964 general election. In Smethwick, a neighbouring constituency, the Tory candidate was challenging Patrick Gordon Walker, the sitting MP, who if Labour was elected would become the Foreign Secretary. Labour activists complained that the Conservative campaign was racist. The 1961 census showed that 24 per cent of births in

---

† Peter Brooke, 'India, Post-Imperialism and the Origins of Enoch Powell's "Rivers Of Blood" Speech', *The Historical Journal* (2007), p. 2.
‡ Ibid, p. 7.

Wolverhampton were to black or Asian mothers although the black population was only 5 per cent. Anonymous campaigners had posted leaflets headed 'If you want a nigger neighbour vote Labour'. In the nearby constituency, Powell told surprised journalists that the biggest issue on the doorstep was immigration. Powell's cure was to control the numbers arriving and integrating those already in Britain.[†] Gordon Walker was defeated and amid the uproar, immigration became for the first time an issue in Westminster.

In 1965, Powell was appointed the shadow Defence Secretary by Heath. Since they shared few ideas about politics and policies except on defence, Powell appreciated the appointment as Heath's method to avoid any unfortunate disagreements.[‡] While Heath remained anxious that Powell would break out and resist sticking to the party's policies, he did not anticipate an argument with Powell about immigration.

In 1965, Powell spoke openly – probably for the first time – about immigration. He was reported by *The Times* saying that it was 'inconceivable' that the rate of immigration into Britain – 75,000 in 1964 – could continue. Some would say he had secretly given up on integration because his real fear was immigrant-only communities. On 30 April 1965, he told a private Conservative Party inquiry that with pressure in his constituency on hospitals and schools, immigration had become a 'flashpoint' and had to be stopped. The party was urged to adopt his policy and 'free us from the humbug, insincerity and self-delusion of what we have said on this subject in government'.[§]

One year later, in a speech on 25 March 1966 during the election campaign, he described immigration as an issue which 'forces itself upon our attention'. It was and should be, he said, an election issue. He stressed the importance of integration: 'I am for my part resolutely determined that they shall, as humanly possible, have the same rights and the same treatment as anyone else ... But all our efforts at integration will be overwhelmed and swept away if the

---

[†] Simon Heffer, *Like the Roman: the Life of Enoch Powell* (Weidenfeld & Nicolson, 1998) p. 360.

[‡] Robert Shepherd, *Enoch Powell* (Pimlico, 1997), p. 297.

[§] Simon Heffer, *Like the Roman: the Life of Enoch Powell* (Weidenfeld & Nicolson, 1998), p. 379.

tide of the immigrants continues to flow in.' At the present rate of entry, he calculated on the basis of official statistics, there would be 2.5 million immigrants in Britain by 2000. His cure was controls and state-assisted repatriation for those immigrants willing to return to their original homes.[†] 'Stopping the further inflow' and promoting repatriation was certainly Conservative Party policy in 1965 under Alec Douglas-Home, not least because Powell wrote the leader's speech advocating those policies. One year later, Conservative policy, he correctly repeated, was that 'the rate of admission must be further and greatly reduced'. The sober advocacy of strict controls was supported by Heath after he became leader.[‡]

By 1967, Powell had developed his opposition to the Labour government's immigration policies. In an article under the headline 'Facing up to Britain's race problem' in the *Daily Telegraph* on 16 February 1967, he pinpointed a deception in the government's presentation of the issue. While ministers could rightly state that immigration was being controlled – entry vouchers were issued to only 7,000 males every year – the government did not announce that annually a further 50,000 dependants of established immigrants were also entering Britain. If that continued, wrote Powell, there would be an additional 1.75 million immigrants in Britain by 2000. By extrapolation, of immigration, emigration and births, he predicted that by 2000, 5 per cent of Britain's population or 3.5 million people would be black. With a nod towards a distinction between immigration and race, Powell explained that his concern was not merely the numbers but the immigrants' concentration in what he called 'self-perpetuating colonies'.

His critics pinpointed a flaw in his argument. As minister of health between 1960 to 1963, he had authorised the NHS to recruit immigrants as doctors and nurses. Although he denied involvement in that policy, many remained unconvinced as his campaign was sharpened.[§]

In what some would consider to be emotional language,

[†] Ibid, p. 404.

[‡] Nicholas Hillman: 'A "chorus of execration"? Enoch Powell's "rivers of blood" forty years on', in *Patterns of Prejudice* (Routledge, 2008), p. 92

[§] Robert Shepherd, *Enoch Powell* (Pimlico, 1997), pp. 222, 351.

Powell described during that year his alarm that 'entire areas' of Wolverhampton were going 'black', affecting the lives of the long-term residents, without any protest or discussion. 'For sale' signs going up in a street, he wrote, 'struck terror into all its inhabitants'. Areas of the city, he continued, were changing as if 'transformed by the bulldozer' and the 'shattering effects on the lives of families' was occurring 'with virtually no physical manifestations of antipathy'. He advocated 'virtually terminating net immigration' by stopping dependants entering Britain and voluntary repatriation so that the numbers would be 'fixed'. With hindsight, he ended with a self-fulfilling prediction: while immigration had fallen down the agenda 'I am going to prophesy that there will be subsequent phases when the problem will resume its place in public concern and in a more intractable form, when it can no longer be dealt with simply by turning the inlet tap down or off.'

The change in tone was partly triggered by the decision of several east African governments – all in former British colonies – to expel their Asian populations. Within Britain, there was a dispute whether the Asians – at least 250,000 people – had been assured of British nationality by a Conservative government in a 1962 Act. Both the Labour government and senior Tory politicians conceded that those guarantees had been made and the Asians were entitled to British passports. If the British government reneged, they explained, the Asians would either have to accept Kenyan nationality or be stateless.

Powell disagreed. He claimed there had been a 'draughtsman's oversight' in the 1962 Act causing an 'unforeseen loophole' and there was no British obligation to the Asians. Allowing their entry, he said, contradicted Tory policy as restated that year. His stance caused unease among senior Conservative politicians. As minister of health at the very Cabinet meeting in 1962, Powell had approved the legislation allowing the Asians to apply legitimately for British passports. His claim about an 'unforeseen loophole' was proven by the records to be disingenuous, but worse, he was alleging a conspiracy among civil servants to wrongly grant British nationality. He would claim that 'no trace of any undertaking having been given in respect of [Asian] passport holders has ever been produced'.[†]

---

† Robert Shepherd, *Enoch Powell* (Pimlico, 1997), p. 336.

The government's official records showed that his accusation was untrue. He was right, however, that no politician envisaged that 250,000 Asians would take up their right to enter Britain.

The possible arrival of 250,000 Asians coincided with an outbreak of serious race riots in America. Although there was no conceivable parallel between the history of Britain's new immigrants and the descendants of America's slaves, Powell relied on the imagery to draw an equivalence. He not only began to speak about the threat of similar destruction of British cities but eased his rhetoric into what his critics would mark as a significant escalation. In December 1967 he spoke not only about the 'folly of immigration' but also race: 'The British people have been told that they must deny that there is any difference between those who belong to this country and "those others". If you persist in asserting what is an undeniable truth, you will be hounded and pilloried as a racialist.'[†]

At the time, Powell's opinions appeared to be unexceptional among Conservatives and were certainly unnoticed within the wider public. Among Wolverhampton's Conservatives, he was speaking to the converted but his sentiments were not transmitted to a wider audience. Unlike most British constituencies, the town had a comparatively large immigrant population and its growth was a natural topic of conversation for local people. Among that group, Powell's sentiments were not seen as racist, not least because he made a point of emphasising numbers. Fewer arrivals, he said, made integration easier and, in his eccentric opinion, minimised the challenge to democracy.

By 1968, immigration and race had become more important at Westminster. In addition to the American riots and the debate about the chances of 250,000 Asians arriving, politicians were divided about the treatment of the immigrants already settled in Britain. For the left, the 1965 Race Relations Act had laid the foundation stone for outlawing discrimination. The right regarded the law as an abomination because it bestowed rights to a minority against the majority. That sentiment was aggravated in 1967 by the Labour government's proposal to strengthen the 1965 Act by creating an offence of discrimination on the grounds of race in employment

† Ibid, p. 329.

and housing. As James Callaghan, the Home Secretary, explained: 'You cannot legislate prejudice out of existence,' but Parliament should prevent overt prejudice which would create bitterness among immigrant school leavers if they were rejected from jobs just because they were black.

The proposed Bill annoyed Powell and most Conservatives. They argued that the new offences, creating racial privileges, would cause injustice and frustration. In practice, a white Englishman would be legally restricted about what he could say, whom he could employ and to whom he could sell his house. The freedom of the majority to be bigoted was to be restricted by a law imposed by so-called liberals who in the right's opinion were 'authoritarian moralists'.

In early 1968, the shadow Cabinet prevaricated about the new Race Relations Bill and its attitude towards immigration. Heath was torn between supporting strict controls, not wanting to condone racism, the demands from the majority of party activists to stop immigration, and his own reservations about the Bill. He felt that Britain had an obligation towards the east African Asians, could not forbid black immigrants settled in Britain to invite their wives and children to join them without appearing racist, and yet wanted to control immigration. Squaring that circle was nearly impossible. Powell, who in general was irritated by Heath, was especially aggravated by the leader's apparent prevarication about the Race Relations Bill.

In theory, Powell's support for equality was unexceptional. He did object, he said, to a black person being refused service in a pub. But there were limits to his sense of equality. In some circumstances, he said, an individual should not be prevented from advertising a job or a home with the caveat 'No coloured person need apply'. Powell placed the right of the individual against the rights of the minority. To many, that distinction amounted to discrimination on the grounds of race. And Powell made the charge of racism against himself credible by categorising even the blacks born in England as immigrants.

In Powell's definition, a racist was 'that man who believes that one race is inherently superior to another', as distinguished from consciousness of differences between peoples, which in Powell's view made everyone a racialist. In Powell's opinion nationalities were 'different' and it was mistaken to ignore that, or believe it was 'racist' to acknowledge differences.

In criticising the Race Relations Bill, Powell spoke about 'one-way privilege'. Regarding those Conservatives who supported the Bill, he scoffed: 'The kindest thing that can be said about those who propose and support it is that "they know not what they do".' His anger had become emotional.

By the beginning of 1968, he was clearly frustrated by Heath's search for consensus with Labour, not least on immigration.[†] Yet his sentiments were unknown among the public, the media or even among some of his colleagues in Westminster. Only the few who were close to the maverick in Wolverhampton seemed to have been aware of his deepening antagonism towards immigration. The statistics for 1967, published in April 1968, showed that while immigration was officially limited to 8,500 permits a year and only 4,078 people had received entry permits, they had been joined by 52,813 dependants. That statistic was given no publicity but the effect was clearly noticed in the Midlands.

The contrast between central London and the poor neighbourhoods in Powell's constituency was stark, and unknown to most power brokers in the capital. The argument for allowing entry to dependants was deemed to be too complicated to debate, not least because Heath and his allies agreed that to prevent immigrants already established in Britain to marry or live with their families was inhumane. Powell disagreed and, like every politician, wanted to show his electorate that he cared for their concerns. Exceptionally, Powell was also addressing a bigger stage.

On 9 February 1968, Powell spoke at a Conservative dinner at Walsall about the 'continued flow' of immigrants. That Britain should have saddled itself with allowing 50,000 dependants to enter Britain in every year was, he said 'crazy ... enough to make one weep and drive one to despair'. Addressing his constituents' concerns, he mentioned the 'sense of hopelessness and helplessness which comes over persons who are trapped or imprisoned when all their efforts to attract attention and assistance bring no response'. Their plight, he noted, was unknown to the vast bulk of white Britons.

---

† Robert Shepherd, *Enoch Powell* (Pimlico, 1997), p. 325.

In subsequent years, Powell and his supporters would suggest that the politician was frustrated by how little attention his Walsall speech attracted. They would argue that his conduct while preparing for his famous speech in Birmingham eight weeks later reflected his disappointment. But others have suggested that his Walsall speech did attract significant attention.[†] Not only did the local newspaper praise Powell for raising 'what has been on so many people's minds' but some fellow frontbenchers criticised his language and tone. Most importantly, Heath asked Powell not to repeat his speech. If Heath expected obedience, he mistook Powell's excitement at finding himself in the spotlight. Immigration attracted the media and was a suitable subject to ride along the high wire to embarrass Heath.

In 1968, few journalists were more respected than Nicholas Tomalin of the *Sunday Times*. With his easy manner, he encouraged those who he interviewed to drop their guard. Powell succumbed to the journalist's charm. 'I deliberately include,' he admitted to Tomalin, 'at least one startling assertion in every speech in order to attract enough attention to give me a power base with the Conservative Party. Provided I keep this going, Ted Heath can never sack me from the shadow Cabinet.' Powell never disputed the accuracy of Tomalin's quotation.

Buoyed by that interview, Powell did not discourage reports of public support for his Walsall speech. In particular, he noted that just three weeks later, the Labour government somersaulted and imposed stricter controls to limit the numbers of east African Asians entering Britain. That concession did not deter James Callaghan, the Home Secretary, from formally introducing the Race Relations Bill in early April. The Tories were divided. Heath supported the Bill so long as there were changes because he feared outright opposition would cast the Conservatives as racist. Nevertheless, at a shadow Cabinet meeting, he proposed a series of amendments. The strategy, implicitly supported by Powell, effectively rejected the Bill. The reason, as Powell said, was that the Bill 'will not in its practical application contribute to the achievement of racial harmony'. Every member of the shadow Cabinet was asked for his opinion. Powell said 'no comment' and joined others in a sub-committee to agree the

---

† Robert Shepherd, *Enoch Powell* (Pimlico, 1997), p. 340.

wording of the amendments to change and effectively oppose the Bill. At the end of the process, everyone had the impression that he supported the party's policy. Powell had been particularly watched during a debate on the Bill on Tuesday 2 April. He could have used the opportunity to challenge Heath. He did not but few were fooled. When he would be asked after his famous Birmingham speech by the *Birmingham Post* about his ultimate ambition, he replied: 'There is no politician who is not ambitious; it is the definition of the animal.' Pressed further whether there was a connection between his speech and his ambitions, he replied: 'No comment.'

Less than two weeks after the shadow Cabinet meeting, without warning, Powell exploded his bomb. As he wrote his speech, Powell's considerable experience could not have precluded his anticipation that his strike would raise the temperature. Yet even he could not have expected its historic influence.

The kernel of his message was that by 2000, 10 per cent of Britain's population – five million to seven million people – would be black or Asian. 'Whole areas,' he predicted, 'towns and parts of towns across England will be occupied by different sections of the immigrant and immigrant-descended population.' The consequences of that transformation, he forecast, were apparent from the messages he received from his own constituents. The whites 'for reasons which they cannot understand ... find themselves made strangers in their own country', resentful about access to schools, hospitals, employment and housing. The milestone in 1985 would be 3.5 million immigrants. His solution was to reduce immigration to 'negligible proportions' and the launch of a programme of 'urgent encouragement of re-emigration'. The alternative, he speculated, was dire.

Until that moment, his speech raised no special alarms. But what followed permanently transformed Britain's debate about immigration. First he described a conversation with a white male constituent. 'In this country,' Powell reported the man saying, 'in fifteen or twenty years' time the black man will have the whip hand over the white man.' Powell attacked the political convention which sought to prevent him repeating that conversation:

Here is a decent, ordinary fellow Englishman who in broad daylight in my own town says to me, his Member of Parliament, that this

country will not be worth living in for his children. I simply do not
have the right to shrug my shoulders and think about something else
... I can already hear the chorus of execration. How dare I say such
a horrible thing? How dare I stir up trouble and inflame feelings by
repeating such a conversation? My answer is that I do not have the
right not to do so.

Ratcheting up a gear, he next referred to a letter from a woman who
described the fate of an elderly widow. 'She is becoming afraid to
go out,' explained Powell. 'Windows are broken. She finds excreta
pushed through her letterbox. When she goes to the shops, she is
followed by children, charming, wide-grinning piccaninnies. They
cannot speak English, but one word they know. "Racialist," they
chant. When the new Race Relations Bill is passed, this woman
is convinced she will go to prison. And is she so wrong? I begin to
wonder.' He concluded: 'The old lady ... lives in fear of violence.'

The Bill, explained Powell, anticipated that immigrants would
integrate into British society but that expectation, he said, was
a 'ludicrous misconception, and a dangerous one to boot'. Sikhs
wanted to maintain their customs and like other immigrant groups
would 'consolidate their members to agitate and campaign against
their fellow citizens, and to overawe and dominate the rest with
legal weapons which the ignorant and ill-informed have provided'.
The ignorant were the white liberals in Westminster and to pass
their race Bill was akin, said Powell, 'to risk throwing a match onto
gunpowder'.

To those who he believed were blinded by their dogma, he
addressed his stark warning:

Those whom the gods wish to destroy, they first make mad. We must
be mad, literally mad, as a nation to be permitting the annual inflow of
some 50,000 dependants ... It is like watching a nation busily engaged
in heaping up its own funeral pyre. So insane are we that we actually
permit unmarried persons to immigrate for the purpose of founding a
family with spouses and fiancées whom they have never seen.

The climax of Powell's oratory, delivered with the conviction of an
evangelical preacher, was a quotation from Virgil's *Aeneid*: 'Like

the Roman, I seem to see the river Tiber foaming with much blood.' Using that emotion, allegedly describing the anguish of an Englishman, Powell placed himself on a pedestal as philosopher, politician, street-corner gossip and classical prophet. Probably no other British politician could hit such a mark in a single speech.[†] Powell was taken seriously because his intelligence and status as a classics scholar bestowed an intellectual credibility upon his rhetoric.

Before nightfall, Powell dominated the media and gossip among politicians. The most important reaction was Heath's. Their relations were strained but Powell certainly did not want to be sidelined. Nevertheless, he had failed to follow the normal procedure of forewarning the Tory leader about his speech by delivering the text in advance to Central Office. Powell would assert that the speech was too insignificant to bother Conservative headquarters but few gave that excuse serious credibility. He had sent the text in advance to his local newspaper and four copies were delivered to the Press Association. Most deduced that his tactics were to maximise his publicity and simultaneously avoid being gagged.

In his first interviews that evening, Powell disingenuously told questioners about his surprise that his speech could have raised so much interest because he had merely been 'speaking the official line'. None of the other members of the shadow Cabinet agreed. Contrary to Conservative policy, Powell wanted to halt the automatic flow of dependants and ultimately favoured 'mass repatriation'. And his tone dramatically separated his approach from the party's. Although the Conservatives were split on immigration, no one else had the taste for equating immigration with 'funeral pyres' and 'rivers foaming with blood'.[‡]

The majority of senior Tory leaders, especially Willie Whitelaw and Quintin Hogg, were appalled, not only by the tone and content of his speech but by a clear declaration of war against Heath by a rival who offered himself to the right wing as a credible, popular leader. Powell, they feared, would 'create hell' for the party's leader. Influenced throughout Sunday by the prominence of the speech in the newspapers and TV news, all agreed with Heath that Powell

---

† Robert Shepherd, *Enoch Powell* (Pimlico, 1997), p. 346.
‡ Hillman, op. cit, p. 92.

should expelled from the shadow Cabinet. In fact some went further and threatened to resign if Powell was not sacked. Only Margaret Thatcher would quietly sympathise with Powell, insisting that he was not a racist but agreeing that his words were 'strong meat'.

On Sunday night, Heath telephoned Powell to announce his decision. The media were told by Heath that Powell's speech was 'racialist in tone and liable to exacerbate racial tensions. This is unacceptable from one of the leaders of the Conservative Party and is incompatible with the responsibility of a member of the shadow Cabinet.' The Conservative Party, continued Heath, 'stands for fairness and decency between races and respect for the dignity of the individual. The words and actions of the party and its leaders must be directed to this end.' But he also added: 'I have repeatedly emphasised that the policy of the Conservative Party is that immigration must be most stringently limited and that immigrants wishing to return to their own countries should be financially helped to do so. But everybody in the country must be treated as equal before the law.'

Effectively, Powell had shot himself in the foot. Contrary to his plan, he had been expelled from the shadow Cabinet and he had been tarnished as a racist. Regardless of whatever explanations he offered in the future, he had become an outsider and a byword for extremism.

Not surprisingly, he defended himself in his reply to Heath's dismissal but could not resist a dig. While promising continued support, he added: 'I believe you will be Prime Minister of this country and that you will be an outstandingly able Prime Minister, perhaps even a great one.' His criticism continued in what some would regard as a smear of Heath's cowardice – for sharing Powell's opinions but lacking the courage to admit it: 'There is one cause of anxiety which I hope time will dispel. It is the impression you often give of playing down and even unsaying policies and views which you hold and believe to be right for fear of clamour from some section of the press or public.' In his own defence, Powell wrote: 'You took occasion to stigmatise my speech in Birmingham as "racialist" when you must surely realise that it was nothing of the kind.'[†]

During Sunday night, Powell returned with his family to London. He could not have been pleased by the media reaction on Monday

---

† Robert Shepherd, *Enoch Powell* (Pimlico, 1997), p. 351.

morning. Reading *The Times* at breakfast must have been a shock. The editorial, headed 'An evil speech', described his utterance as 'disgraceful', 'racialist' and 'shameful'. The speech was condemned for making 'a deliberate appeal to racial hatred. This is the first time that a serious British politician has appealed to racial hatred in this direct way in our post-war history.' Even the *Express and Star*, his local newspaper, which had supported his Walsall speech, criticised him for being 'unnecessarily extravagant in his language', which had incurred 'damage to a cause'. The comparisons between himself and Oswald Mosley reinforced the damage. While his apologists suggested that the anger was about the speech's tone rather than the content, and his intention was to cause maximum embarrassment, others saw a more profound division. Powell's advocacy of repatriation was directly targeted at non-whites and, as such, overtly racial.

The critical sections of the media and Westminster were confronted by a dilemma: the majority of the public supported Powell. Opinion polls found that up to 82 per cent of those asked endorsed his sentiments. Over 100,000 Britons individually wrote letters to Powell expressing their agreement. Very few letters were outright racist. Only 800 wrote disapproving letters. Among Conservatives there was anger that Heath had sacked Powell. Even more remarkable was working-class sympathy for the free-market Tory. The focus of Labour's anguish was the strike by 4,000 London dockers, leaving twenty-nine ships idle, and a widely publicised spontaneous march by 800 dockers along the Embankment to Westminster singing 'I'm Dreaming of a White Christmas'. They were joined by Smithfield meat porters. Outside Parliament, the workers booed the Kenyan high commissioner, who was visiting the palace, and, more surprisingly, heckled Ian Mikardo, the left-wing east London Member of Parliament. The popular MP was clearly staggered by the sentiments of his bedrock constituents. His experience underlined Powell's warning about Westminster's isolation from reality, and justified Powell's need to speak in halls around the country because both the Labour and Conservative parties refused to debate immigration in the Commons.† 'The supreme function of statesmanship', Powell

---

† Simon Heffer, *Like the Roman: the Life of Enoch Powell* (Weidenfeld & Nicolson, 1998), p. 526.

would say, 'is to provide against preventable evils.' Powell spoke about his 'need to speak out' to avoid the 'curses of those who come after' because they had 'knowingly ... shirked warning of the truth'.

Nevertheless, on his arrival in Westminster later that Monday, Powell was met by the genuine anger of the Tory front bench. Powell, they unanimously said, had overstated his case and lost parliamentary support. Apparently, he did get support from Keith Joseph, who blamed the 'honourable short-sightedness of the last Tory government in allowing a flood of immigrants in exacerbated by the passion of the Labour Party to allow floods of immigrants', but that was limited consolation.[†] Shunned by many of his former colleagues, he could find parliamentary support only among the Conservative Party's few extreme right-wingers, who lacked credibility among the party's mainstream membership. Naturally, at the peak of the heady emotions during those days, the weakness of his position remained obscured. It would take some weeks before he gradually discovered that his popularity had declined in the one place he sought more influence.

In the immediate aftermath, Powell was caught in a pincer. On the one hand, he delighted in justifying his arguments and the truth of his warnings. A letter from thirty-nine immigration officers at Heathrow confirmed the government's duplicity: 'Were you to pay a weekend visit here to witness the Asian influx, your fears for the future of this country would doubtless be increased. We are fed up with the corruption and deceit that goes on to get immigrants into this country. This has been going on for years.' Powell released the letter, prompting a Home Office investigation and a witch-hunt for the organisers. Revealingly, the Home Office denied the officers' accusations and refused to implement a remedy.

The downside for Powell was to deny the allegations of racism. His defence would become, some would say, inconsistent, both about the fundamental issue and about the forecasts of numbers of immigrants arriving in Britain.

One foundation of his denial of racism was his expressed surprise about the 'earthquake'. Emphatically he denied that he had ever predicted the outcry. He denied the quotation about contriving a

---

† Simon Heffer, *Like the Roman*, p. 505.

'rocket'.[†] He minimised the sentiments expressed in his interview with Nicholas Tomalin. He ridiculed the idea that his speech had 'rocked the boat'. And he distanced himself from the overt racists who embraced him as their leader by presenting himself as a mere messenger. 'Decisions appear to present themselves fully dressed at the door,' he told the *Daily Mail* in July 1968. 'There is a knock at the door and I open it, and there is the decision. And so it was with that speech.' In summary, Powell denied playing the race card to win popularity and possibly the party's leadership.

In making speeches, Powell explained in another article, politicians try 'to provide people with words and ideas which will fit their predicament'. He presented himself as an interpreter to crystallise people's opinions rather than change them. 'You cannot be the Member for Wolverhampton South West without this matter having been on your mind for the past 10 or 12 years.'[‡] To a similar question, he replied: 'How dare I stir up trouble and inflame feelings by repeating such a conversation? I do not have the right not to do so.' When urged during a particularly robust TV cross-examination by David Frost to bear responsibility for the racial violence [especially in Birmingham] sparked by his speech, he replied: 'I'm not going to be put in the absurd position of dissociating myself from people with whom you know perfectly well I am in no way associated.' To his critics, the wordsmith had merely begged the question: can a politician shirk responsibility for the consequences of his words and deeds? Did Powell not have a duty to anticipate the reaction to his intentionally widely publicised speech? Could he be excused of presenting his prejudices as irrefutable wisdom? Was he a clever agent provocateur, a brilliant conspirator or merely a deluded academic? His denial of any accountability suggested naiveté, dishonesty or cowardice.

Powell's only expressed regrets were misjudging the Conservative Party's opposition to the Race Relations Bill and, more superficially, for translating the Virgil quotation about the Tiber from Latin in the press hand-out. Improbably, he believed, 'nobody would have bothered to translate it' and that would have avoided 'unnecessary

---

† Hillman, op. cit., p. 85.

‡ *Birmingham Post.*

misunderstandings'. For years, he denied being a racist, especially Paul Foot's judgement in 1998: 'The most important thing by far about Enoch Powell was that he was a racist pig of the most despicable variety.'[†] Foot's left-wing judgement, based on his book published in 1969 which had presented Powell's immigration policies at best as opportunistic, gave no credibility to Powell's distinction between 'race' and 'identity'. Others accepted Powell was an intelligent educated observer and chose not to ignore his distinctions and definitions. 'What I take "racialist" to mean,' he explained, 'is a person who believes the inferiority of one race of mankind to another, and so acts and speaks in that belief.' He denied being a racialist except perhaps in reverse: 'I regard many of the peoples in India as being superior in many respects – intellectually for example, and in other respects – to Europeans.' That argument pleased his supporters although he was probably at his most honest in a TV documentary in 1995: 'What's wrong with racism?' he asked. 'Racism is the basis of nationality.'[‡] And since he believed that immigration undermined the nation's cohesion, especially the population's concern for democracy, he could clothe his opposition to immigration, especially from the sub-continent, as principled and not racist.

His credibility suffered once his 'facts' were subjected to forensic scrutiny. In his speech he had mentioned a school where a white girl was the only one in a class of immigrants. Inquiries produced an official explanation that it was an exceptional occurrence on one day. Six other white children in the class happened to be sick that day. At best Powell had been misled by an unchecked anecdote.[§] Others searched for the old woman – the only white in her Wolverhampton street – who had suffered excrement being pushed through her letter box. She could not be found. Pertinently, Powell admitted during the Frost TV interview that he had never spoken to the woman, nor could he personally vouch for her existence. His best defence was 'that it is true as it is typical'. Pressed, he could only refer to official reports of what happens in circumstances

---

† Hillman, op cit., p. 89.

‡ Ibid, p. 89.

§ Simon Heffer, *Like the Roman: the Life of Enoch Powell* (Weidenfeld & Nicolson, 1998), p. 445.

of 'pushing out the native population'. He spoke on behalf of those who ask: '"Why does nobody speak to us? Are we alone? Are we trapped?"' Those sentiments, his characterisation of his constituents bearing a 'sense of oppression, the sense of being victimised', describing his constituents as 'strangers in their own country' when only 2 per cent of Britain was black, were precisely the words suggesting racism to his critics.

On *Panorama*, Ted Heath emphasised that Powell's dismissal was triggered by his perceived racism. The speech, said Heath, was 'inflammatory and liable to damage race relations'. The majority of Britons, he continued, believed that the question 'must be treated with moderation and with tolerance' and do not 'share Mr Powell's way of putting his views'. Powell was unapologetic. He had chosen his words, he insisted, 'very carefully indeed … I didn't wish to be misunderstood and I believe there is no room for misunderstanding.'[†] Within days he had the pleasure of witnessing Heath retreat.

In response to the party activists' support for Powell, Heath advocated that the numbers of immigrants entering Britain should be 'severely curtailed' and his opposition to the Race Relations Bill hardened. Bowing to the right wing during the debate on 23 April 1968, Heath rejected James Callaghan's appeal for 'leadership and nobility' to end the threat of racism and opposed the Bill because it would fail to 'contribute to the achievement of racial harmony'. He was preparing the ground for a speech in Dudley. On 27 April, the leader listed the Tories' proposals for greater controls, albeit matched by demands of debating the issue 'calmly and reasonably'. Responding to Heath, but really to Powellism, the government agreed to fund repatriation, limit immigration to 5,000 entries every year and announced its intention to introduce tighter controls.

Regardless of the criticism, Powell had successfully compelled the country to debate immigration. As *The Observer* conceded, until then 'race [had] become a taboo subject' which lamentably had prevented a civilised public discussion.[‡] Under the sub-headlines 'A sense of betrayal' and 'Remedy for grievances' *The Observer*, which

---

[†] ITV, 21 April.
[‡] *The Observer*, 28 April 1968.

had supported Tory proposals in 1961 and 1962 to 'limit the flow' of immigrants, admitted: 'There are in many cases very real problems of schooling and accommodation.' Labour, reported the newspaper, had ignored its supporters' concerns. 'A lot of white Britons feel that the coloured immigrants are interlopers. Whereas Americans of every sort are Americans, it is much harder for our people to see a turbaned Sikh or African as an Englishman, or even quite convincingly British.' On controlling or even stopping immigration, the newspaper's editorial was forthright: 'Every community has the right to control its own immigration policy; therefore the demand for a complete stop is not in itself disreputable.' But *The Observer*'s support was tempered. Past pledges to Asians and dependants must be honoured, it said, and the country should improve the immigrants' conditions and integration. The similarly left-supporting *Daily Mirror*, having castigated Powell in its editorials, could not ignore the huge post bag from its readers overwhelmingly in support of Powell. Repeatedly, the letters complained that Powell was right and the debate about the subject was suppressed. The newspaper admitted that MPs had dismissed 'the genuine fears that exist and behave as though the electorate lack the right to defend peacefully their established way of life'.[†]

By contrast, *The Sun* was critical of Powell, supporting Heath for refusing to be 'tarred with a racialist brush'. In reply, Powell described *The Sun* as being 'sincere' but also 'misguided, prejudiced and emotionally overheated'. The *Daily Telegraph* was even more critical, suggesting that Powell's statistics projecting the numbers of immigrants was an 'indefensible hypothesis that both the immigration of dependants and the immigrants' birth rate will continue at the rate of the past few years.'[‡]

The numbers of immigrants and Powell's suspicion that the official statistics were at best unreliable were at the heart of the debate. Powell argued that excessive numbers of immigrants would prevent integration and provoke strife. His opponents, while advocating integration, minimised the number of immigrants in Britain to justify their conviction that mention of any problem was unjustified and therefore racist.

---

† *Daily Mirror*, 25 April 1968.
‡ *Daily Telegraph*, 22 April 1968.

Based on the statistics provided by the Registrar General, Powell had projected in his speech that in fifteen or twenty years (1985) there would be 3,500,000 immigrants and their dependants and descendants in Britain. Thereafter, his estimates varied. Partly because the official statistician predicted that Britain's population in 2000 would be seventy million, Powell predicted that 6 per cent of the population would be 'immigrants' and that meant five million to seven million. On other occasions. he forecast 4.5 million immigrants.

David Ennals, a Home Office minister, called Powell's projections of immigrants' growth 'sheer fantasy'. The government believed there would be 2.5 million immigrants by 1988, one million less than Powell's forecast.[†] Two academics, Bill Smithies and Peter Fiddick, respected by Labour, insisted that 3.5 million 'won't happen'. Mark Bonham Carter, the chairman of the Race Relations Board, predicted that only 4 per cent of Britain would be immigrants by 2000.

Proving that all those forecasts were guesswork, a study at Sussex University declared there would be three million immigrants by 2000, while the Conservative Research Department estimated there would be between 1.4 million and 2.1 million, and 'at the outside' 2.5 million. The Conservative Party's leaders were told by their own researcher that Powell was mistaken to believe that immigration was not on the decline. 'We can look forward to a dramatically decreasing intake,' the researcher apparently asserted.[‡]

Dubious about the statistics, Powell delivered his estimate based on empirical evidence. The birth rate in Wolverhampton, he said at Eastbourne on 16 November 1968, illustrated his argument. The town's population was 267,000. Of that, 5.13 per cent were immigrants yet they were producing 23 per cent of the births. On that day, he predicted that the total number of immigrants in the UK in 2002 would be 4.5 million.

During 1969, Powell realised what he perceived to be a flaw in the statistics. The numbers of immigrants and their dependants excluded their children who were born in the UK. He therefore revived his estimate of 5–7 million immigrants in 2000. That shift

---

† Hillman, op. cit., p. 102.
‡ Simon Heffer, *Like the Roman: the Life of Enoch Powell* (Weidenfeld & Nicolson, 1998), pp. 523–5.

revealed his attitude. By showing his primary interest to be the sheer numbers of blacks in English cities, he was implying that a black born in Wolverhampton could not be English but permanently remained an immigrant.

Two speeches during that year suggested that he did not genuinely believe in integration. In Bradford in July he told his audience: 'We are left with the prospect that ... a fifth or a quarter of some of our major towns and cities ... will be coloured.' In November he told the House of Commons that within twenty-five years in central London, 'there will be whole areas which are entirely occupied by an alien ... I have to tell the House that in my opinion, for which I take full responsibility, such a prospect is fraught with the gravest danger of internecine violence.' In his opinion, immigration was no longer driven by mere economic self-improvement but was part of a wider agenda by Britain's race relations practitioners. By encouraging immigration, they 'wanted a race problem in order to destabilise society'. He added: 'There are some whose intention is to destroy society as we know it and "race" or "colour" is one of those crowbars they intend to use for the work of demolition.'[†]

In 1970, increasingly cut off from the party, Powell's predictions became more extreme. Convinced that British cities would soon experience violence, he nevertheless condemned any extra financial expenditure to improve conditions of housing and schools in immigrant areas as waste, instead suggesting that the government spend £300 million on repatriation.[‡]

That nihilism undermined his genuine discovery. Namely, that the first publication by the Registrar General of births based on parents' place of birth in 1970 stated that there were 1.5 million immigrants in Britain whereas the real number was nearer two million. His suggestion of an underestimate was based on the Registrar's admission that immigrants' birth rate was higher than previously stated.[§] In 1969, the government predicted, the immigrant community would have 35,000 births but Powell estimated the real figure

---

† Simon Heffer, *Like the Roman: the Life of Enoch Powell* (Weidenfeld & Nicolson, 1998), p. 523, 9 June 1969.
‡ Ibid, p. 540.
§ Ibid, p. 549.

would be at least 52,000.[†] That discrepancy influenced the numbers in 2000. Powell projected that the immigrant community would rise from two million to four million, or 6 per cent of the population, by 1985. While Richard Crossman, the Labour minister, in public condemned Powell's extrapolation as 'untrue, alarmist and totally irresponsible', in private he confided in his diary that he had persuaded the government's statisticians to distort the true figures, which would confirm Powell's argument.[‡]

Powell's derided predictions proved as 'correct' or as 'wrong' as his opponents' and the Registrar General's. Immigrants made up 6.6 per cent of the population in 2000, albeit 3.6 million people. Accordingly, Powell's estimate in 1968 of five million to seven million in 2000 (one tenth of the population) was wrong but that was based on the official prediction of a higher birth rate, leading to an estimated population of seventy million. In the event, the 2001 census showed that Britain's population was just under sixty million and the black and Asian population was 8.1 per cent (4.46 million) – and that depended on immigrants accurately declaring their ethnic background in the census. Accordingly, Powell was more 'right' than his critics but his message was lost amid questions about his belief and motives.

During the 1970 election campaign, Powell said: 'The people of this country have been misled, cruelly and persistently.' Although the Conservative Party election manifesto promised 'no further large-scale permanent immigration', Powell focused his argument not only on those established in Britain but those born in the country. In a speech in Scarborough, he described even those babies as 'aliens'. By defining them as 'alien', he explained, he meant people 'who consider themselves strangers here, as sojourners in a strange land. To describe the great majority of that "second generation" as English in everything but colour is as false as it is cruel and insulting to them.' That argument, focused entirely on the colour of the skin, ignored integration by self-improvement and the chance that the immigrants' children could assume Britain's cultural identity.

---

† Ibid, p. 584.
‡ Ibid, p. 549.

At the outset, Heath's chance of electoral victory was unlikely. In the event, he won a majority of thirty. In the immediate aftermath, the party was instinctively resistant to accept that Powell had attracted more voters to the Conservative Party. But subsequent research suggests that the Tories gained an extra swing of 1.5 per cent from Powellism, which was sufficient to turn a notional Labour majority of twenty-five into a Tory majority of thirty.[†] Yet Powell's influence over Heath's administration is questionable. While Powell's supporters quote the 1971 Immigration Act, which restricted immigration, as Heath's appeasement of Powell, the Prime Minister ignored the outsider by allowing the entry into Britain of Ugandan Asians and Pakistani refugees.

By September 1971, three years since his speech, at least 180,000 new immigrants had arrived in Britain, and in the Conservative Party's first year of office, the rate of net immigration had actually increased by 17 per cent. But even that statistic probably underestimated the inward flow. The government's claim that many immigrants would eventually leave the country was dubious and the 1971 Act, complained Powell, deliberately omitted a proper definition of British citizenship which would have excluded other Asians applying for British passports. As a result, in 1976 Powell asked in the Commons why Portuguese-speaking Goans who were Indian citizens were suddenly allowed to enter Britain from east Africa as British citizens. The Labour government replied that they were entitled to enter the country because they possessed British passports.

By then, Powell was the odd man out, speaking from the fringe of the debate. The only cure to the growing immigrant population, he told the Commons, was 'massive repatriation'.[‡] Rejecting the possibility that immigrants could become integrated British citizens, adopting British customs and participating as equals in all British institutions, he was accused of 'relish[ing] … a council of despair'. To the majority, including those anxious to limit immigration, Powell appeared to be hysterical and out of touch with the tolerant English, who did not sympathise with the discrimination which Powell's policies of repatriation and a ban on allowing dependants

---

† Hillman, op cit., p. 98.

‡ Hansard, HC Deb, 8 July 1976, vol. 914, col. 1666.

entry would encourage. Even if he proved right about numbers, most Englishmen did not believe that their streets would be 'foaming with much blood'. Common sense, as so often, prevailed.

In 1976, a Labour backbench MP, in a bid to prevent discrimination, proposed that employers should be compelled to compile a register of employees categorising their colour, race, nationality, ethnic or national origins. During the Commons debate, Powell lampooned the proposed legislations as 'satirical'. Would employers, he asked, be required to compile a chart measuring the darkness of the employee's skin and how would a person's race be defined? And since trade unions and schools opposed keeping records because the compilation itself would be discriminatory, how could keeping records help race relations? The proposal was dropped. On the mainstream, the focus was to prevent discrimination, encourage toleration and facilitate integration while limiting immigration. The unanswered problem was to find a solution for those already in Britain who, as Powell predicted, lived in isolation within their own communities.

The deep-rooted problem was that Powellism and the association with racism were preventing the moderate majority curbing the extremist demands from what developed into an aggressive race relations industry. Rules, incentives and codes about the treatment of minorities and multiculturalism were being implemented although they were not only offensive to the majority but also, many believed, proving to be self-defeating and even destructive for the prospective beneficiaries. However, any rational debate which would have diagnosed and prevented the extremists was silenced by Powell's legacy.

Yet one of Powell's predictions proved to be truer than he could have imagined. In May 2011, the Office for National Statistics announced that Britain's ethnic minority population had risen by 40 per cent in eight years. In England and Wales, 9.1 million people, one in six of the population, were non-white. Officially, London's ethnic minority population is just over 40 per cent. Empirically, it is well over 50 per cent and in some boroughs over 80 per cent. Were Powell alive today, he might well have said '*Quod erat demonstrandum*'.

'Rivers of Blood'

Annual General Meeting of the West Midlands Area Conservative Political Centre at the Midland Hotel, Birmingham, 20 April 1968

The supreme function of statesmanship is to provide against preventable evils. In seeking to do so, it encounters obstacles which are deeply rooted in human nature. One is that by the very order of things such evils are not demonstrable until they have occurred: at each stage in their onset there is room for doubt and for dispute whether they be real or imaginary. By the same token, they attract little attention in comparison with current troubles, which are both indisputable and pressing; whence the besotting temptation of all politics to concern itself with the immediate present at the expense of the future. Above all, people are disposed to mistake predicting troubles for causing troubles and even for desiring troubles; 'if only', they love to think, 'if only people wouldn't talk about it, it probably wouldn't happen'. Perhaps this habit goes back to the primitive belief that the word and the thing, the name and the object, are identical. At all events, the discussion of future grave but, with effort now, avoidable evils is the most unpopular and at the same time the most necessary occupation for the politician. Those who knowingly shirk it deserve, and not infrequently receive, the curses of those who come after.

A week or two ago I fell into conversation with a constituent, a middle aged, quite ordinary working man employed in one of our nationalised industries. After a sentence or two about the weather, he suddenly said: 'If I had the money to go, I wouldn't stay in this country.' I made some deprecatory reply, to the effect that even this government wouldn't last forever; but he took no notice, and continued: 'I have three children, all of them been through grammar school and two of them married now, with family. I shan't be satisfied till I have seen them all settled overseas. In this country in fifteen or twenty years' time the black man will have the whip hand over the white man.' I can already hear the chorus of execration. How dare I say such a horrible thing? How dare I stir up trouble and inflame feelings by repeating such a conversation? The answer is that I do not have the right not to do so. Here is a decent, ordinary fellow Englishman, who in broad daylight in my own town says to me, his Member of Parliament, that this country will not be worth living in for his children. I simply do not have the right to shrug my shoulders and think about something else. What he is saying, thousands and hundreds of thousands are saying and thinking – not throughout Great Britain, perhaps, but in the areas that are already undergoing the total transformation to which there is no parallel in a thousand years of English history.

In fifteen or twenty years, on present trends, there will be in this country three and a half million Commonwealth immigrants and their descendants. That is not my figure. That is the official figure given to Parliament by the spokesman of the Registrar General's office. There is no comparable official figure for the year 2000; but it must be in the region of 5–7 million, approximately one-tenth of the whole population, and approaching that of Greater London. Of course, it will not be evenly distributed from Margate to Aberystwyth and from Penzance to Aberdeen. Whole areas, towns and parts of towns across England will be occupied largely and wholly by different sections of the immigrant and immigrant-descended population.

As time goes on, the proportion of this total who are immigrant-descendants, those born in England, those who arrived here by exactly the same route as the rest of us, will rapidly increase. Already by 1985 the native-born would constitute the majority. It is this fact above all which creates the extreme urgency of action now, of just that kind of action which is hardest for politicians to take, action where the difficulties lie in the present but the evils to be prevented or minimised lie several parliaments ahead.

The natural and rational first question, with the nation confronted by such a prospect, is to ask: 'How can its dimensions be reduced?' 'Granted it be not wholly preventable, can it be limited, bearing in mind that numbers are of the essence?' The significance and conse-quences of an alien element introduced into a country or population are profoundly different according to whether that element is 1 per cent or 10 per cent. The answers to the simple and rational question are equally simple and rational: by stopping, or virtually stopping, further inflow, and by promoting the maximum outflow. Both answers are part of the official policy of the Conservative Party.

It almost passes belief that at this moment twenty or thirty additional immigrant children are arriving from overseas in Wolverhampton alone every week – and that means fifteen or twenty additional families of a decade or two hence. Those whom the gods wish to destroy, they first make mad. We must be mad, literally mad, as a nation to be permitting the annual inflow of some 50,000 dependants, who are for the most part the material of the future growth of the immigrant-descended population. It is like watching a nation busily engaged in heaping up its own funeral pyre. So insane are we that we actually permit unmarried persons to immigrate for the purpose of founding a family with spouses and fiancés whom they have never seen. Let no one suppose that this flow of dependants is about to tail off automatically. On the contrary, even at the present admission rate of only 5,000 year by voucher, there is sufficient for a further 25,000 dependents per annum ad infinitum, without taking into account the huge reservoir of existing relations in this country – and I am making no allowance at all for fraudulent entry. In these circumstances nothing will suffice but that the total inflow for settlement should be reduced at once to negligible proportions, and that the necessary legislative and administrative measures be taken without delay. I stress the words 'for settlement'. This has nothing to do with the entry of Commonwealth citizens, any more than of aliens, into this country, for the purposes of study or of improving their qualifications, like (for instance) the Commonwealth doctors who, to the advantage of their own countries, have enabled our hospital service to be expanded faster than would otherwise have been possible. These are not, and never have been, immigrants.

I turn to re-emigration. If all immigration ended tomorrow, the rate of growth of the immigrant and immigrant-descended population would be substantially reduced, but the prospective size of this element in the population would still leave the basic character of the national danger unaffected. This can only be tackled while a considerable proportion of the total still comprises persons who entered this country during the last ten years or so. Hence the urgency of implementing now the second element of the Conservative Party's policy: the encouragement of re-emigration. Nobody can make an estimate of the numbers which, with generous grants and assistance, would choose either to return to their countries of origin or to go to other countries anxious to receive the manpower and the skills they represent. Nobody knows, because no such policy has yet been attempted. I can only say that, even at present, immigrants in my own constituency from time to time come to me, asking if I can find them assistance to return home. If such a policy were adopted and pursued with the determination which the gravity of the alternative justifies, the resultant outflow could appreciably alter the prospects for the future.

It can be no part of any policy that existing families should be kept divided; but there are two directions in which families can be reunited, and if our former and present immigration laws have brought about the division of families, albeit voluntary or semi-voluntarily, we ought to be prepared to arrange for them to be reunited in their countries of origin. In short, suspension of immigration and encouragement of re-emigration hang together, logically and humanely, as two aspects of the same approach.

The third element of the Conservative Party's policy is that all who are in this country as citizens shall be equal before the law and that there shall be no discrimination or difference made between them by public authority. As Mr Heath has put it, we will have no 'first-class citizens' and 'second-class citizens'. This does not mean that the immigrant and his descendants should be elevated into a privileged or special class or that any citizen should be denied his right to discriminate in the management of his own affairs between one fellow citizen and another, or that he should be subjected to inquisition as to his reasons and motives for behaving in one lawful manner rather than another.

There could be no grosser misconception of the realities than is entertained by those who vociferously demand legislation (as they call it) 'against discrimination', whether they be leader-writers of the same kidney and sometimes on the same newspapers as those which year after year in the 1930s tried to blind this country to the rising peril which confronted it, or archbishops who live in palaces, faring delicately with the bedclothes pulled right up over their heads. They have got it exactly and diametrically wrong. The discrimination and the deprivation, the sense of alarm and resentment, lie not with the immigrant population but with those among whom they have come and are still coming. This is why to enact legislation of the kind before Parliament at this moment is to risk throwing a match onto gunpowder. The kindest thing that can be said about those who propose and support it is that they know not what they do.

Nothing is more misleading than to compare the Commonwealth immigrant in Britain with the American negro. The negro population of the United States, which was already in existence before the United States became a nation, started literally as slaves and were later given the franchise and other rights of citizenship, to the exercise of which they have only gradually and still incompletely come. The Commonwealth immigrant came to Britain as a full citizen, to a country which knew no discrimination between one citizen and another, and he entered instantly into the possession of the full rights of every citizen, from the vote to free treatment under the National Health Service. Whatever drawbacks attended the immigrants – and they were drawbacks which did not, and do not, make admission into Britain by hook or by crook appear less than desirable – arose not from the law or from public policy or from administration but from those personal circumstances and accidents which cause, and always will cause, the fortunes and experience of one man to be different from another's.

But while to the immigrant entry to this country was admission to privileges and opportunities eagerly sought, the impact upon the existing population was very different. For reasons which they could not comprehend, and in pursuance of a decision by default, on which they were never consulted, they found themselves made strangers in their own country. They found their wives unable to obtain hospital beds in childbirth, their children unable to obtain school places, their homes and neighbourhoods changed beyond recognition, their plans and prospects for the future defeated; at work they found that employers hesitated to apply to the immigrant worker the standards of discipline and competence required of the native-born worker; they began to hear, as time went by, more and more voices which told them that they were now the unwanted. On top of this they now learn that a one-way privilege is to be established by act of Parliament: a law, which cannot and is not intended to operate to protect them or redress their grievances, is to be enacted to give the stranger, the disgruntled and the agent provocateur the power to pillory them for their private actions.

In the hundreds upon hundreds of letters I received when I last spoke on this subject two or three months ago, there was one striking feature which was largely new and which I find ominous. All Members of Parliament are used to the typical anonymous correspondent; but what surprised and alarmed me was the high proportion of ordinary, decent, sensible people, writing a rational and often well-educated letter, who believed that they had to omit their address because it was dangerous to have committed themselves to paper to a Member of Parliament agreeing with the views I had expressed, and that they would risk either penalties or reprisals if they were known to have done so. The sense of being a persecuted minority which is growing among ordinary English people in the areas of the country which are affected is something that those without direct experience can hardly imagine. I am going to allow just one of those hundreds of people to speak for me. She did give her name and address, which I have detached from the letter which I am about to read. She was writing from Northumberland about something which is happening at this moment in my own constituency.

Eight years ago in a respectable street in Wolverhampton a house was sold to a negro. Now only one white (a woman old-age pensioner) lives there. This is her story. She lost her husband and both her sons in the war. So she turned her seven-roomed house, her only asset, into a boarding house. She worked hard and did well, paid off her mortgage and began to put something by for her old age. Then the immigrants moved in. With growing fear, she saw one house after another taken over. The quiet street became a place of noise and confusion. Regretfully, her white tenants moved out.

The day after the last one left, she was wakened at 7 a.m. by two negroes who wanted to use her phone to contact their employer. When she refused, as she would have refused any stranger at such an hour, she was abused and feared she would have been attacked but for the chain on her door. Immigrant families have tried to rent rooms in her house, but she always refused. Her little store of money went and, after paying her rates, she has less than £2 per week. She went to apply for a rate reduction and was seen by a young girl, who on hearing she had a seven-roomed house, suggested she should let part of it. When she said the only people she could get were negroes, the girl said 'racial prejudice won't get you anywhere in this country'. So she went home.

The telephone is her lifeline. Her family pay the bill, and help her out as best they can. Immigrants have offered to buy her house at a price which the prospective landlord would be able to recover from his tenants in weeks, or at most a few months. She is becoming afraid to go out. Windows are broken. She finds excreta pushed through her letterbox. When she goes to the shops, she is followed by children, charming, wide-grinning piccaninnies. They cannot speak English, but one word they know. 'Racialist', they chant. When the new Race Relations Bill is passed, this woman is convinced she will go to prison. And is she so wrong? I begin to wonder.

The other dangerous delusion from which those who are wilfully or otherwise blind to realities suffer, is summed up in the word 'integration'. To be integrated into a population means to become for all practical purposes indistinguishable from its other members. Now, at all times, where there are marked physical differences, especially of colour, integration is difficult, though, over a period, not impossible. There are among the Commonwealth immigrants who have come to live here in the last fifteen years or so, many thousands whose wish and purpose is to be integrated and whose every thought and endeavour is bent in that direction. But to imagine that such a thing enters the heads of a great and growing majority of immigrants and their descendants is a ludicrous misconception, and a dangerous one to boot.

We are on the verge here of a change. Hitherto it has been force of circumstance and of background which has rendered the very idea of integration inaccessible to the greater part of the immigrant population – that they never conceived or intended such a thing, and that their numbers and physical concentration meant that pressures towards integration which normally bear upon any small minority did not operate. Now we are seeing the growth of positive forces acting against integration, of vested interests in the preservation and sharpening of racial and religious differences, with a view to the exercise of actual domination, first over fellow immigrants and then over the rest of the population. The cloud no bigger than a man's hand, that can so rapidly overcast the sky, has been visible recently in Wolverhampton and has shown signs of spreading quickly. The words I am about to use, verbatim as they appeared in the local press on 17 February, are not mine, but those of a Labour Member of Parliament who is a Minister in the present Government. 'The Sikh community's campaign to maintain customs inappropriate in Britain is much to be regretted. Working in Britain, particularly in the public services, they should be prepared to accept the terms and conditions of their employment. To claim special communal rights (or should one say rites?) leads to dangerous fragmentation within society. This communalism is a canker; whether practised by one colour or another it is to be strongly condemned.' All credit to John Stonehouse for having had the insight to perceive that, and the courage to say it.

For these dangerous and divisive elements the legislation proposed in the Race Relations Bill is the very pabulum they need to flourish on. Here is their means of showing that the immigrant communities can organise to consolidate their members, to agitate and campaign against their follow citizens, and to overawe and dominate the rest with the legal weapons which the ignorant and the ill-informed have provided. As I look ahead, I am filled with foreboding. Like the Roman, I seem to see 'the River Tiber foaming with much blood'. That tragic and intractable phenomenon which we watch with horror on the other side of the Atlantic but which there is interwoven with the history and existence of the States itself, is coming upon us here by our own volition and our own neglect. Indeed, it has all but come. In numerical terms, it will be of American proportions long before the end of the century. Only resolute and urgent action will avert it even now. Whether there will be the public will to demand and obtain that action, I do not know. All I know is that to see, and not to speak, would be the great betrayal.

Defence and Foreign Policy

Andrew Alexander

Enoch Powell never occupied the post of Defence Secretary. He had only the shadow role. But his formidable power of analysis, during his time in that role and afterwards from the back benches, was regarded by military thinkers of the period as remarkably expert and foresighted – certainly well ahead of anything which had originated previously in Tory frontbench thinking. During his early years as the party's official defence spokesman he tried, though not very hard, to avoid upsetting too many of his colleagues in the shadow Cabinet or within the party generally. Once out of his shadow office following his famous 1968 immigration speech, he could talk and write more freely. His influence, once seen by his political colleagues as dangerous, was highest among the military thinkers of the day.

At the end of the Second World War, Britain was uniquely susceptible to illusions. In the greatest conflict the world had ever known, Britain had indisputably been one of the Big Three. Now it was, at best, the 'half' in the Big Two-and-a-Half. The empire, which had once exercised dominion over one fifth of the world's population, was beginning to break up. India and Pakistan became independent in 1948. A call, later a demand, for self-rule was rising throughout the colonies. Britain itself was hamstrung by its debts, mainly to the United States. The country's overseas business assets had been largely sold off to pay for war materials from America. The Labour Party, in office from 1945 to 1951, was constantly constrained by the size of the debts, but it could celebrate the prospective end of empire as cheerfully as Conservatives deplored it – in so far as they acknowledged it at all. Anti-colonialism had long been part of Labour's rhetoric. The Colonial Office's function became that of guiding the colonies towards self-government.

This function did not undergo much change officially when the Tories returned to power in 1951, though the speed of this move to self-government slowed down. There was no longer pressure from the top to hurry the process. The empire itself was plainly smaller. But the colonies were still numerous if sometimes small and scattered across the globe, and many of them contained military bases of one sort or another. These became of serious importance with the onset of the Cold War. The romanticised view of the white man's burden could linger on. Churchill himself, with his enormous international prestige, could still say soon after regaining his post as Prime Minister in 1951 that he had not become the Queen's first minister in order to preside over the 'liquidation' of the British Empire. A very few Conservatives could see the inevitable but it was not safe to say so within the hearing of their local parties.

The Suez venture in 1956 was a moment of disillusionment. Britain and France colluded secretly in an attack on Egypt when President Nasser's government – causing trouble for French North Africa – nationalised the canal. The swift collapse of the venture and the humiliating withdrawal resulted from Washington's refusal to support sterling's exchange rate, which soon came under assault. Harold Macmillan, who took over from a sick Sir Anthony Eden in early 1957, toured the Third World in 1960 in an attempt to mend bridges with the various nations that had been outraged by the Suez affair. He gave his 'winds of change' speech in South Africa, which a large portion of the Conservative Party read with deep foreboding.

Still the imperial theme lingered on. To the bulk of Tory MPs, the geographic extent of the colonies and the USA's eagerness for access to them gave serious comfort. Retreat to the role of a second-class power seemed unthinkable. In any case, two delusions were created to provide the appearance of strength and importance. The first was the new British Commonwealth with much emphasis on the national adjective. As colonies became independent they were happy to join this meaningless institution. It cost them nothing, pleased whichever party was in power at that moment and helped in their constant call for financial aid. It had no military significance, though it might supply an illusion of power or at any rate influence.

The other and more important area of national delusion was the supposed 'special relationship' with the USA, above and beyond the sharing of bases. By virtue of this hangover from wartime, both the Conservative and Labour parties could convince themselves that they were unique allies of the all-powerful USA. They were able to contribute the wise advice which could only come from a long history of experience and diplomacy. Washington was happy to perpetuate this illusion. It ensured that the old imperial bases still in being should be shared in the supposedly vital task of containing Communism.

President Truman had launched the Cold War in 1945, regarding the Soviet Union, as he later recorded, as bent on 'world conquest'. The USA was the world's only nuclear power as well as the only country to emerge from the war richer than when it started. It held the purse strings, particularly important to Britain while sterling wobbled perpetually on its fixed exchange rate. The irony about this was that the current account of the balance of payments – the key to the strength of the exchange rate – was constantly under pressure through the cost of maintaining the overseas bases and their British contingents.

Understanding of the cost, worth and purpose of Britain's overseas bases, generally denominated as the 'east of Suez' policy, was very slow to adjust inside or outside Parliament. It was into this issue that the newly appointed shadow Defence Secretary threw himself with a passionate claim that Britain should face the reality of its changed situation. He had himself come a long way since his days in India where he had been a keen, even a romantic, supporter of empire. When he became an MP and had to think about basic issues, he emerged with the zeal of a convert.

One thing which did not change was his dislike and distrust of the USA. He maintained though not on any public platform that the Americans had always been intent on ending the British Empire. It seemed to his Tory colleagues at best an exaggeration, at worst a downright nonsense, part of Powell's typically eccentric view of the world. Yet Elliot Roosevelt in a life of his father, FDR, wrote that the demise of the British Empire was something he was determined to achieve, alongside an end to the French and Dutch empires. There had been real clashes between the President and Churchill, ignored in the great war leader's version of the Anglo-American relationship. Powell's dislike of the USA was reinforced by his only visit there in 1966. He admired the vigorous entrepreneurial spirit but saw the Americans as dangerously aggressive and a natural foe. By contrast he saw Russia by virtue of its position and its history as a natural ally. The Soviet Union's top priority was to curb Germany, which had launched two invasions of its territory in twenty-seven years with devastating consequences. To this end it was clear that Russia would keep hold of the territory through which the German attack had come. The constant demand of Washington that it should give up control of these nations reinforced Soviet fears, particularly once the rearmament of West Germany became such an important American cause.

Powell's views on the United States were later to be strongly voiced in his comments, though from the back benches, on the war in Vietnam. He saw that as combining both military and political folly. His views were clearly at odds with those of most Tories and certainly Ted Heath as leader. His problem about achieving any influence for his views seemed to have a solution when Heath, coming to the party leadership in 1965, offered him a choice of shadow appointments. Powell could hardly be left out since he was such an admired figure in the party and had been in the Macmillan Cabinet as Health Minister. Somewhat to Heath's surprise and relief Powell chose Defence. It would in practice allow him to discourse on the foreign policy which Defence would have to serve. Powell himself was under the impression that his leader, with his impatience about tradition and nostalgia, would support an end to post-imperial links.

The appointment to this particular position of the man who had once been the youngest brigadier in the British army also seemed natural enough. Besides, the parliamentary politics of defence seemed so safely dull. Much of the interparty tussling was confined to technical points about the worth of aircraft carriers, or one sort of jet aircraft against another. Powell could safely be left to use his acknowledged powers of analysis to deal with these essentially operational problems and to score points over Denis Healey, Labour's Defence Secretary. Powell was a risk which Heath did not appreciate at the time of his appointment. His enthusiasm for the post was never in doubt. To many others it seemed the least exciting area of parliamentary activity since there were, they thought, only minor differences between the two parties on these matters. Defence debates in the Commons were not much reported in the media. Asked at a lunch with political journalists if he did not find his post and its problems rather boring, he replied: 'Not at all; the danger is that I love it too much.' The political journalists were soon to find out how exciting the post could be.

Once in his post, Powell embarked on a policy of gradually re-educating his party. His colleagues on the Opposition Defence Committee might have been thought easy to handle. Many of them had been serving officers during the war or had since seen service under the regime of conscription. But nearly all of them had only been regimental officers. They knew little about strategic issues and had given them equally little thought. Progress in teaching them to think strategically proved slow.

To Powell, the 'east of Suez' issue was both obvious and urgent since clarifying it was the key to Britain's role in the world as well as its defence policy. A clear line was needed from the start. He used the 1965 party conference in his new role to plant a stick of dynamite. He addressed the conference and duly evoked an enthusiastic ovation – such admirable language, such an impressive intellect. It was left to the media to tell the cheering party faithful what he had actually called for.

One of the party's rising stars, David Howell, shortly to become MP for Guildford, arrived late for the conference and bustled into the press room, asking urgently for a copy of Powell's speech. 'I gather,' he explained, 'that Enoch has taken us out of east of Suez, nobody noticed and they all got up and cheered.' Both comments were true. But Powell had used somewhat elliptical language. He could not denounce the official party policy but he could leave the press to point out what he was driving at. And he had, indeed, received an enthusiastic ovation.

The relevant passage in his speech ran:

> However much we may do to safeguard and reassure the new independent countries in Asia and Africa, the eventual limits of Russian and Chinese advance in those directions will be fixed by a balance of power which will itself be Asiatic and African. The two Communist empires are already in a state of mutual antagonism; but every

advance or threat of advance by one or the other calls into existence countervailing forces, sometimes nationalist in character, some
expansionist, which will ultimately check it. We have to reckon with
the harsh fact that the attainment of this ultimate equilibrium of
forces may at some point be delayed rather than hastened by western
military presence

Had he said bluntly that overseas bases were potentially dangerous (and foolishly costly in foreign exchange), the same audience
would have been baffled by the audacity of the claim. To them, any
projection of British power was reassuring – and needful in the
uncertainties of the time and the obvious, to them, importance of
supporting the Americans and NATO. He was, however, to defend
the NATO alliance in a cautious way, which soothed a little of the
unease in the party about him:

An alliance which can successfully defend western Europe against
an attack from the east – the only present direction from which
danger is apprehended – is central to our defence policy. Forces
and materials which are needed for the purposes of that alliance
have an overriding claim on the resources which we can devote to
our defence.

This sounded reassuringly orthodox. It was not until much later
that he voiced his concern about America's role as leader of NATO.
Heath was challenged by the press about Powell's out-of-line
views at the conference. He provided what were to become his two
stock answers. Either Powell was posing questions or he was looking at future possible developments. Privately of course Heath was
furious. And he became more furious when Powell strayed from
defence into other areas of policy. Powell argued that in opposition,
shadow ministers were free to range outside their portfolios. Only in
government did unity become essential. The anger at Powell airing
his radical views was not confined to Heath or indeed his shadow
Cabinet colleagues. Backbenchers were alarmed and, it must be said,
puzzled. All sorts of other issues – prices and incomes, inflation,
foreign policy, trade unions' affairs – these had been comfortably
settled at the 1966 election, surely? But Powell was undaunted.

Powell's views on the foreign exchange costs of 'east of Suez' aroused more interest on the Labour benches than among the Tories, who reckoned that a Conservative government would mean greater national prosperity and an ability to shoulder what they regarded as the normal costs of being a world power. For the Labour government the costs were a serious and practical issue. Powell took up the argument in a Commons defence debate in 1966:

We have to measure our outlays against the return which they produce in terms of security. Everyone who has spoken in this debate from different points of view has reiterated the simple but basic point. Only those military obligations must be undertaken by a nation which it can and will perform; to do so otherwise is to court disaster and disgrace for others as well as ourselves ...

I doubt if it is realised at all widely how large a part of our balance of payments is played by military expenditure which we undertake in foreign currency. Last year for example we ... earned a surplus of £271 million after investing abroad a further huge sum of £160 million. What converted this surplus into a deficit of £354 million was the government's expenditure in foreign currency, of which the largest item (£280 million) was military.

Thus our growing burden of external debt is not, as is often falsely alleged, to enable us at home to live beyond our means, but to finance our effort, and principally our military effort, overseas. No other nation in the world except the United States is comparably situated for the simple reason that the military effort of other nations is normally nearly all within their own frontiers.

Our defence expenditure in foreign currency falls into three main areas: Europe, the Far East and the Middle East, in the ratio of 4:4:3. In other words Europe represents just under 40 per cent and the rest just over 60 per cent. I regret, however, to mention that there is a large fourth item just round the corner with which we shall soon be confronted. This is the cost of all the American aircraft which the government is buying on the never-never.

Our outlays in Europe, of course, arise from our commitments under the North Atlantic Alliance, which reflects the basic and indefeasible interests of this country in the security of western Europe. The rest of our commitments, historically speaking, are the result directly or indirectly of our former imperial presence outside Europe, very largely of our one-time Indian Empire.

Powell was to make other references to the importance of Britain's European commitment which were later raised as evidence that he had once, at least, been committed to the importance of Europe and thus its development as a political union, initially as the Common Market. But as he was to point out, a military alliance does not and cannot foreshadow political integration.

The point he made in the Commons debate – that Britain's constantly precarious financial position was due to overseas commitments – unsurprisingly intrigued the Labour backbenchers, who complained constantly about the regular failure of the Wilson government to implement its election promises because of financial problems. The later diaries of Richard Crossman, a senior Cabinet minister in each Wilson government, show that the cost of overseas bases was always a problem. But Wilson remained very much under the influence of Washington.

When it came to the so-called independent nuclear deterrent, Powell decided at first to go along with the existing party policy, that is, the pretence that the weapon might be usable and the independence was real. This was an important factor in the mind of the average Tory voter and the average Tory MP. It fitted alongside the illusions about 'global power'. But he did so with a certain element of caution while a Tory frontbencher.

> Our right to control the use of our own strategic nuclear weapon must be retained to the limit of our ability, at least until military and political circumstances are profoundly different to what they are today. It is the merest casuistry to argue that if the weapon and the means of using it are purchased in part, or even altogether, from another nation, therefore the independent right to use it has no reality. With a weapon so catastrophic it is possession and the right to use which count.

As a proposition that would be true. But he omitted the fact that the weapon could not be used without the United States, through a fail-safe procedure, pressing the right button. It was part of the grand delusion that we were a nuclear power in the sense that the French were to become.

Powell had long believed that the danger of a war, conventional or otherwise, as seen at the time was not real. The Russians had no desire to commit suicide in a nuclear conflict. As for a conventional conflict, a Russian attack could only result at worst in the Soviet Union occupying Europe but remaining at war with the Americans across 3,000 miles of ocean – 'the ultimate unwinnable war – a military planners' nightmare,' he observed. But to say that the Soviets were no real threat would have left his own colleagues (and not only them) baffled in the state of opinion which prevailed so long as the Soviet Union continued to exist.

He used the general belief that there might be a threat from the east to declare that British military power had to be attuned to Europe and to the possibility of the forces on the Continent one day throwing up the traditional danger of a single power coming to dominate the area. Of the possibilities of such a development, he said:

> We do not know in what form or in what circumstances a future threat to our existence may present itself. History is littered with the wars which everybody knew would never happen. A computer has not yet been invented which will tell us the future pattern in the world at large, or even in our own turbulent continent ... commonly known as Europe. We do not know. We do know, however, the essential requirements of our country's defence in a form sufficiently general to meet all cases.
>
> Those requirements of our defence are basically two. The first is to retain for ourselves and deny to an enemy the means of access to these islands. The second is to maintain, and if it is lost, to restore the balance of power on the mainland which will prevent an enemy from dominating western Europe successfully.

Expelled from the shadow Cabinet in 1968, Powell had become free to express his thoughts more fully from the back benches. This freedom continued after Ted Heath won the 1970 general election, though this time from the government back benches. He rounded off what he called 'the nuclear hypothesis', which was also being challenged in the USA by military thinkers.

The nuclear mushroom cloud which has hung over national defence policy for two decades is at last rising into the stratosphere and dispersing. As it clears away it discloses a landscape not unfamiliar. For years now the opposition have been saying that we cannot, must not, allow ourselves to be drugged with the idea that any war which threatened the safety and existence of this country would be bound to go nuclear almost at once.

For 'the opposition' we should perhaps read the former Defence Secretary, voices from the Labour side and the more serious military commentators. There remained a strong feeling among Conservative MPs that a war meant nuclear or nothing. Since he had first become shadow Defence Secretary, Powell said,

a profound change of opinion on this subject [a nuclear war] has been gaining ground. So far as our principal ally, the United States, is concerned it has won through to open and official acceptance. I might summarise it in a sentence from Mr McNamara's [US Defence Secretary Robert McNamara] statement to Congress two months ago: 'The threat of an incredible action is not an effective deterrent.'

Powell had met with McNamara in Washington. No doubt they found much to agree on. Powell wanted a British retreat from empire. McNamara had had a grim time trying to curb the gung-ho attitude of President Johnson and the generals in the Vietnam struggle. When he came to write his self-excoriating memoirs, his views on the innate futility of Vietnam were much the same as Powell's.

Powell went on in 1971, now just an observer of his party in office, to raise the issue of the navy's role in a conventional war, still so woefully misunderstood in his own party. He had complained of the Labour mismanagement of the Royal Navy. Why was it so comfortably assumed that a Continental war was the only conventional threat?

The last two decades have been the first period for 300 years when the maritime forces of this country have not had it as a prime object and capability to prevent an enemy from blockading these islands or gaining access by sea. This has happened because we had persuaded ourselves that a long war at sea, such as we have had to face several times in our history, was no longer to be reckoned with ... The very possibility was scouted; we slept secure in our hammocks between the assumed alternatives of no war or nuclear suicide ... It has now been abandoned by our principal ally, the United States, which now officially envisages the possibility of what they call 'an all-out war at sea', lasting months if not years, which would be fought and could be won without going nuclear at all.

A corresponding and almost more dramatic change of scene has taken place on land. Hitherto the alternative of no serious war or nuclear suicide was accepted because it was assumed that a potential enemy had overwhelming superiority of non-nuclear forces and that any ordinary resistance to his onslaught would be impossible for more than a matter of hours. This assumption has been torn up

In short he now found strategic thinking in the USA moving ahead of that in Britain, certainly ahead of his own party.

Powell constantly tried his best to educate his own colleagues and public opinion on the basics of military strategy. The Arab–Israeli war of 1967 provided him with the ideal moment to remind his colleagues about the crucial issue of distance – and with that the need to forget old illusions.

The mere fact of Britain's relatively small size and resources ... is nothing new. What is new is that in the last twenty years one of the axioms of military power has been forgotten or denied. This is the axiom that military power is relative to distance: it is effective in inverse ratio to the distance at which it is exercised. [Perhaps, he was to muse later, military power even falls off as the square of the distance.] Why this basic axiom has fallen into disregard is not difficult to explain. The world has been mesmerised since 1945 by the spectacle of nuclear power and the conquest of space. The megaton weapon and the satellite in orbit, not to mention the development of the rocket, have made it easy for the cliché to be mouthed and believed, that space has been annihilated. Indeed, for some purposes, space has virtually been annihilated; but not for military purposes. For military purposes, short of mutual suicide … distance and geography are as significant today as they have ever been.

But Britain has been more predisposed than any other nation to make the wrong deduction about the military importance of distance because of her recent past – or rather, her misinterpretation of her recent past; for Britain's geography has changed since World War II to a far greater extent than that of any other great power. Until twenty years ago, Britain was also India … consequently the Indian Ocean stood in the same relation to Britain as the Eastern Atlantic…

Thus, the British got into the habit of thinking in what are sometimes called global terms. They were used to finding it as easy, if not easier, and much more common, to apply military power in the Persian Gulf or the Malacca straits than in the Skagerrak or the Straits of Gibraltar … Hence it was easy for them to fail to draw the military conclusions from that profound change in Britain's military geography which occurred – so far as such events can be precisely dated at all – in 1947 … In the last few years, however, there have been sharp reminders that military power does not exist in the abstract but is a function of place … Israel inflicted a decisive defeat on Egypt and Jordan. She did what Britain could probably not have done, and even what the United States would have had the greatest difficulty in doing … This does not mean that Israel is a greater military power than Britain. It only means, what we could see anyhow, by looking at a map, that Israel lives there and we do not. Israel is now the principal military power in the Middle East excluding Turkey. But she has no military power at all on the Straits of Dover or in the Low Countries. She doesn't live there.

Powell launched another attack on the delusions occasioned by the Arab–Israeli war:

In the last two years we have had the Prime Minister [Harold Wilson] and his colleagues informing not only the Labour Party in well-reported private meetings but Parliament and the world at large that Britain is to have a worldwide peace-keeping role and hold forces available to put out 'brush fires' wherever peace is threatened. Well, in the last month all this has been put to the test of reality. As soon as peace was threatened in the Middle East area on both sides of which British forces are actually stationed, an area of what is supposed to be 'traditional British influence', it promptly appeared that we could do nothing about it … we were determined not to be involved. As for our bases, Cyprus, Libya and even Malta, we were informed that we should not be permitted to use them; and the only thing that was heard about our naval forces in the Mediterranean was an official protestation that the carriers were moored 1,000 miles away from the fighting … the so-called British presence, either in the Mediterranean or in the Persian Gulf, was powerless to protect our interests either in oil or in sterling.

The oil producers had 'just turned the taps off' … We of course never dreamt that we could do anything to prevent it by our military presence any more than we could have used forces in the area to prevent sterling deposits being withdrawn.

Powell's approach had long been the opposite of the USA's policy, in which a physical presence was seen as the surest safeguard for a nation's interests. He went on: 'It was just because we were physically present that our oil and our reserves were in danger.' This was entirely in keeping with his stated views that the safeguard for access to raw materials was the simple one of the willing seller on the one hand and the willing buyer on the other. As for brush fires,

by a strange irony it so happened that, almost unnoticed, a perfectly classic post-colonial brush fire was blazing at the same time in west Africa, to the detriment of all manner of commercial interests and to the threatened break-up of a country which Britain had literally brought into existence. I refer to Nigeria. Yet it never occurred to anyone, and rightly not, that Britain had any other role to play in the matter than to avoid involvement and maintain a position as far as possible diplomatically correct. We had in the past launched the Federation of Nigeria to the best of our ability as a well-administered and viable country. In its future fortunes we would have had no greater hand than any other well-wishers.

He attacked the line that there was such a thing as 'the Big Four', a label attached to the two great powers plus France and Britain, as 'arithmetically insoluble'.

But between the little two – between France and Britain – there was the difference, this vital difference. France, after years of suffering and effort often derided by others as *folie de grandeur*, had won through to self-knowledge and so was able to act in the light of her real power, a not discreditable minor part. Britain on the other hand … behaved like King Lear: 'I will do such things – what they are yet I know not – but they shall be the terrors of the earth.'

If Powell was clear what Britain's defence policy should not be, what approach was he advocating? It was a question to which his own puzzled colleagues pressed him for an answer. He defined the main aim as 'the maintenance of such balance of power as will prevent hostile use of the adjacent mainland'.

The issue of distance, on which he often spoke, inevitably raised the question of the American frustrations in Vietnam.

It is not that the mere distance imposes unacceptable limitations on the exercise of American physical power across the Pacific: on the contrary, the Ocean in a sense links their advanced bases in the Western Pacific and in South-East Asia with the home country. The point is that the Americans do not live in South-East Asia, whereas the North Vietnamese and their neighbours do. Consequently, since the Americans do not intend to set up shop permanently in South-East Asia – in effect to conquer it – hardly any degree of military force, however great, could produce that decisive effect on their opponents' will which is the meaning of victory.

Here at any rate Powell gained some support in Washington. As mentioned earlier, he had a talk with Robert McNamara, whose views on nuclear warfare and on Vietnam, eventually aired in his remarkably frank memoirs, had come round to a close similarity with Powell's. McNamara had had to tell the American generals that any belief in measured and escalating nuclear warfare was wholly misguided. Once a nuclear weapon was used, he argued, escalation would be rapid, indeed uncontrollable. On Vietnam McNamara was at that time envisaging his own resignation. He had been responsible for the conflict since the time of his appointment by President Kennedy.

Powell constantly faced the argument from his own colleagues that the Malayan emergency showed that Communist terrorists could be eliminated by military force and wise governance. He pointed out that when the emergency was getting into its stride, Britain was seen as the sovereign power, though he admitted that the dating was a fine thing. It was different in Vietnam, where the populace knew that one day the Americans, who had no roots in the country, would go away. Britain had been lucky in the sense that the path to Malayan independence had not been forged while the campaign was in progress.

He was later to achieve a major success on the Vietnam issue which he did not appreciate at the time. He was prompted in this by the head of the Conservative Research Department, Sir Michael Fraser, who said that there was a rumour that the Ministry of Defence was preparing to raise a token contingent to aid the Americans in Vietnam. This was something, he was assured, that Heath wanted him to take up. With the 1966 general election at hand, Powell was only too happy to do so, though with some caution. He declared that he would 'not be surprised' if the rumour were true and that Wilson was succumbing to pressure from Washington. 'If such a step is even remotely in contemplation, the Prime Minister ought to tell the country one way or another before polling day.'

Very oddly, Conservative Central Office disowned Powell, who was 'speaking on his own behalf'. Denis Healey denied the rumour and called on Heath to sack Powell, who then called in Wilson for a categorical assurance that there would be no aid for the Americans. He gave one and dismissed Powell's comments as a 'last-minute scare' before polling day. President Johnson, as was later learnt, had indeed pressed Wilson for support – 'even one kilted bagpiper' would do.

Powell was told during the 1970 election of the view of Washington correspondents that his intervention in 1966 had been effective in curbing Wilson's plans. Powell reflected on this as 'the greatest service I have performed for my country, if that is so'. True or not, the Vietnam issue was for him another example of British weakness in its dealings with Washington. When the USA started bombing North Vietnam, London issued a comment of support. When the bombing was temporarily stopped, the British government again issued a note of approval. When it was resumed, London again declared its support. This was the way, Powell commented, the Soviet Union expected her satrapies to behave.

On and off his party's front bench, Powell maintained his call for a radical overhaul of Conservative defence policy – and the foreign policy which it was intended to serve. But however forceful his arguments, they seem to have had no effect. The two interventions in Afghanistan and Iraq proved ill judged – as he would have predicted – and counter-effective. In both cases, the opposition front bench did not just support but positively acclaimed the assaults. It was hard to decide who was the more eager supporter of the Labour government's new found sense of militarism, shadow Foreign Secretary William Hague or shadow Defence Secretary Liam Fox.

They not only took no notice of Powell's warning about the axiom of military power falling off as the distance increased, they also cast aside any doubts about the value of the so-called special relationship. Britain was once again to be entangled in conflicts started by the United States. Both wars ended in ignominy. The Iraq conflict, launched in 2003, did not last the few months that Washington expected, but until 2011. Even then US forces left the country in a state of near civil war, even though – or possibly because – an apparent democracy had been established. A belief that because of advanced technology war could be affectively waged at an immense distance was shown to be as false as when Powell originally denounced it.

The Afghanistan conflict started with an American attack on the country's Taliban government in the wake of the 9/11 atrocity of 2001, claimed by Al-Qaeda as its own work. This terror group was allowed to exist and train in Afghanistan and an assault on Kabul was already being secretly planned by the US military. Again American hopes that the country would be awed by the NATO contingent which the USA mustered proved false. The prospect of another retreat was finally accepted by Washington in 2011. The promise was made that the troops would be out by the end of 2014. The regime which had been established was nominally democratic but was widely denounced as corrupt and ineffective. The rule of President Hamid Karzai seemed not to run far from Kabul.

But the faith in power through technology was still hard to

dislodge. American pilotless 'drones' were constantly deployed in the area of the country bordering on north-west Pakistan. The Islamabad government was dragged into the conflict and the political instability of Pakistan was heightened. Henry Kissinger, former US Secretary of State, was to declare that Pakistan had become what the Balkans were to the First World War.

The Americans were reduced within three years of their scheduled withdrawal to seeking a truce with the Taliban, whose regime had been the original target of Washington's attack. No such truce appeared to be in prospect as the US presidential elections loomed. Britain's role in both the Iraq and the Afghanistan wars made it an easy target for claims that the two transatlantic allies were waging a war against Islam itself. Spain had already withdrawn its modest contingent after a terrorist attack on a train in Madrid. In London, terrorists mounted attacks on the Underground and on a bus in July 2005. Had not Britain involved itself as it did in the Middle East conflicts these incidents would not have taken place. Nor would the constant and costly (in terms of manpower) surveillance, which became a feature of British life.

The refusal by the British government to heed the axiom about distance meant that the British effort put a great strain on the Army without effective results. The impact on morale is difficult to measure. But the regular assurances by British generals of a whole variety of successes which did not materialise undoubtedly led to a lowering of confidence in the Army leadership. The high expense for Britain of the intervention made it ever harder for the Ministry of Defence either to save money as successive British governments asked or to formulate a defence policy which made sense.

Powell's warnings had gone unheard. The old postures and prejudices remain intact, however skilfully Powell had analysed them and argued for radical change.

Defence and Foreign Policy

Monday Club Dinner at the Painters' Hall,
7 December 1967

It is not only in economic affairs that Britain has been haunted during the last twenty years by a severe inferiority complex, which came to a recent climax over devaluation. We have suffered from a similar, and equally severe, complex in our thinking about defence; and this, I fear, has not yet reached its climax. Just as economically we are overawed by the staggering statistical 'growth rates' of other countries, so in defence we have been overawed by the size and visible power of the United States and the Soviet Union. This has induced a dangerous kind of paralysis; for when the idea gains ground that our defence effort is foredoomed to be ineffectual, it becomes easy to persuade people – particularly under a Labour government, and a Labour government with a left wing such as this one – that therefore a British defence effort cannot be worth paying for.

This state of natural dejection has been fostered by causes peculiar to our time. The mere fact of Britain's relatively small size and resources does not account for it, because that fact is nothing new. What is new is that in the last twenty years one of the axioms of military power has been forgotten or denied. This is the axiom that military power is relative to distance: it is effective in inverse ratio to the distance at which it is exercised.

Why this basic axiom has fallen into disregard is not difficult to explain. The world has been mesmerized since 1945 by the spectacle of nuclear power and the conquest of space. The megaton weapon and the satellite in orbit, not to mention the development of the rocket, have made it easy for the cliché to be mouthed and believed, that space has been annihilated. Indeed, for some purposes, space virtually has been annihilated; but not for military purposes. For military purposes, short of mutual suicide (and that is the very opposite of the controlled and disciplined use of force which we call war) distance and geography are as significant today as they have ever been.

But Britain has been more predisposed than any other nation to make the wrong deduction about the military importance of distance because of her recent past – or rather, her misinterpretation of her recent past; for Britain's geography has changed since World War II to a far greater extent than that of any other great power. Until twenty years ago, Britain was also India, and her military geography and location was that of India as well as of the British Isles. Consequently the Indian Ocean stood in the same relation to Britain as the Eastern Atlantic, and South-East Asia in the same relation as (shall I say?) the Balkans and the Baltic Sea. Thus, the British got into the habit of thinking in what are sometimes called global terms. They were used to finding it as easy, if not easier, and much more common, to apply military power in the Persian Gulf or the Malacca straits than in the Skagerrak or the Straits of Gibraltar. They fell into the not unnatural error of supposing that this military power was exercised from and by the United Kingdom as such, and consequently that there had been a special dispensation of providence in their favour, whereby the law of the inverse ratio did not apply to the products of the British public school system. Hence it was an easy step for them to fail to draw the military conclusions from that profound change in Britain's military geography which occurred – so far as such events can be precisely dated at all - in 1947.

So what with nuclear fission, and the Koh-i-noor, we have contrived – to our own discomfiture – to ignore the military axiom of power and distance. In the last few years, however, there have been sharp reminders that military power does not exist in the abstract but is a function of place. 'All these things happened for ensamples: and they are written for our admonition, upon whom the ends of the world are come' (1 Cor.10.11). There was one this year. Israel inflicted a decisive defeat on Egypt and Jordan. She did what Britain could probably not have done, and even what the United States would have had the greatest difficulty in doing. Certainly we would have taken longer about it, and it would have been a mercy if the work had not been botched. This does not mean that Israel is a greater military power than Britain. It only means, what we could see anyhow, by looking at a map, that Israel lives there and we do not. Israel is now the principal military power in the Middle East excluding Turkey. But she has no military power at all on the Straits of Dover or in the Low Countries. She doesn't live there.

Khruschev's brinkmanship in 1962, given that Russia did not regard the establishment of missile sites in Cuba as an adequate occasion for nuclear self-extermination, was resolved without a single pawn being taken off the chessboard. The United States could indisputably sink any vessel trying to get to Cuba and, if necessary, could occupy the island; so as soon as it became clear they were ready to do so the show was at an end. It is no use having a long arm if the fingers and the hand at the end of it can be chopped off. Otherwise, either one's bluff is called or one loses.

Conversely, observe the importance of geography in frustrating the American arms in Vietnam. It is not that the mere distance imposes unacceptable limitations on the exercise of American physical power across the Pacific: on the contrary, the Ocean in a sense links their advanced bases in the Western Pacific and in South-East Asia with the home country. The point is that the Americans do not live in South-East Asia, whereas the North Vietnamese and their neighbours do. Consequently, since the Americans do not intend to set up shop permanently in South-East Asia – in effect, to conquer – hardly any degree of military force, however great, could produce that decisive effect on their opponents' will which is the meaning of victory. If you can't win and you don't live there, you lose.

Finally, to take an example of our own: Rhodesia. This country's policy towards Rhodesia since U.D.I. has been so calamitous, exposing us to loss and derision, because we overlooked the basic fact that Britain is incapable of exercising physical power in central Africa. We have behaved as though Rhodesia and Rutland were for practical purposes interchangeable. When socialists, pacifists and Liberals call for force to be used against Rhodesia, they are disclosing the fundamental misconception on which the whole policy was based. Militarily speaking, we aren't there and we can't get there.

This insight into the relationship between geography and military power is vital to a restoration of our confidence in ourselves and of a rational basis for our armed forces. It means that a nation's military strength and effectiveness is not absolute – so that it could

be read off on a list of forces compiled out of reference books like
Brassey's Annual or *Jane's Fighting Ships* and arranged in order of
size – but is relative, relative to its situation and environment. A
nation which is strong where it can be, and needs to be, strong and
has successfully married place with force, may be as formidable and
as secure as those numerically much larger.

The application of this principle to the United Kingdom produces
what ought to be a truism. That it sounds more like a paradox is a
measure of our neglect or oblivion of the axiom of the inverse ratio.
The United Kingdom is potentially strongest and most effective
militarily in the Eastern Atlantic and Western Europe. A pound
spent on the arms and preparations relevant to those theatres
produces a higher return in military strength than a pound spent
otherwise. The principle of superiority of force implies that in any
theatre policy will aim at operating with the maximum alliance;
yet still it remains true that for a given outlay of resources upon
defence, the greatest influence upon allies and the greatest insurance
against their absence, defeat or defection is obtained by investment
in the theatres where force is maximised by position.

It is possible to go further. Out of the various forms of armament
and preparation applicable to a given theatre of war, those will yield
the greatest return in strength which derive the most reinforce-
ment from the military geography. For example, Switzerland would
derive more power from a given investment in fortifications and
mountain troops than in armoured divisions. This observation in
turn is reinforced by the principle that in strategic terms aggression
is much more expensive than defence.

All this adds up to something particularly important for Britain
at all times and especially at the present time. We have an inveterate
love of falling between all the possible stools and of doing a bit
of everything with superb competence on a completely inadequate
scale. Nothing is therefore more salutary and necessary than the
discipline of priorities and the obligation to concentrate. We have
to counteract in our defence policy a long habit and tradition of
dilettantism, derived from distant wars against military inferiors
and flag-showing cruises in neutral waters. War is about winning.
War is about striking what matters most with all one's might. Our
present sense of inferiority, economic as well as military, is closely

linked with our inability or reluctance to concentrate – and concentration involves renunciation, renunciation of many objectives to concentrate upon a few, renunciation of what one does mediocrely to concentrate on what one does supremely.

Let me sum up. The defence forces of a major power must keep some touch with every branch of the military art. But a Britain which concentrated its defensive investment overwhelmingly upon the means of victory in the areas of its natural strength – the Atlantic and Western Europe – would find itself, relative to its situation, to be a military power not inferior to any. The true antithesis is not balance in East of Suez and West of Suez but balance in strength and weakness. Weakness is not productive of influence. You can no more exert power with inferior force than you can invest a deficit. In recent years we have too often to buttress our self-esteem by talking about our role and importance in the world. It has not been a proud or edifying spectacle. If we would provide ourselves with those forces in which we are capable of being strong we shall not need to talk about our role and importance in the world. We should have them.

A Personal Recollection

Anne Robinson

My first awareness of the existence of Enoch Powell came, like many other things in my life, from my mother. She was fascinated by politics: a frustrating world away from her everyday life, even though that in itself was extraordinary. In post-war Britain, when it appeared the rest of womankind had been firmly returned to their domestic boxes, my mother was doing the polar opposite. In food-rationed Britain she'd created and was running an ever-expanding poultry business. Her alarming skill at money-making was sufficient to move her young family to the grandeur of a large mansion in Blundellsands in the suburbs of Liverpool.

She naturally voted Tory. Not that she took any active role in local politics. Indeed she held most politicians in contempt. She even distrusted Winston Churchill. But there were two exceptions: Michael Foot, and Enoch Powell. A socialist and a Tory, but significantly both fiercely independent and hard to pigeonhole. She singled them out because they excelled in what mattered to her most – oratory and advocacy. Powell's and Foot's flair, she would frequently declare, was second to none.

Thus, their names reverberated around our home. The fact that these two men appeared to have little in common politically mattered not a jot to her. They were the intellectuals of their day with the skill to convey their views. From a small child I was taught that it was far more instructive to listen to or read the opinions of Foot and Powell than either of their respective leaders.

In the 1950s you'd have needed to have a keen interest in politics to follow Enoch Powell's career. I was barely fourteen when he first made headlines in 1958 having resigned from the government in protest at the level of public spending. A rebel or, if you were looking on from our vantage point in Blundellsands, a hero – since naturally my mother adored Enoch even more for his magnificent display of awkwardness.

His next act of swimming against the tide left no one ignorant of his name. The furore following the famous immigration speech of April 1968 encompassed the whole country. By then, I was a young *Sunday Times* news reporter working for the legendary Harry Evans. It was a paper which prided itself on its liberal, campaigning reputation. Its condemnation of the speech (and Enoch Powell's motives in making it) was so pronounced that, before the year was out, he and the *Sunday Times* would be head to head in an acrimonious legal dispute.

Looking back, it is hard to think of a year as important politically as 1968. Almost every day produced a spine-tingling newspaper headline. There were the assassinations of Martin Luther King and then Robert Kennedy, the Paris riots, the invasion of Czechoslovakia, the continuing horror of the Vietnam War, and Richard Nixon's election as US President.

The new heroes of the decade were those who had sacrificed their lives in the name of liberty. In contrast Enoch Powell had become a figure of hate in the world of the London glitterati. A young journalist on the *Sunday Times* had little reason to question this conclusion. My mother, however, was under no such constraints. She believed Enoch had had the nerve to say out loud what everyone was thinking – except, of course, for the small political and journalistic elite in which her daughter now mixed. Significantly, Liverpool was a city with a history of immigration going back far beyond that of the Midlands. The difference was that Liverpool's immigrant population, referred to unashamedly at that time as 'darkies' and 'half-castes', was almost exclusively confined to ghettos on the edge of the city. For my parents, the idea that their own rather grand area of suburbia (Liverpool 23) – where there were 'in' and 'out' drives and plentiful employment for cooks and gardeners – might become akin to Liverpool 7 and 8 would have been every bit as distressing as it was proving to be for the long-term white residents in Wolverhampton.

In fact the marking down of the second half of the 1960s as a time of huge change – delivering a much-welcomed freedom in behaviour and outlook for young people – is an almost comically lopsided picture. There were so many aspects of everyday life which today would be correctly judged abhorrent and totally unacceptable. Certainly not just the language of Enoch Powell. This was the decade when young boys – my brother Peter was one of them – were still being shipped off at the tender age of six or seven to the harsh regimes of prep school where corporal punishment and bullying were the norm and where, today, Esther Rantzen's helpline would be permanently engaged. For women, there was no equality of pay or opportunity. The Pill was not available for unmarried women. Abortion was a luxury for rich girls. Babies were called illegitimate (or worse) if born out of wedlock and it was still the practice to send unmarried mothers away to give birth and within a few weeks to have the babies forcibly removed for adoption. A woman crying 'rape' could expect to be disbelieved or told she was 'asking for it'. So much so that a woman who experienced rape would not have considered it anything other than her own stupid fault.

Apart from in a few large organisations, maternity leave was unheard of. In 1968, a woman wishing to rent a television set required the supporting signature of a man. Any man! A woman requiring an overdraft or applying for a mortgage needed to have the conditions read aloud to her by her bank manager. The Married Women's Property Act of 1964, for the first time giving married woman a legal share of the matrimonial home, was in its infancy. There were remarkably few female accountants, estate agents, barristers or senior police officers. As late as 1980, BBC Radio 2 had a policy of never playing two female singers back to back. The Sexual Offences Act, which decriminalised homosexual acts in private between consenting males over twenty-one, was less than a year old. Indeed those in the 1960s who forecast new laws against racial discrimination and sexual discrimination were dismissed as scaremongers.

Much of the above seems barbaric and jaw-dropping today. But it is muddle-headed to suppose that all the politicians who accepted the status quo were 'sexists' any more than people like my mother were 'racists'. Equally, expressions which today are offensive and racist were commonplace in that decade, but not normally with that intention. I didn't judge my parents as racists for supporting Enoch Powell. Like many others, my mother and father felt they had not come through a war in order to see neighbourhoods transformed and property values threatened.

Furthermore, as a fully paid-up capitalist, my mother would have considered the notion of state interference when it came to selling her home – leaving her unable to make the final choice of purchaser – deplorable. Her sympathies were with Enoch Powell's constituents. And in this context, it's interesting to note that only a few years ago Brian Walden, who at the time of the speech was the Labour Member of Parliament for nearby Birmingham All Saints, admitted on a Radio 4 programme that he and his party hugely misjudged the fears and anxieties of homeowners.

Of course when rereading today the 'Rivers of Blood' speech in full (and how many do?), there is no doubt over the distasteful, even odious wording it includes. Much the same could be said of Churchill in the 1930s, when on occasions he referred to people as 'savages'. And to be called a warmonger in the 1930s wasn't much better than being called a racist in the 1960s. Nevertheless, after the immigration speech Enoch was entrenched in the public psyche as a formidable, forbidding creature; his dark aura assisted by the pencil-thin moustache, the mostly unsmiling countenance and the scary black Homburg hat.

It was a few years later, in the mid-1970s, that I found myself at the House of Commons interviewing him for a newspaper profile. He was famous for not having an office in the House and our chat was conducted on one of those green benches in the proximity of the central lobby.

Anyone who met Enoch Powell remembers the first occasion. Those penetrating blue eyes and his manner of speech were intimidating (even for a girl whose own mother was regarded as terrifying by most people). Naturally, the moment I mentioned 'rivers of blood' my tutorial commenced. The expression never appeared in the speech, he said. And he went on to explain from where the quotation derived and why, when viewed in its context, it should hardly have caused offence to any reasonable person. It was a nerve-racking start. But the fact that he bothered to go into detail and did so in a gentle, respectful manner convinced me that beneath the forbidding exterior he was actually courteous, kind, painstaking.

As I left, he asked if I'd bring my completed work to him. He

didn't, he insisted, wish to alter my opinion, only to correct any
errors of fact. Accordingly, a few days later I turned up at his house
in South Eaton Place. He answered the door and led me to the
basement where we sat at a tiny kitchen table. Saying a private
prayer, I handed him the finished profile. It felt like being at school
again. Thank goodness for the unexpected interruption. He'd only
just started reading my copy when Pamela Powell, his wife, bustled
in with an apology for disturbing us but she had some important
instructions. 'Your lunch, Enoch,' she said, 'is in the fridge. There
is apple pie to finish. The cream is in a jug at the top of the fridge.
Do *not* spill the cream.' The great Enoch Powell nodded meekly.
For one who had grown up in a matriarchal home, the scene was
reassuringly familiar. I relaxed. Mr Powell even smiled for the first
time, and then, having corrected the grammar (inevitably), said,
'Very good. Thank you for coming along.' I left his house much
endeared to him.

In the early 1980s, I moved to Hampstead, where Michael and
Jill Foot were my neighbours, like me besotted dog owners. And
thanks to Jill's daughter Julie, a *Sunday Times* colleague, I formed a
close friendship with the Foots, to the extent that I came to regard
them as secondary parents. Jill was an exceptional cook and endear-
ingly hospitable both to young journalists and to her husband's
favourite political colleagues. Thus to my great amusement I learnt
that the Powells were frequent supper guests. Scholarship clearly
took precedence over political views. And significantly Michael
was another person who, despite his disagreement with Enoch on
immigration, never ever believed he was in any way a racist. How
my mother, who had so often been ridiculed for her twin support
of Enoch Powell and Michael Foot, would have enjoyed knowing
there was nothing foolish in her choice of heroes.

I have one final memory of Enoch. Shortly after I'd made the
transition to television as the presenter of the BBC's *Points of View*,
I dipped my toe for the first time into the world of TV current
affairs. My chance came with Southern Television, which, at the
time, was launching a programme of a similar format to today's
Question Time. It appeared once a week in a different venue along
the south-east coast. The series coincided with the First Gulf War
of 1990. Enoch had ceased to be an MP. But he was still a 'very good

booking' and we considered ourselves lucky to have him as a guest on the first programme. Another guest on the panel of four was the *Daily Mail* journalist Ann Leslie.

Before the start I wandered into the makeshift make-up room to say my hellos and found them deep in conversation. Not that I could understand a word. They were speaking Swahili to each other. This bizarre scene did nothing for my mounting anxiety. As a relative newcomer to television, I had ahead the tricky task of conducting proceedings from the middle of the audience with a hand-held microphone. The show was live. There was much to deal with. There was much that could go wrong. And as the guests made their way to the stage, I whispered to Enoch that I remembered his saying that, before a major speech in Parliament or elsewhere, he always made it a point to perform on a half-full bladder. 'I've taken your advice,' I hissed, 'because I'm petrified.'

The programme began with the four guests on the stage and myself in the middle of the audience. We got through the first question, and then, with the camera solely on me, I caught Enoch, out of sight of the viewers at home. He suddenly smiled and then, to my utter astonishment, he gave me a 'thumbs up'. It was charming. An adorable gesture I've never forgotten.

Yes, Enoch was a controversial figure. His language was ill judged. But to come to a satisfactory verdict on any of his pronouncements, you need to read the small print. Enoch's intellectual force, or maybe his pig-headedness, or maybe a mixture of both meant he failed to make allowances for the fact that many people would not do so. But to ascribe racist motives to a politician simply because he used language which, for many of his listeners, was normal is sloppy logic. Enoch deserves better. My mother was right. He was a worthy hero. And to have had the opportunity to meet and spend time with Enoch Powell I regard as one of the great pleasures and privileges of my journalistic life.

Energy and the Environment

Richard Ritchie

> It appears to be accepted on all sides as axiomatic that Britain ought
> to have an energy policy [and] that over and above this there
> ought to be an international energy policy, with the IEA as its agency
> ... These notions are ill conceived and pernicious.

These words of Enoch Powell, spoken at an energy conference
in London in 1976, dramatise the gulf between his and today's
prevailing attitude towards the role of government. There are few in
politics, and even fewer in the energy industries, who would challenge
the need for an interventionist energy policy at the moment. The last
person of major political authority to do so was Nigel Lawson, who, as
Secretary of State for Energy, was one of those rare politicians more
concerned to reduce his power than increase it. But subsequently,
Lawson's legacy has been eroded, partly because of environmental
concerns, and partly because of anxieties – real or unreal – over the
market's capacity to deliver security of supply. Today, energy policy
is higher up the political agenda than ever before. Moreover, the
alleged scientific consensus surrounding climate change has provided
a perfect excuse for politicians with an appetite for interference to
indulge their statist enthusiasms. It is no coincidence that the 'left'
of politics has adopted climate change as one of its favourite causes.
Given that politicians of all parties are becoming increasingly interventionist, some with the professed intention of addressing 'market
failures' and others with a more acute sense of what they judge to be
'fair' or 'green', energy policy could reasonably be regarded as falling
into the category Powell described as follows:

> At the end of a lifetime in politics, when a man looks back, he discov-
> ers that the things he most opposed have come to pass and that nearly

all the objects he set out with are not merely not accomplished, but seem to belong to a different world from the one he lives in.

Thus, it is possible that Powell, if alive today, would have been the first to concede that his past remarks on energy policy have little relevance now. Nor would he necessarily have been ashamed to say so, given his attitude towards the realities and nature of politics. He would have had an admirable excuse for belonging 'to a different world'. For most energy commentators, climate change is a game changer: it presents problems and issues which Powell was not called upon to address during his time in active politics, and which are assumed today as requiring a totally novel policy response of a much more interventionist character.

One purpose of this chapter is to speculate on how Powell would have responded to this challenge, given what he said on energy and other related subjects. Granted, he disputed the need for an energy policy. Would he have disputed the same for climate change as well? The answer is not clear cut, as will become evident. Powell's views on the environment were not as *laissez-faire* as sometimes imagined. Indeed, contrary to what is often supposed, Powell saw an active role for government in many areas of policy.

To begin with, however, it is necessary to consider the issue of energy policy alone, without its environmental dimension, since it is widely assumed today that the state's obligation to guarantee security of energy supplies is sufficient in itself to justify political intervention. Powell would not have agreed, and would have stuck to his guns in respect of his major critique of 'the whole conception of energy policy':

At least one voice ought to be raised at this conference, if only for an instant, to denounce the whole conception of energy policy. It appears to be accepted on all sides as axiomatic that Britain ought to have an energy policy; that over and above this there ought to be an international energy policy, with the IEA [International Energy Agency] as its agency; and for good measure that the superstate of which Britain is provisionally a province, the European Economic Community, ought to have an energy policy.

I assert that all these notions are ill conceived and pernicious. And that their result must be to maximise error and consequently the waste of human effort. I prove my thesis in three minutes as follows.

The meaning of energy policy is that governments, individually or collectively, will act to alter what would otherwise have been the price, production and distribution of energy from various sources. It is an admitted fact that the supply and demand for energy from various sources has been subject to severe, rapid and unanticipated changes, and official forecasts have been consistent only in being wildly wrong. There is no reason to suppose that in this respect the future will differ from the past.

Erroneous anticipations, and decisions based upon them, are abandoned more slowly and reluctantly by governments than by the rest of mankind, for the following reasons among others. Governments are able to persist in error longer than the rest of us, because they have the power of coercion, e.g. control of prices, imports, production etc. Governments are by definition politically and not economically motivated. They have a vested interest in actions which are popular in the short term and especially those which preserve the status quo. Unlike other investors, they have no interest in being proved right five, let alone twenty-five, years later.

Only God knows how the supply and demand for energy from various sources is going to change in the future. Waste of human effort will therefore be minimised if the erroneous assumptions which we cannot help making are modified as quickly as possible, if abortive decisions are abandoned promptly, and if old anticipations are replaced by new ones, however unpalatable, with the minimum delay.

These conditions will only be met if decisions are dispersed, unconstrained and economically motivated – in short, if governments neither interfere with them nor usurp them nor alter the data of changing supply and demand on which they have to be based. Energy policy is worse than the search for an illusion: it is a prescription for frustration.[†]

If ever there were a succinct critique of the whole philosophy of government intervention in an economy, it is this. This three-minute

---

† Speech to a national energy conference, Church House, Westminster, 22 June 1976.

diatribe against the very idea of an energy policy could equally be applied to any attempt by government to intervene in the economy and, as such, could reasonably be said to comprise all that Powell had to say on the subject. Powell would surely have hoped that these words were timeless and relevant not just to energy but to the role of government in the economy as a whole. But three minutes was not sufficient time to encapsulate everything that Powell thought or said about energy, and is not by itself an adequate response to the question posed by Powell himself as to whether or not his views 'belong to a different world from the one he lives in'.

It is fashionable today for many advocates of a market approach to the economy to exclude energy on the grounds of its strategic importance, and because oil and gas resources are almost entirely owned and controlled by national governments. But while Powell did make some concessions in this area – possibly more than is often supposed – he would have contested strongly the notion that 'energy' was too important to be left to the market.

His hostile attitude towards energy policy is also rooted in the economic principles which, if he were alive today, he would still contend are valid and important. Perhaps the most important of these was Powell's championing of 'less government' and his fundamental belief in the capacity of politicians to make things worse, rather than better. He set out exactly what he meant by 'less government' in an important speech in November 1970, in which he was very clear that '"less government" does not mean less government everywhere ... If *laissez-faire* means that government withdraws from those functions in society which the citizens must not or cannot try to perform for themselves, then the Tory Party is not, never has been, and never can be, the party of *laissez-faire*.'

As examples of such functions, Powell cited public order and the administration of justice; social and welfare services; health and education. But in choosing these, Powell was adamant in making a distinction between economic and non-economic forces:

> There is a mixture of what economic forces can and will do, and what they cannot do. Unfortunately, we have tried in this country to achieve the non-economic purposes by forms of nationalisation which, like all forms of nationalisation, tend of their own nature

towards an arrogant and exclusive monopoly. In this spirit therefore the Conservative urge towards 'less government' does not mean denying the non-economic purpose: it does not mean dismantling the National Health Service or the state education system or withdrawing the state's ultimate guarantee of security against want. It does not deny that we may wish to see more security against want, more education, more medical aid than would be chosen on purely economic grounds. What it *does* mean is that where economic forces will provide services within this area, we shall see to it that they are not choked or driven out by the ever-growing appetite of the state, but rather that the state withdraws in proportion as the action of individuals, expressing itself through market forces, advances.

When it came, however, to the field of business, commerce and industry, 'where the economic motive reigns supreme', Powell was very clear that the case was different:

There is no point in using the effort and savings to dig coal or build ships if the same effort and savings would yield more economic good if used for something else. We do not do these things for fun or as religious exercises, but for the measurable, material benefit we expect to get. The Conservative Party, being a capitalist party and a party of free enterprise, accepts the market – price, profit and loss – as the arbiter of measurable material benefit, and rejects the state.

Powell is then emphatic that this calls for an all-or-nothing approach:

There is no choice here but to go the whole hog. From exchange rates to production subsidies, from little Neddies[†] to nationalised industries we are obliged to put the state in all its guises under 'notice to quit'. Until that notice can be enforced – and it will take much time and much work to do it – we shall continue to suffer

---

† 'Little Neddies' operated under the umbrella of the National Economic Development Council, and represented attempts to plan and to stimulate economic activity in various industry sectors by bringing together businessmen, trade unionists and officials.

such absurd spectacles as that of our Cabinet deciding on the rival commercial merits of one airliner against another, with the Treasury and the Foreign Office putting their oars into questions which are no more fit to be their business than the makes of motor car or the range of goods in Marks and Spencer ... You can neither intervene, nor withdraw from intervention, by half-measures.[†]

It is this distinction between 'economic' and 'non-economic' purposes which goes to the heart of today's debate over energy policy and which largely determines whether or not Powell's past remarks are in any way relevant to the problems which now confront us. First and foremost, does climate change fall into the economic or non-economic category? Powell once said that the debate over 'guns or butter' was a political debate, concerning solely the extent to which a country wished to defend itself. That was something the 'market' shouldn't be called upon to decide. It was beyond its capacity and purpose. But there are those today who argue that climate change is equally an issue of survival, and one which calls for an array of rationing and controls hitherto associated with wartime. It is necessary to consider how Powell would have addressed this argument, if we are to relate his past remarks to the present.

Also to be taken into account is the crucial importance to a national economy of the nation's basic infrastructure, including its physical energy networks. Many would argue that government has the primary, if not sole, responsibility for ensuring its provision and good repair. In a little-noted speech which Powell made in January 1981, he addressed the seemingly parochial issue of the Liverpool–Belfast ferry in a way which is relevant to the entire energy debate:

Communication is the essence of all government: it is not for nothing that the mail is the Royal Mail. How much more is the essence of the Union of Great Britain and Northern Ireland ... for no sooner was the Union created in 1800 that almost feverish energy was applied to improving, strengthening and accelerating the communications between Ireland and the seat of Parliament and of government. Anybody who imagines that those communications are

---

† Speech to South Kensington Young Conservatives, 30 November 1970.

not a political matter is too innocent to be allowed out alone. Side by
side with the more visible and violent campaign against the Union, a
quieter and more subtle campaign is being waged with the object of
reducing the facility of movement and transport between Ulster and
Great Britain and rendering Ulster increasingly dependent upon
lines running through the Irish Republic and consequently vulnerable to pressure and blackmail. The failure to provide Northern
Ireland with those energy links to the mainland which alone make
sense in the long run is not a consequence of economics ...

Nobody in Ulster, I am sure, begrudges channelling British gas
or British electricity to our southern neighbours wherever and
whenever that is economic. In fact, we would welcome the expansion of British trade and exports. But any fool can see what would
be Ulster's situation if the link were the other way and if our access
to the electricity grid of Great Britain and the Continent or to the
resource of natural gas around the British Isles were at the mercy of
the Irish Republic and of the Union's enemies whom it harbours.[†]

If true of the Irish Republic, why not of Russia? This short extract
is illuminating for many reasons. First, it reveals how some of
Powell's free-market views were moderated once he became an
Ulster MP. As a Tory MP, for example, Powell would seldom have
been heard welcoming 'the expansion of British trade and exports'
as an objective in itself. But more important for energy policy, if
Powell believed it was politically vital for Ulster to have access to
the electricity grid of Great Britain in order to avoid 'blackmail'
from the Irish Republic, why do not similar considerations apply to
the UK as a whole in terms of the Middle East or other sensitive
areas of the world? As any oil or gas company knows, the existence and direction of an oil and gas pipeline is a highly political
matter. The discovery of oil and gas is only the beginning. Access
to the market is crucial if the investment risk is to be undertaken.
Pipelines and networks have major implications for the revenues
of governments but also, and more important in this context, the
security of energy supplies. And while no oil or gas company would
willingly invest in a pipeline for which there was no economic

† Speech at Helen's Bay, Co. Down, 7 January 1981.

rationale, it would be rare indeed for such an investment to escape profound political considerations. Already, therefore, the question arises as to whether the supply of energy can be regarded as merely 'economic'. The pipeline issue is just one example. The fact that access to energy resources such as oil and gas is exclusively a matter for governments to permit or to obstruct is another reason why their geographical and political location is relevant to governments and consumers alike.

Powell's speech on 7 January 1981, quoted above, suggests that over time he moderated somewhat his objection to government intervention, despite his earlier criticism of the whole idea of an energy policy and his assertion that 'you can neither intervene, nor withdraw from intervention, by half-measures'. He still believed that was true, but only in terms of merely 'economic' issues. This was also relevant to the new energy policy (or lack of it) articulated by Nigel Lawson in 1982 (six years after Powell's dismissal of the whole idea) which led to the privatisations of the gas and electricity industries, the break-up of British Gas and the liberalisations of domestic energy markets. This was followed by Cecil Parkinson's announcement at the Conservative Party conference in 1988 that 'coal will be privatised', as indeed eventually it was under the Coal Industry Act 1994. Even Powell in his Morecambe Budget of 1968 had assumed that coal would remain in public ownership.

The characteristics of the energy market which Lawson inherited are significant. As Dieter Helm has explained in his analysis of British energy policy,[†] 'For most of the post-war period, the energy sector was run by the state through integrated monopolies.' Coal, electricity, gas, nuclear, and even parts of BP were all under public ownership. The British National Oil Company had been established to ensure that the state had a vehicle through which the development and exploitation of the United Kingdom continental shelf (UKCS) could be controlled and managed by politicians. To quote Helm again, 'Energy was part of the planned economy, and the task of government was to improve its performance within that overall structure.'

---

† Dieter Helm, *Energy, the State and the Market: British Energy Policy since 1979* (Oxford: Oxford University Press, 2003).

Powell was a fervent opponent of the 'planned economy'. Indeed, in his adoption speech as far back as the general election of October 1964, he actually chose energy to embellish the point:

> Two or three years ago, no one, except perhaps a few scientists, even suspected that we were about to see sources of power opened up on our very doorstep in the North Sea which will change the power economics not only of Britain and Europe but of the world. The influence of those events on this country's whole economy, industry and population pattern will be immense. Not being a socialist, I do not pretend to foresee what that influence will be precisely, or indeed even in outline. But this I do know, that economic plans drawn up a year or two ago will soon be out of date from this one cause alone, and that plans attempted now will look absurd before we are much older.

It is no surprise therefore that, in his earlier speeches, Powell's denunciation of an energy policy was just one battle among many in his war against the type of planned economy largely favoured by 'planners' – of whom there were many – in the Labour and Conservative parties at the time. It was under the Conservative government of Margaret Thatcher, and especially through the determination of Nigel Lawson, who was appointed Secretary of State for Energy in September 1981, that the post-war planned approach to energy policy was progressively dismantled. But even Lawson's policy of disengagement did not, in Powell's words, 'go the whole hog', mainly because the policy of denationalisation (as Powell would have described it) was not accompanied by a similar faith in the unfettered workings of the market and competition. There was still a political sense that energy was different in kind from other 'essentials', and that the existence of an energy regulator, operating under objectives and criteria prescribed by Parliament, was an essential element in overseeing the UK's energy mix and performance. This was not Lawson's fault. A temporary approach he devised to oversee the transition to competition became under future Labour ministers a permanent fixture.

In debating whether or not this was inevitable, it is of interest to go back to the attitudes prevailing during the period when UK oil and gas was first discovered in the North Sea and when Powell discussed the implications in purely economic terms. He did so with a special eye to the balance-of-payments implications, which for him, before the pound floated, were almost an obsession. Indeed, for many years his energy speeches were more about the balance of payments than the security of energy supplies. But he also foresaw, especially in terms of oil, the potential downsides as well as the ups which the discovery of natural resources can bring. Powell was not joking when he said 'The happiest countries are those which have no natural resources',[†] although this was in contradiction to what he had said on an earlier occasion:

> I do not know whether in Scotland you now include in your prayers of thanksgiving a reference to offshore oil and gas; but I do know that if you don't, you ought … [However,] the bonus or bonanza of offshore oil and gas is the resultant difference in cost – real cost, human effort expended – in getting that amount of energy to the point where we use it. Take no notice for this purpose of the striking fact that the sources are on our own continental shelf: being in our own soil has not prevented coal from becoming relatively more and more expensive. We still have to expend effort in getting energy from the surrounding sea, as we have in making Staffordshire pottery or whisky or air-conditioning equipment to exchange for the sheikhly petroleum of the Middle East or for that matter in producing, or obtaining by exchange, energy from any other source, here or elsewhere. The question is simply how much less effort in the one case than the other.

So for Powell, the potential benefit of North Sea oil and gas should be judged entirely on its price. The other considerations were dismissed:

> Do not, please, talk about the security of oil supplies. It would be a greater prophet than we have who could tell you how we shall fare for offshore oil and gas in a future war. Still more, I beg you, do not talk about saving imports, or hard currency, or whatnot. Now that other currencies are exchanged for sterling at their free-market value of the moment, it matters not whether you obtain what you want

---

† 1 December 1978.

by exchanging a given product of your effort with an Englishman or with an Arab. Finally, do not gloat over the £100 million a year in royalties and rents which it is expected will accrue to the state as landlord by 1980. That is a share of the value produced which is taken by the state, as it takes a share of the value produced by potters, or distillers or air-conditioning manufacturers aforesaid. It may, or may not, be nice to contemplate so large a slice going to the Exchequer; but to treat it as additional gain is, I am afraid, just double-counting. No: the bonus is the reduction in real costs, or if you like, the increase in productivity, which has occurred and will occur through the rise of offshore gas and oil. That is the asset of which we are to be stewards.[†]

As the costs of this oil and gas became more apparent, Powell adapted his argument. He regarded North Sea gas as a cheap source of energy, and therefore a benefit: but because North Sea oil was 'dear energy' he was, by 1978, describing it as a curse. This was a contentious point, because in proclaiming this view he was assuming that foreign sources of oil would remain cheaper, despite perceptions of scarcity and the efforts of OPEC to keep the price high. And although he was always enthusiastic to pour scorn on forecasts ('Not just recently, but since the middle of the nineteenth century and earlier, energy forecasts have been wildly, and in retrospect ludicrously, wrong,' he said in March 1979), in questioning the value of North Sea oil he was inevitably forming a view on the future world price of oil. Actually, in respect of his chosen timescale, he got it right:

Let me put my cards on the table face upwards straight away. There ain't gonna be no Ice Age. The real price of oil-based energy will be on a downward trend during the years ahead. So plentiful and so fiercely competitive will be the sources of energy in general that many of those who are now investing heavily on the contrary assumption will be ruined if they are private persons and discredited if they are governments. Attempts will of course be made – both by politicians and by cartels – to restrain competition; and states

† Speech to the Central Fife Conservative Association, Markinch, 27 January 1973.

which have made foolish investments will do their best to compel
their citizens to use dear energy instead of cheap energy. So strong,
however, will be the focus of sheer plenty that these puny efforts are
not likely to succeed for long.

As this graph shows, the real price of oil was indeed on a downward trend following July 1980, so Powell was correct in one sense,
though not in predicting ruin as a consequence. New North Sea
investments became increasingly marginal and challenging, a trend
which has only been reversed in recent years as the real oil price has
again risen to new heights. Life in the North Sea became therefore
more difficult, but private enterprise coped, assisted – it must be
admitted – by positive changes to the North Sea's fiscal regime.
Nevertheless, Powell forecast the oil price better than many energy
professionals.

The so-called collapse of OPEC (noted in the above graph) was
also foreseen by Powell in this same speech:

> The strangest of all the strange delusions of these years since 1973
> has been the belief that the Middle East oil producers can – as the
> metaphor goes – 'hold the world to ransom' because their output
> is so large and their own economies so narrow apart from oil. The
> opposite is the truth. Their very superfluity of riches renders them
> vulnerable and guarantees the fall in the world real price which
> would have been predictable anyhow.

As again predicted by Powell, however, the adjustment in North
Sea production was not immediate and this would have implications for the UK economy as a whole:

But if – or rather, when – the world real price of oil falls, UK production will not be turned down again in a hurry, nor will the other submarine fields which the same transitory conditions have stimulated and are stimulating still. They will make a fight of it to survive. Likewise, the investment which is going into the production of energy from other sources will not be written off hastily but will be brought into production and kept in production as long as possible – if not longer.[†]

It was in a different speech that Powell discussed the implications of domestic oil and gas production for the economy as a whole and in a spirit which is especially pertinent today, given the current policy drive to 'rebalance' the UK economy in favour of manufacturing. In February 1986, Powell described the 'plunge in oil prices' as 'specially good' news because 'it marks the reversal of that abrupt switch from current deficit to current surplus on our balance of payments which in recent years has been helping to force unemployment up and manufacturing production down.' He continued:

> The artificially high price our oil commanded gave us an overdose of leisure which we were quite unprepared to absorb. Thank goodness, we can now look forward, with any luck, to some decent trading deficits. Yes, you heard me right the first time: I said 'decent *deficits*'. With a current account surplus it is we who export our capital; with a current deficit it is the rest of the world which invests in us … Like most of my fellow countrymen, I am not too keen on foreigners: but I have no objection to their money … If [for example] it takes the fancy of the Japanese to export their savings, that's their affair. From our point of view it all helps to keep our disastrous surplus with the outside world within limits and so to stem the outflow of capital from Britain. Too much of it has flowed to the United States.[‡]

This extract is but one of many where Powell's remarks on energy constitute an equal, if not greater, interest in discussing the benefits of a floating currency. To repeat, Powell regarded domestic oil and

---

† Speech to the Heating and Ventilating Contractors' Association, 9 July 1980.
‡ Speech in Grimsby, 21 February 1986.

gas as only having value in so far as they were cheaper than the alternatives. He did not see domestic energy production beneficial even for reasons of tax:

> 'Oh, but' the nation owns the North Sea oil and can get revenues from it like the dukes of old from their estates. How stupid can people be? If this was so, all we should need to do in order to be as rich as Croesus would be to nationalise the land – or, better still, nationalise everything. Alas, we all know that at the best we should not be one penny better off ... The wealth of a state is the taxable capacity of the people within its jurisdiction ... Taxes can take many forms, and new ones can always be invented; but what matters, as kings and princes have always discovered to their sorrow, is how much income there is to tax.[†]

Much of this will sound academic and fanciful to a generation brought up on the belief that taxes on energy can help fill the government's depleted coffers and 'save the planet' at the same time. Moreover, while a considerable amount of academic attention has been given to assessing the economic significance to a nation of possessing abundant energy resources – and there are arguments on both sides – most countries would probably disagree with Powell that they would be better off without them. Powell placed almost exclusive reliance upon price. But he said very little about the uncertainties created by volatility of price or the political threat posed by the arbitrary decision of a belligerent nation to disrupt the supplies of oil.

While there is evidence to sustain Powell's belief that in the end the laws of supply and demand cannot be baulked, the world has also seen how the political disruption of a commodity as essential as oil or gas can bring a country to its knees within days. True, this disruption could be caused as much by internal forces such as domestic terrorism or trade union militancy as by an external act, and to this extent the geographical ownership of the oil and gas is an irrelevance. But there is an apparent inconsistency in Powell's concern over excessive energy dependence on the Republic of

---

[†] Speech in Edinburgh, 7 December 1977.

Ireland (see above) and his relative indifference to potential hostile acts from other countries.

This indifference was due in part – and surprisingly so, in light of Powell's dismissal of the geographical dimension – to the UK's self-sufficiency in oil and gas. ('If the present input from the Gulf into the world's oil consumption were eliminated, Britain would be "quids in" on the rise in price that would still further increase our already disgustingly large surplus on current trading account.') But the main point Powell was determined to make (and would be making still, were he alive) was that the protection of oil and gas resources in the Middle East was no excuse for going to war. In March 1984, Powell addressed the specific issue of blocking the Strait of Hormuz. In light of what has happened since, and what is happening today, it makes interesting reading:

> The declared objects are twofold: to protect something called 'that part of the world', and to protect 'the oil supplies which are so vital to the west'. The first thing to attract attention is the word 'protect', which induces the question 'From whom?' ... Even Russia, whom it is conventional to credit with dreams of dominating Iraq and/or Iran, has not manifested the slightest inclination to intervene, not being as mad as that or perhaps not even mad at all ... If the oil supplies really are 'vital' to anybody, it is to Iran and Iraq themselves as producers and foreign currency earners ... So what would we be doing with Her Majesty's ships that would 'protect that part of the world and the oil supplies that are so vital to the west'? ... In order to command or keep open a narrow strait, it is indispensable to hold if not both of the shores at least one of them, sufficiently to be able to dominate the other. The assertion of an intention to open or keep open the Straits of Hormuz by naval and naval-based air power is a military absurdity ... The Persian Gulf, I realise, has historical and emotional echoes for the British. Perhaps those echoes make our perception of American insanities more myopic than it otherwise might be ... The American administration is as obtuse and irresponsible in its blundering threat to intrude into the Gulf as it was in its blundering series of successive interventions in the Levant.[†]

---

† Speech to Warwick University Conservative Association, 9 March 1984.

It should now be apparent that Powell addressed energy policy almost exclusively in terms of its economic impact, and rejected the notion that because energy was so important, it required a different economic approach from other essential commodities. In contrast, government involvement today in energy markets is justified as much, if not more, on environmental as on energy grounds. While some would argue that there is an inherent conflict between the policies required to safeguard energy supplies on the one hand, and the duty to protect the planet on the other, this view is hardly fashionable. Most governments and commentators assume that policies to promote low-carbon energy complement 'keeping on the lights' because fossil fuels are finite and will eventually 'run out'. Perhaps, although this argument would not have appealed to Powell at all. But at the end of the day, it is in any case hard to believe that – were the science surrounding climate change to be dismissed and discredited unequivocally – there would still be enthusiasm for the renewable subsidies, incentives, taxes and distortions which constitute current energy policy, which deliberately increase energy costs and which discriminate against fossil fuels. If it were just an economic matter, renewable energy could be left to fight its own corner without interference from the state; indeed, capitalists (if there are any left) will argue that the market itself can guard against too great a dependence upon any single source of energy, without the advice of governments.

The situation is different, however, if for non-economic reasons it is proposed that cheap and plentiful supplies of energy are no longer the objective. In essence, this is the current assumption upon which the UK government and European Union's energy policy is based. Its foundation is the belief that the 'science' of climate change demands an interventionist energy policy which increases the costs of fossil fuels in order to provide an energy mix and low-carbon infrastructure which the market on its own could not possibly justify.

Against this background, it is difficult for politicians to avoid the scientific issues of climate change, although this probably would have been Powell's inclination. As he once explained to David Frost in a different context:

There are many scientific facts and disputes on which I have no opinion and have not been concerned to form an opinion ... You surely can understand that there can be questions, very important in the relevant sciences, on which a politician not only is entitled not to have an opinion, but as a politician has no business to form an opinion.[†]

It is far from clear that Powell could have held this line in respect of climate change; more likely, he would have been tempted to follow Nigel Lawson's example in throwing doubt upon the apparent scientific unanimity surrounding the subject (or at least upon how the science was 'spun'). What is certain is that he would have dismissed the idea that scientists are the best people to determine the necessary policies to deal with a problem which, on their authority alone, is said to exist. The experience of 'unusual weather' is not yet of such a magnitude as to arouse the everyday anxieties of the electorate; it is the scientists who are making the running and keeping it on the agenda. Politicians are left with deciding whether or not the scientific concern over global warming is sufficient to thrust the energy debate from the economic into the non-economic dimension, especially in terms of future generations.

If Powell's view had been in the affirmative, he would have considered a greater role for government, albeit in accordance with market principles. Remarks which he made in other areas have a bearing on this aspect of energy policy. First, there is his attitude to environmental issues generally, which he summarised when in March 1977 he addressed an audience of builders:

Conservation, gentlemen: wherever you look, wherever you listen, in every group from pub to pulpit – I bet they do it in pulpits – you will find them talking about conservation. However, conservation's no good for you. You're not conservers – the Lord bless you; you're destroyers and replacers. Your great Victorian predecessors, indeed your great predecessors in every great age of construction, have also been the great destroyers, men with so proud a contempt for what it was that they destroyed that they did not interest themselves to know whether it was Romanesque or Perpendicular; they just pulled it down. That's the kind of age for you; that's the environment you

---

† *Frost on Friday*, 3 January 1969.

need in the construction industry, the great age of Baroque, for instance, when in San Gallen, without a second thought, they would remove a Carolingian monastery, complete, eighth, ninth century; *swoosh!* it was gone, and that exhilarating fabric the Rococo cathedral rose in its place. The great Victorians had much of the same spirit. It's true what they put in its place was, they were sure, better Gothic than what the Middle Ages had ever built. Certainly much of it was better constructed. But they destroyed first, and built afterwards.[†]

Here, it is clear that Powell's approach to the environment was as distinctive and as combative as in any other area of policy. He stated what is obvious, but often overlooked, that economic activity of any kind is bound to have an environmental effect and that some of the most cherished or necessary developments of today were considered environmentally detrimental in the past. Indeed, Powell went further when he argued that 'Man's endeavours to survive in the environment where he finds himself have bequeathed to us the wild places of our own country and of the earth,' and he cited examples such as the Broads of East Anglia, the 'bareness' of the South Downs, and the New Forest as environmental beauty spots created by man's intervention in nature. 'Outside these islands how often are the wildest wildernesses of the earth the monuments to man's past cultivation and pasturage.'

This does not mean, however, that Powell was blind or unsympathetic to the detrimental environmental implications of economic activity:

So we find ourselves confronted, as not infrequently when dealing with *Homo sapiens*, by a paradox. He, the great destroyer, the great wilderness maker, looks on in amazement when we cry out to him: 'Stay your hand and halt just where you are.' Paradox it may be, joking I am not; for this is the paradox which stares in the face all lovers and would-be preservers of wildlife. The wildest of all wildlife is man, and to him we must address ourselves first, if we want to preserve wildlife. So what shall we say to him, as he removes the tropical rainforests or creates nuclear power stations and disposes

---

† Speech to a builders' conference, 9 March 1977.

of their waste products, and then turns upon us, when we protest and use *force majeure* to stay his hand, and with a quizzical, bewildered expression says to us: 'But this is how I have behaved since my species first came into existence, and wherever I went nature has followed in my tracks and clothed the wilderness with glory. Why suddenly rise up in front of me now with your committees and your legislation and your international busybodies and do-gooders, crying out "Hold, enough!"?'

Powell poses this question as much to himself as to others, because he was second to none in honouring and enjoying the beauty of nature and the heritage of our past. He often said, for example, that his one great political inconsistency was in supporting subsidies to the British Museum when, on libertarian grounds, he should have opposed them. So he answered his own question thus:

> What we are looking for is a compromise ... between curiosity and destruction, between a museum or an encyclopaedia and the urge to use and devastate. We would not presume to limit or control your ceaseless urge to use, to use up, to destroy ... All we say is: do not deny or defeat your other urge, the urge to satisfy your curiosity. Whatever is the reasonable minimum necessary to meet the demand to understand, to study, to observe, let that suffice and let that survive. Whole continents – not even the forbidding continent of Antarctica – we do not seek to deny you. Whole oceans – even the secret depths of the Pacific – we do not want to put out of bounds. Curiosity, the natural curiosity of our common nature, has cunning enough to find ways of satisfying itself with what little needs to be withheld from mankind's other uses.[†]

In short, Powell would not have allowed climate change to become an excuse for arresting economic development, any more than he would have allowed it to impinge upon individual freedom of choice. But equally, as he demonstrated when discussing the role of the state in land, he stood for more than just *laissez-faire*:

---

† Speech to Yorkshire Wildlife Trust, 6 December 1991.

We just do not have the same emotional links with the other goods and services that are traded in the market as we have with land. The effect on me of the vision of the skyline of the South Downs is something quite separate from many of the considerations which would be brought to bear upon its planning, its preservation or its utilisation for the extraction of chalk or for an east–west route. There is a socio-aesthetic, a socio-emotional significance of land ... I want to try to identify some of the roles in which society has re-entered or sought to re-enter the scene in the second and third thirds of this twentieth century. Perhaps the easiest to identify is that of guardian, as the guardian of the community's land, its common possession, against spoliation: a prohibitive, regulatory or, if you like, negative role, the State saying, on behalf of society, 'No, that use shall not be made of that land; that extraction shall not take place from that land; that land shall be left unused.' It is the community, vocalised by the state, protecting its own; and the powers which are claimed derive from the admission, not merely of a common interest – there is a common interest in traffic control, there is a common interest in control of industrial safety, there is a common interest in the control of epidemic diseases – but of a common interest deriving from a common and essential possession. It is that which brings the state on to the stage in terms of prohibition.

I find it useful myself to contrast that role as strictly as possible with its role whereby, also in a representative capacity, it says not what shall *not* be done with land, but what *shall be done* ... Both these roles of the State, negative and positive, come into essential conflict with the private ownership of land and of rights in land and with the processes of the market ... All market values are speculative, because they are all concerned with what is going to happen in the future ... But when the State says no, or when the State says yes, it does away with the process of evaluating collective assumptions ...

Alas! Alas! Mankind has been trying to settle the future since mankind existed. But you haven't got the plan into its first draft before you discover it was wrong. The mistake does not and should not disincline those who act on behalf of the community to cease to do so; for after all, the argument for protecting, for example, amenity against an *unforeseen* threat is just as good as the argument for protecting it against a *foreseen* threat. But since the threats cannot be foreseen, (as nothing else can be foreseen,) you cannot deal with the problem by a universal plan.[†]

This extract contains three important indications of Powell's thinking towards climate change. First, climate change is clearly relevant to land, and therefore belongs to a special category from Powell's perspective. Second, Powell concedes the case for prohibitive regulations and taxes, but not positive or prescriptive intervention. But finally, Powell would have been very sceptical of attempts by governments or international bodies to address the issue globally: 'since the threats cannot be foreseen, (as nothing else can be foreseen,) you cannot deal with the problem by a universal plan.' He would have had to reconcile this view with the fact that – if climate change is indeed a problem – no country can unilaterally solve it.

All that one can surmise is that, if convinced of the need for action, Powell would have proposed policies of the 'negative' rather than the 'positive' variety. He would still have been sceptical of the state's role in finding a solution; he would still have thought that politicians were more likely to make the problem worse, rather than better; and from his attitude to economic development generally, it is likely that he would have been much more enthusiastic for policies of an 'adaptive' nature (such as the Thames Barrier) than in covering his beloved 'wilderness' with wind farms. But it is not inconceivable that he would have admitted the case for a carbon tax!

However, it was when addressing the Royal Society of Health Congress under the theme 'Health and the Environment: Whose Responsibility?' that Powell came closest to addressing the concerns which exist today over climate change. It is, in more ways than one, another significant contribution to today's debate:

'Health and the Environment: Whose Responsibility?' This is a political and not a medical subject, otherwise indeed I would not be presuming to address you on it. It belongs to my professional field, and not to yours. My reason for making this assertion thus boldly

---

[†] 'Land: The Role of the State', 19 March 1980.

is the word 'responsibility' in the title. There is no such thing as responsibility without power; responsibility and control are precisely coterminous. Wherever, therefore, responsibility is claimed or asserted, there also power is claimed or asserted. Moreover, where that power or control is not the power or control of an adult individual over his person or property, it must mean the power to coerce others in the disposal of their persons or property. Now, in any condition but that of naked violence, coercion is clothed in forms which render it more or less acceptable, or at least accepted; and the function of directing that coercion is entrusted to a specialised organ of society, whose operators are the rulers or, in a more comfortable and familiar idiom, the politicians. Thus the innocent-seeming question in the title, 'Whose responsibility?', translates itself into the more menacing terms 'How much politics?' or, synonymously, 'How much compulsion?'

Having established his credentials, Powell returns to one of his favourite themes, namely the justification or not for a degree of state 'coercion' – and this is very relevant to today's debate on climate change:

Let us now start looking at health and the environment from the end where coercion is least problematic, that namely where the behaviour of one individual creates a danger to other members of society: we do not hesitate to take any measures necessary for restraining those who menace the safety of their fellows by reason of mental condition or infectious disease. We justify the coercion doubly – by the requirements of the survival of the community itself and by the principle that personal liberty does not include the liberty to injure others. Nor would we decline in principle to coerce, or exercise surveillance over, those who render noxious the environment in which the community lives, or who purvey noxious substances to their fellows, even when the purveyance is a voluntary transaction between the individuals concerned.

Observe, however, that the term 'noxious' covers an extremely broad band of meaning, extending from strychnine to tobacco, and that it imports considerations both of degree and of circumstance, since almost any substance is capable, under given conditions, of producing harmful effects. Political debate has for many years, in this country and elsewhere, been exploring the labyrinthine complexities underlying the apparently simple proposition that the citizen should be restrained from purveying noxious substances to his fellows: the question 'What is harm?' can prove in practice either unanswerable with precision or liable to be differently answered in different states of knowledge. Witness the warning on the cigarette packet, or the controversy about 'pot'. The difficulties are no less when the harm to individuals is indirect through what is called 'the environment', rather than direct ...

The difficulties of giving precision, setting limits, to the notion of 'harm' are profound and far-reaching; responsibility for preventing actual harm to the health of individuals, either directly or through their environment, therefore opens up a potentially vast field of political action. These difficulties, however, are as nothing to the explosive rate at which coercion multiplies if for the prevention of 'harm' is substituted the promotion of 'benefit'. Since all activity aims at benefit of some kind or other, and since much of that benefit can be related to the individual's physical well-being, let alone to that virtually unlimited concept, 'the environment', it follows that the scope of coercion would theoretically be extended to coincide with the greater part of the life, actions and decisions of all members of the community.

Here, Powell is speaking mainly about health. But what he says could apply also to the impact on individuals of global warming. Those who take the most pessimistic view of its implications and effects are already calling for the sort of coercion which impinges upon 'the greater part of the life, actions and decisions of all members of the community'. In another respect, Powell was alluding to the current obsession with 'health and safety':

If the meaning of 'injuring others' is given the widest possible extension, the scope of individual responsibility is reduced to zero, and a compelling case is made for unlimited coercion over all aspects of individual behaviour that could have an effect upon the individual's physical or mental well-being ... It is a totalitarian society, exerting unlimited claims over the totality of the individuals composing it.

Finally, Powell returns to the distinction between 'negative' and 'positive' policies already referred to above:

> If collective responsibility is to protect, then coercion ought in princi-
> ple to be confined as far as possible to the enforcement of a negative, a
> prohibition, a 'thou shalt not'. This is a method which has been applied
> with great success to the prevention of pollution of the environment:
> compulsion is authorised by defining what is not permissible, lines
> which must not be crossed, limits which must not be exceeded. One
> advantage of the negative approach is that, while excluding one course
> of action, it leaves all others open: the consequences to be drawn from
> the prohibition, the rearrangement or redeployment of resources
> and effort are not prejudiced; no one single pattern of behaviour is
> imposed – only one pattern is eliminated ...
>
> The history of legislation and administration to reduce pollution
> of rivers is an object lesson in the efficacy of the negative method. It
> can be appreciated by contrasting what would have been the effect
> of the alternative approach, if a general and positive responsibil-
> ity for the condition of rivers had been placed upon the state. The
> approach by prohibition is not only a safeguard against unlimited
> encroachment by coercion and supersession of individual by state
> responsibility; it is also, despite its description, the truly creative
> approach, because it automatically enlists the efforts of the community
> as a whole in achieving the desired result as economically and effi-
> ciently as possible. Perhaps it might be added, as a rider, that the
> approach by prohibition does least to weaken the responsibility of
> the individuals and bodies corporate as enforceable through the
> courts: not the least important contributions to the improvement of
> the condition of Britain's rivers have been made by successful action
> for damages and injunction.
>
> While I have chosen the relatively limited illustration of
> river pollution, the same considerations would be found to apply
> throughout the whole environmental field ... coercion and the use
> of the criminal law are justified to prevent clear and acknowledged
> harm or danger to the life and health of the individual arising from
> the acts or omissions of others, but that compulsion is not justifiable
> for the purpose of enforcing a diversion of effort towards one aspect
> of individual well-being and consequently away from others; and

further that the normal adult individual's responsibility for his own health and safety is not qualified, and ought not to be removed from him, by any consideration of the indirect effects, however serious, which are implicit in his relations with the rest of the community.

In other words, assumption by the state of responsibility either for the general improvement and well-being of its members, or the consequences to the individual of his personal decisions, is incompatible with a non-totalitarian society

The relevance of this for current policies towards climate change is clear. First, if persuaded that there was a problem to deal with, Powell would not be opposed in principle to legal limits on carbon emissions or, for example, lower speed limits. He might question their efficacy or their cost, but not the state's right to intervene in this manner. On the other hand, he would be fundamentally opposed to current attempts to promote renewable energy by subsidies, or to 'rig' the market in order to arrive at a pre-ordained solution. Above all, he would be mindful that 'total resources being limited, some choices can only be met at the expense of others'.

Taking together all that Powell said upon energy specifically and the environment generally, one can conclude the following. He would not deny that there are areas of energy policy where political intervention is inevitable – such as the location of a nuclear power station, or the building of an oil pipeline. He *would* deny that the importance of energy demands the suspension of market forces and he would abhor what many categorise today as an amazingly *dirigiste* and old-fashioned energy regime which governments in Europe are in the process of creating. He probably would accept that scientific concern over climate change justifies political interest and involvement. But he would be extremely nervous that this was used as an excuse for 'coercion', state planning and the sort of controls which are only justified in wartime.

Above all, Powell would hold constant to his fundamental distrust of politicians and their capacity to make things better. He knew state intervention in many areas was inevitable; but he also knew that the priorities of any politician were almost guaranteed to deliver a short-term and distorted decision which failed to serve the public interest. This was true of both economic and non-economic areas of policy. So he tried to keep such areas for intervention to a minimum – a totally contrary instinct and approach to what is commonplace today on both sides of the political divide. 'We are all interventionists now' might accurately describe the attitude of contemporary politicians; if so, Powell would indeed have concluded that 'at the end of a lifetime in politics, when a man looks back, he discovers that the things he most opposed have come to pass and that nearly all the objects he set out with are not merely not accomplished, but seem to belong to a different world from the one he lives in.' However, in the case of energy, the jury is still out. There are still enough advocates of a market approach for Powell, were he alive today, not to despair.

Energy and the Environment

Connaught Rooms, London, 20 November 1973

All of us, and especially we politicians, persistently underestimate how many of our problems price would solve for us, without our having so much as to lift a finger, if only we would stand back and let it do its work.

Take the case of oil. Now, if the interruption of oil supplies is brief and temporary, due to an act of war or a catastrophe of nature, price will do nothing to remedy it. When a city is closely invested by the enemy, the rise in the price of corn does not bring one single additional grain within the walls. In such circumstances as those, control by the authorities – rationing, control of price, and even subsidy which helps to share the hardship between different classes – is entirely rational and justified. Not so, if the scarcity is of a different sort – if it is due to a long-term rise in demand or diminution of supplies. In that event, control will prove disastrous and only price can work salvation.

Those who ought to know advise that the present shortage of oil is only incidentally a result of the Arab-Israel war, and that the oil-producing countries of the Middle East have embarked on a long-term policy of keeping more of their oil in the ground for the future, while the oil consumption of the world continues to soar. If this is right, then rationing and price controls – except perhaps during the actual wartime emergency – will be not merely futile and self-defeating but harmful. What we imperatively need is that the price of oil should be allowed to rise towards the point when the restricted supply and the growing demand are brought back into balance. 'Rationing-by-the-purse' is the true good fairy, whose wand will in the shortest possible time ease our pains and pour balm upon our hurts.

There are sources of energy, both petrochemical and other sources, which at this moment lie just beyond the economic threshold of exploitation. Let the market price rise not necessarily very far – and the threshold is shifted, the exploitation becomes economic. What is more, once the resources are unlocked, the force of competitive production starts to drive the economic break-even point downwards again: mass production, technical progress and sheer improvement in efficiency bring forward the new supplies in larger quantity and at lower price than had in theory been anticipated. That is how it always happens. Unless the price is first allowed to rise freely, the additional resources remain out of reach. It is the rise in price of the existing supplies which calls the new ones into production and, through the medium of profits, provides the new capital for their development.

Something else happens as well. There is only one way to defeat the speculator. That way is not controls or rationing, nor laws and penalties. Controls and rationing, in other words prices artificially held down, are the very culture in which speculation flourishes – or rather I should say, since speculation (which only means the intelligent attempt to anticipate the future) is inherently a good thing and not a bad thing, 'in which speculation flourishes to the public harm instead of the public benefit'. As soon as those who have been holding off the market or limiting supplies with a view to obtaining a higher price for them in the future, perceive that prices are rising towards the new break-even point, they make haste to unload: the speculative reward for waiting has vanished, and those who are holding on to resources face an evenly balanced risk that the next price movement may be down and not up. It is not gunboats or diplomacy that brings reluctant sheikhs to heel, but economics.

I have no desire to spoil a nice lunch by bringing in that most odious subject of inflation; but I am afraid there is no escape. Otherwise some silly fool (not here of course, but elsewhere) will interpose the objection: 'But if the Government let oil prices rise, that will make inflation worse!' One really does wonder where some people get their education. The fact that some articles, including so-called essential ones, get scarcer can no more cause inflation than the fact that some articles get more plentiful can cause deflation. The scarcity and the plenty belong to the real world, not to the money world; and the penalties of not allowing scarcity and plenty to be spelt out by price are just the same when inflation is going on at the rate of 10 per cent a year as when there is no inflation at all.

A rise in the price of petroleum leaves less purchasing power to spread over everything else. If petroleum becomes relatively scarcer, then everything else becomes relatively more plentiful; and if petroleum becomes relatively dearer, everything else becomes relatively cheaper. If the price of petroleum goes up, the price of everything else must correspondingly fall – unless of course total purchasing power is also being increased at the same time so as to enable, and indeed compel, all prices to rise simultaneously. That is why the Government are taking measures to control the supply of money, which would be perfectly futile if inflation were due to world scarcities, of petroleum or anything else. So let us not be deterred from using price as Slave of the lamp to overcome scarcities, by confusing it with the Evil Genius of inflation.

Enoch Powell as a Classicist

Margaret Mountford

As someone who was born in Northern Ireland in the 1950s, I was aware of Enoch Powell's career in politics, particularly his so-called 'Rivers of Blood' speech in Birmingham in 1968 and his arrival as an Ulster Unionist candidate for South Down in 1974, a seat which he held for thirteen years, and I knew that he was reputed to have been a brilliant classicist before he turned to politics. When I went back to university in 1999 to study classics, it was Powell's edition of the text of Thucydides that I used and his lexicon to Herodotus that I consulted. When I became interested in papyrology (the study of documents written in Greek on papyrus, most of which were found in Egypt) I was surprised to discover that he had also edited a collection of papyri. So I was delighted when the opportunity arose for me to write this chapter.

Powell's prowess as a classicist is the stuff of which legends are made: first taught Greek by his mother (herself self-taught), translating Herodotus while still a schoolboy, winning a scholarship to Trinity College, Cambridge and every available prize while an undergraduate there, a Fellow of Trinity at twenty-two and Professor of Greek at the University of Sydney at twenty-five. Classics influenced his name – he chose to be known as J. Enoch rather than John E. Powell in order to avoid confusion with a classicist called John U. Powell – and his reading of the Greek New Testament, in particular St. Paul's epistle to the Galatians, was a major cause of his becoming an atheist in his teens.[†] Yet he gave up classics as a profession on the outbreak of the Second World War,

---

† Simon Heffer, *Like the Roman: The Life of Enoch Powell* (London: Weidenfeld and Nicolson, 1998), pp. 7, 10.

rejecting the professorship at Durham University which he had been offered, and returned to the field only sporadically thereafter.

Powell was an outstandingly gifted linguist. To complete a Greek prose paper (translation from English into Greek) acceptably within the time limit would be an achievement for most students; Powell needed only half of the three hours set for one of his scholarship examinations for Trinity to translate the piece twice, in the styles of Herodotus and Thucydides. Another paper, translation of an extract from Bede, was also completed twice, once in the Greek of Plato and once in Herodotean Ionic Greek. By the time he left school he was also fluent in French and German and competent in Italian and while a Fellow of Trinity he taught himself medieval Welsh.[†]

Powell's first major publication in the classics field was an edition of the Rendel Harris papyri of Woodbrooke College, Birmingham, published in 1936 and now known as P. Harris I. James Rendel Harris, a classical and biblical scholar and palaeographer, had purchased these papyri from dealers during a visit to Egypt in 1922–3 and, as it was then illegal to take such documents out of the country, smuggled them out in hat boxes belonging to his female travelling companions.[‡] Most date from the third and fourth centuries AD and come from Oxyrhynchus, the town a hundred miles south of Cairo made famous by the excavation of thousands of papyrus fragments by two Oxford scholars, Grenfell and Hunt, in the late nineteenth and early twentieth centuries. Powell had discovered the existence of the papyri in his long vacation in 1932, when he was researching Thucydides in the library of the Selly Oak Colleges in Birmingham, and began working on them while still an undergraduate. He deciphered, translated and commented in full on 128 papyri, and summarised another thirty-six. Most were fragments of literary works, including Homer, Euripides, Plato and Demosthenes, but there were also a number of documentary papyri including documents concerning property, loans of money, runaway slaves, guardianship of minors, compulsory labour on the Nile dykes, private letters and magic spells. While some experts complained that

---

[†] Heffer, *Like the Roman*, p. 29.
[‡] Interview with Martyn Kelly, *Times Higher Education Supplement*, 1 September 1995.

the commentaries were too short, and others that the identification of letters unclear in the original text was insufficient (papyrologists mark these with a dot below the line), the comments of H. I. Bell, an eminent papyrologist and Keeper of Manuscripts at the British Museum, in his review in 1938 are still true today.

> Decipherment and editing of Greek papyri, particularly of a miscellaneous collection containing many fragmentary and defaced texts, is a task which usually requires many months, if not years, of training, even if the editor be a good classical scholar. To tackle successfully such an undertaking as an 'autodidact', and in the midst of other exacting work is an achievement given to few men, and one can but wonder at the tour de force which Mr Powell has accomplished in this volume.[†]

Powell was then only twenty-four.

Emphasis on the precise written word is the distinguishing characteristic of most of the rest of Powell's scholarship. Greece itself did not interest him greatly, although he admitted to feeling some emotion when flying over, en route to Australia, its 'unfamiliar places to which names so familiar belong'.[‡] That emphasis is made clear by his inaugural lecture, 'Greek in the University', given in Sydney on 7 May 1938 (he had been offered the chair the previous year) and subsequently published. Rather than speaking on a topic arising from his research, primarily then on Herodotus and Thucydides, he chose to defend the teaching of Greek; in the words of E. R. Dodds, 'Here once again is the familiar but always interesting spectacle of a professor of Greek endeavouring to justify his own existence.'[§] Powell acknowledged that people wanted to learn about classical Greece because 'culture, as we understand it, is connected by a direct line of descent with Greek civilisation' and that Greek studies would give 'an insight into the history of culture

---

[†] H. I. Bell, *Journal of Egyptian Archaeology*, vol. 24 (1938), pp. 141–3. Bruno Snell agreed, in *Gnomon*, vol. 13 (1937), pp. 577–86: '*Als erste Arbeit auf diesem Gebiet ist diese Ausgabe trotz mancherlei Mängeln staunenswert.*' [As a first piece of work in this field this offering is despite some deficiencies astonishing.]

[‡] Heffer, *Like the Roman*, p. 36.

[§] E. R. Dodds, review of Greek in the University, *Classical Review*, vol. 53 (1939), p. 37.

as a whole' and therefore an antidote to barbarism, but his reasons why it should be taught were largely based on the benefits of textual criticism (striving to work out what the original words and meaning of a text would have been, when confronted with alternative manuscript traditions and damaged or unclear documents), which he considered demanded 'the constant exercise of taste'. Students should 'cultivate not only an independent and critical judgement, but a historical sense' and should acquire

> in general a disposition to treat statements on their own merits and not on those of the authorities from whom they emanate, an eye sharpened to detect special pleading, false argumentation and hocuspocus, and a healthy freedom from the prevalent though often entirely subconscious superstition that the printed word and the established opinion have some mysterious and inherent claim to be believed.

One would hope that the study of any subject at a higher level would lead to such a healthy degree of scepticism. However, Powell also claimed that the 'qualities of taste and discrimination are trained and strengthened by the exercise of Greek composition', which should also lead to the writing of better English. Latin authors he dismissed as inferior to their Greek prototypes, claiming that the Romans did not possess 'the instinctive good taste and self-restraint which distinguished the classical Greeks'. Even then this was regarded as a conservative approach,[†] and I would not categorise an audience revelling in the bawdy comedies of Aristophanes against the backdrop of a brightly painted Parthenon as showing good taste and self-restraint, but the main thrust of Powell's argument, influenced by A. E. Housman (whose lectures Powell had attended at Cambridge and who was also a Fellow of Trinity) but which to judge from his early writings had always been his main interest, was the value of textual criticism.[‡] The degree to which this was self-taught is shown by his apparent surprise, when he met

---

[†] Dodds, op. cit.

[‡] His first published article, written in German in the *Philologische Wochenschrift* in August 1931, when he was still an undergraduate, was a textual comment on Herodotus VII 139.5.

Paul Maas, a renowned classical scholar, in Florence in 1935, to learn that 'someone else had made discoveries and established principles of which I had thought myself the exclusive owner.'†

Four of Powell's major publications on Greek texts relate to Herodotus, the 'father of history'. In 1937 he completed *A Lexicon to Herodotus*, which was published by Cambridge University Press in 1938 and which lists every reference to every word in the text, including the various forms of the definite article (23,341 instances), except καί, for which he identified 4,267 instances, the remaining 3,284 having all the simple connecting meaning 'and'. Powell had purchased for 600 marks a collection of word slips made in 1912–14 by two German scholars, Kalpers and Nawak, and used these as the basis for the work. He was praised at the time for the 'amazing industry, much thought and care and fine scholarship' which had gone into the making of an 'exemplary' lexicon,‡ which was greeted as 'a quite invaluable addition to our equipment for the study of Herodotus'.§ The lexicon is much more than an index: translations are given, references classified by meaning and construction and compound verbs are listed at the end of the entry for the main verb. Robin Lane Fox's description of it as 'an entirely mechanical production with no intellectual power' is in my view unfair, although he conceded that it is 'nonetheless valuable' and showed the strength of Powell's 'sharp, clear and nit-picking mind' as a classicist.¶ Described as a 'prodigious feat', an 'astonishingly focused and accurate achievement' and 'an indispensable resource for those who work on this author',** it is astounding when one considers that Powell, then only twenty-six, had already published a volume of

---

† M. L. West, 'Herodotus at Cambridge: With Samuel Butler and Enoch Powell', *Greece and Rome*, vol. 56, 2nd series (2009), p. 244, n. 3, citing a 1984 letter from Powell to Eckhart Mensching.

‡ W. L. Lorimer, review of *A Lexicon to Herodotus*, *Classical Review*, vol. 52 (1938), pp. 178–9.

§ J. L. Myres, review of *A Lexicon to Herodotus*, *Journal of Hellenic Studies*, vol. 58 (1938), p. 284.

¶ Heffer, *Like the Roman*, p. 28, quoting a private interview.

** Simon Hornblower, personal communication; Alan Griffiths, personal communication; West, 'Herodotus at Cambridge'.

papyri and was also working on a critical text of Thucydides and a translation of Herodotus.[†]

The lexicon was followed, in 1939, by *The History of Herodotus*, not as wide-ranging a work as its title might suggest but 'limited to the problem of composition', namely in what order, and where, Herodotus composed his work. Despite his comments about German scholarship (see below), Powell was influenced by Nietzsche, and in the preface claimed to have constantly borne in mind his exhortation '*Wir wollen die Feinheit und Strengheit der Mathematik in alle Wissenschaften hineintreiben, soweit dies nur irgend möglich ist*': to apply the fine attention to detail and stringent approach of the field of mathematics to all fields of knowledge. Powell's hypothesis was that Herodotus's work was written in three main periods and that the book as we now have it resulted from his decision to tack a history of the wars between Greece and Persia onto an earlier, separately published text on Persian history, to which he had added in the intervening period stories about Scythia, and the consequent, although not complete, remoulding of the original work. The theory was based almost exclusively on an analysis of cross-references in the text. Intellectual arrogance, possibly but I think unlikely that of youth, shows through in the preface: 'As I care more about the soundness than the novelty of my reasoning and conclusions, acknowledgment to predecessors is rare. I have, besides, profited much more often from their mistakes than their successes.' He praised Kirchhoff as his only predecessor in the compositional analysis of Herodotus whose work had stood the test of time, and mentioned Jacoby, who is still acknowledged to be one of the greatest scholars of Greek, only once or twice, although 'any discussion of Herodotus' life must owe a very substantial debt to Jacoby's magisterial treatment'.[‡] Prepared to meet his critics head on, Powell's preface ended:

[†] Lorimer expressed the hope that when he had finished these, Powell would go on to compile a similar lexicon to Thucydides.

[‡] S. R. West at p. 27, n. 82, in Herodotus, *Histories Book VIII*, ed. A. M. Bowie (Cambridge: Cambridge University Press, 2007).

I make myself no illusions about the unpopularity to which a work of dissection is doomed – in England especially. That most longer works of literature must have come into being piecemeal over a period of many years, and that some traces of this process must remain in the finished productions, everybody will admit. But the moment anyone attempts to trace out such a process in one particular case, he finds himself face to face with the whole forces of prejudice and thoughtlessness.

One reviewer described Powell's work as the 'first really systematic attempt to apply the study of cross-references in Herodotus to the problem of the composition of his history', his reasoning as 'subtle and compact' and his conclusions as 'stated with admirable clarity', and asserted that the book 'will certainly form the basis of all future study of the subject'. His criticisms (which he maintained were 'not intended to herald the attack of those "forces of prejudice and thoughtlessness" which P. so confidently predicts') included the failure to take account of the possibility that parts could have been written for independent oral publication as well as for inclusion in the whole work, and of too frequently explaining apparent differences in the text by accusing Herodotus of imperfect recollection of the narrative.[†] Other reviewers were less kind. While Powell brought to his subject 'the requisite learning, no mean analytical skill and a profound knowledge of his basic text', he was criticised for the importance placed on cross-references, the assumption that all were original to their contexts and the deliberate ignoring of predecessors such as Jacoby, who in his turn called Powell a 'revenant' from the age of Kirchoff.[‡] Another praised his 'intricate and ingenious reasoning' but concluded, as is generally accepted, that his main hypothesis remained unproven.[§]

Powell's next Herodotean publication, a commentary on Book VIII, also appeared in 1939. It contains little historical information and, with few translations and many illustrative or parallel passages

---

[†] A. W. Harrison, 'The Composition of Herodotus' History', *Classical Review*, vol. 53 (1939), pp. 123–5.

[‡] Alfred Gudeman, review of *The History of Herodotus*, *Classical Weekly*, vol. 33 (1939), pp. 32–33.

[§] M. Cary, review of *The History of Herodotus*, *Journal of Hellenic Studies*, vol. 59 (1939), p. 173.

quoted in Greek and also untranslated, it is, perhaps unsurprisingly in view of the uncompromising approach of its author, not an easy read for a student.[†] A more recent commentary on Book VIII, seemingly aimed at the same audience, gives much more historical background and explanation, and 151 pages of commentary to Powell's 85, but follows Powell on a number of textual amendments, including quoting with agreement his view that a certain insertion by one of his predecessors was 'delirious Greek'.[‡] As was noted in one review, Powell was primarily concerned with problems of style and language: the book contained 'many sound and brilliant comments' because of his wide knowledge of Herodotus's vocabulary. 'It is for its philological accuracy that his commentary is especially valuable' and the 'short survey of the dialect (pp. xvi ff.) is a brilliant and stimulating piece of work'.[§]

In 1938, while he was in Sydney, Powell had returned to revise the translation of Herodotus which he had started as a schoolboy and continued while an undergraduate, working on it at Trinity for the first hour of every day (his day started at 5.30).[¶] That thorough revision, 'almost complete rewriting', was interrupted by the war, and Powell recommenced work on it in 1946, by which time he had left classics for politics. He acknowledges in the preface the role of his mother, 'my first Greek teacher as well as my first teacher'. The translation was published in two volumes in 1949. Powell wrote it in the English of the King James Bible, believing that 'a certain quaintness and archaism thereby imparted make an impression not dissimilar from that which the Ionic original must have made upon Attic readers in the twenties of the fifth century BC'. How much an archaising translation would give its readers the 'feel' of the original is a moot point. Herodotus was writing in the Greek which he and other Ionian Greeks then spoke, and the fact that the language or dialect might have appeared slightly strange to the ears of a fifth-century Athenian audience

---

[†] See Amy L. Barbour's comments in *Classical Weekly*, vol. 34 (1941), p. 219. It was, however, less common to include translations seventy years ago than today, when it is widely recognised that many if not most readers will not be experts in the ancient languages.

[‡] Bowie's commentary.

[§] P. Treves, 'Herodotus Book VIII', *Classical Review*, vol. 54 (1940), pp. 19–20.

[¶] Heffer, *Like the Roman*, pp. 14, 117.

does not mean that it needs to be made to sound strange to ours, although another more recent translation, Grene's in 1987, attempts something not dissimilar, claiming that the English needed to sound 'a little odd' and to be given a traditional, literary flavour like Homer.[†] (Powell himself gently chided Grene, in a newspaper review, for not mentioning his own earlier effort in the same vein.) The reviews of Powell's translation were mixed. Powell had claimed that the 'first duty of a translator is to be intelligible' and it was acknowledged that he had succeeded in that, but his readiness to adopt emendations and deletions (frequently his own) of the acknowledged standard Greek text (there are thirty-five pages of textual amendments) and his tendency to label passages as interpolations or late additions to the text by Herodotus himself were criticised by some, and he was accused of being too willing to distort the sense of the original in his desire to make the translation readily understandable.[‡] But any serious student of Herodotus will find it useful to compare translations, and Powell's will always be interesting.

In 1942 Oxford University Press published a new two-volume edition of the Greek text of Thucydides, comprising Stuart Jones's 1898 version of the text with the notes on it (the *apparatus criticus*) corrected and augmented by Powell. Two main groups of manuscripts of Thucydides, which themselves derive from one single long-lost manuscript, have come down to us from the tenth and eleventh centuries and Powell had undertaken research on some of the oldest manuscripts during a number of trips to Italy between 1933 and 1936. He also took account of the much earlier papyri containing fragments of the text which had then been published and included a very useful 36-page index of proper names. Powell had deliberately not emended the Stuart Jones text and in the preface (written in 1938 and in Latin, as was then the norm) he had noted his intention, not in the event carried out, to produce a revised version of the text itself. This explains the reference in a

---

† David Grene, 'Introduction', in Herodotus, *The History* (Chicago: University of Chicago Press, 1987). This translation also met with a mixed response.

‡ See August Großkinsky, review of *Herodotus, Gnomon*, vol. 24 (1952), pp. 268–9; J. Tate, 'Herodotus in Jacobean Dress', *Classical Review*, new series, vol. 2 (1952), pp. 23–4; Chauncey E. Finch, review of *Herodotus, Classical Weekly*, vol. 44 (1950), p. 42.

contemporary review to the edition being a 'stop-gap',[†] and why the version is not as full as might have been desirable, and possibly also why Powell did not take account in it of Valla's fifteenth-century Latin translation, which is acknowledged to be a valuable early source. But notwithstanding that, this version of the text was the one used by most English scholars for more than fifty years.

Powell also published a number of articles in classical journals between 1931 and 1939. Most were on textual amendments (to authors as wide-ranging as Sophocles and Demosthenes as well as to Herodotus) but he also wrote on the manuscript tradition of both Herodotus and Thucydides and on the sources of Plutarch's biography of Alexander the Great. His feeling for language was shown by an article on puns in Herodotus, where he wrote of the 'irresistible impression of gentle irony' created by Herodotus's use of the same sound or series of sounds twice in the same context but with different senses or implications.[‡] That sense of humour is reflected in his translation into Greek of an amusing description of rowing at St. John's College, Cambridge, written by Samuel Butler in the mid-nineteenth century in the style of Herodotean ethnography, which Powell sent to a colleague for use in teaching undergraduates.[§]

In his reviews of others Powell showed intellectual arrogance and little restraint. 'P. [Patzer] has a firm grasp of the problem and its literature, and he expounds his views with a logic and clarity which put his book above the average of German dissertations. But his siege-train is inadequate to the fortress he has undertaken to demolish.' Parts of Patzer's argument were 'misconstrued', some remarks were 'nonsense', one interpretation 'monstrous'. 'An average of one misprint to a page is too high.'[¶] In relation to another work on Thucydides's statement about speech-writing, he describes Großkinsky as writing 'at dreadful length' but concludes,

---

[†] W. L. Lorimer, 'An Interim Edition of Thucydides', *Classical Review*, vol. 57 (1943), pp. 14-15. Despite that, the reviewer regarded it as 'indispensable' even if for certain information it was still necessary to go back to the much larger Hude version.

[‡] J. Enoch Powell, 'Puns in Herodotus', *Classical Review*, vol. 51 (1937), pp. 103-5.

[§] M. L. West, 'Herodotus at Cambridge'.

[¶] J. Enoch Powell, 'The Thucydidean Question', *Classical Review*, vol. 51 (1937), pp. 173-4.

mindful I assume of the code by which a reviewer is supposed to find something to praise: 'The book itself ... is well printed and tastefully produced.'[†] While praising a work on *metabole* or *variatio* in Thucydides (the avoidance of repetition at short intervals of the same word or expression) for the accuracy of its collection of examples, a purely mechanical exercise, he writes 'But Dr Ros has a weakness. He does not know the meaning of textual criticism' and (correctly) demolishes Ros's statement that the preservation of so much *metabole* shows how good (in the sense of close to the original) the text must be.[‡] One hapless scholar 'brings to his task [a commentary on Herodotus Book IX] a wide acquaintance with recent foreign literature on the subject, but unfortunately little Greek and no judgement. His edition is therefore valueless to scholars and will be a snare to students.' Powell criticises him for adopting an 'undergraduate fatuity' he (Powell) had published but had since retracted, and even 'the printing and production of the book are disgraceful'.[§] 'Will the Germans ever learn to spell Liddell's name?'[¶]

The Evolution of the Gospel, Powell's translation of and commentary on the gospel of Matthew, appeared in 1994, when he was eighty-two. It was controversial for a number of reasons. Powell's expressed view was that Matthew (and not, as is generally accepted, Mark) was the oldest of the gospels, a 'unique and primary document' which was used by, and arguably was the sole source for, Luke, while Mark used Matthew and Luke. He suggested (not as

---

[†] J. Enoch Powell, 'The Programme of Thucydides', *Classical Review*, vol. 50 (1936), pp. 174–5. The interpretation of Thucydides's claim (I 22 1) to have written what it was necessary or appropriate for his speakers to have said, while keeping as close as possible to the general purport of what was actually said, has exercised scholars for years, and continues to do so. Powell's review caused A. R. W. Harrison to write ('Thucydides 1, 22', *Classical Review*, vol. 51 (1937), pp. 6–7) that Powell was unfair to Großkinsky and had been too hasty in his analysis.

[‡] J. Enoch Powell, 'Variation in Thucydides', *Classical Review*, vol. 53 (1939), p. 13.

[§] J. Enoch Powell, 'The Ninth Book of Herodotus', *Classical Review*, vol. 53 (1939), pp. 124–5.

[¶] J. Enoch Powell, review of Rose Zahn, *Die erste Periklesrede*, *Classical Review*, vol. 48 (1934), p. 238. Liddell is one of the compilers of the leading classical Greek-English dictionary.

a headline but in his analysis of the text) that there was an original 'Urtext', an underlying historical narrative in which Christ was not crucified but was stoned by the Jews for allowing himself to be called 'the son of God', and that the crucifixion at the hands of the Romans was a later substitution produced for a more Judaising wing of the early church. Perhaps it is not surprising that Powell seems to have taken a similar approach to Matthew as he had taken to Herodotus in the *History* over fifty years earlier; in the preface he wrote:

> The scholarship of centuries has been devoted to the document which forms the subject of this book. It was my method in studying it to clear the mind as far as possible of preconceptions or conclusions arrived at earlier by others; and I have deliberately therefore neither ascertained nor recorded previous agreement or disagreement with the results I propose.

Even before its publication the book had aroused media interest; under the headline 'Gospel according to Powell: Christ stoned to death', Dr Tom Wright, then Dean of Lichfield and a member of the Church of England's Doctrine Commission, who had himself obtained a first in Greats at Oxford, was quoted as describing it as 'a work of great erudition, which seems to have lost touch with the distinction between that which is possible and that which is plausible'. He added: 'There is something to be said for starting again from scratch, but the catty answer is that he has chosen to ignore everyone else, so he can't grumble if they return the compliment.'[†] John Baker, quoted in the same article, described him 'as a great classicist but theology is out of his academic field', and the old tendency to overemend and delete the commonly accepted text is also evident. Heffer describes a 'savage' review in the *Daily Telegraph* on 18 September 1994.[‡]

In April 1968 in Birmingham Powell made the speech on immigration that was to change his career, known afterwards as the

---

[†] Andrew Brown, 'Gospel according to Powell: Christ stoned to death', *The Independent*, 16 August 1994.

[‡] Heffer, *Like the Roman*, p. 943.

'Rivers of Blood' speech after his final statement: 'As I look ahead, I am filled with foreboding. Like the Roman, I seem to see "the river Tiber foaming with much blood".' This was an allusion to *Aeneid* VI 87 and the prophecy of the Sibyl of Cumae to Aeneas: 'I see wars, horrible wars, and the Tiber foaming with much blood.' (*'et Thybrim multo spumantem sanguine cerno.'*) It is not clear who Powell meant by 'the Roman'. In Virgil's version of the legend, Aeneas was a Trojan hero who escaped to Italy and through his descend-ants was the founder of Rome. Julius Caesar had claimed Aeneas (and Venus) as ancestors and Augustus, in whose time Virgil was writing, therefore also claimed descent from Aeneas. According to Mary Beard, reconciling the violence with support for Roman imperialism, Virgil was offering a long-term message about ethni-cally mixed states; Rome would become a joint, shared community after all the bloodshed. The prophecy was of the battles Aeneas would face before he would be able to found his brand new multicultural city.[†] On that basis it was a strange line for Powell to quote. While he may have been suggesting that the wave of immigration would lead to fighting and bloodshed, I doubt that he intended to signify that eventually the immigrants would prevail and the resulting state would be better than what went before. More likely he took the view, shared by a number of scholars, that Virgil was challenging Rome's expansionist policy on the grounds that it led not to reason and order but to their dissolution. He may have chosen the line to be sensational, although according to Heffer Powell himself only regretted that he had translated it rather than leaving it in Latin, where it would doubtless have made less of an impact.[‡] Possibly, as Beard suggests, Powell may merely 'have been going for classical legitimation for his own Sibylline prophecy about immigration'.[§] He would not have chosen it lightly or carelessly: his response to one critic was 'The quotation came easily to me, as I am a classical scholar and you are not'.[¶] One wonders whether the impact of the speech would have been as great without the quotation and what

---

[†] Mary Beard, 'A Don's Life', *Times Literary Supplement*, 5 November 2007; she described Powell as 'a first-rate classicist'.

[‡] Heffer, *Like the Roman*, p. 454.

[§] Beard, op. cit.

[¶] Heffer, *Like the Roman*, p. 454.

political office Powell might have attained had he not been a classical scholar.

There is a strong sense of self-confidence in most of Powell's classical work, and a deliberate disregard of the views of his predecessors. His approach to Greek texts was one of extreme precision and rigour, combined with certainty in his own interpretations, which resulted in him suggesting amendments to the 'original' more often than most other scholars, in order to make it mean what he felt it should. He himself acknowledged that his approach had been too narrow. Heffer quotes a letter from Powell to his parents, sent from Sydney in May 1938, when he thought war was imminent, saying that he had grown ashamed of spending so much of his time upon his Greek scholarship, 'a hobby', that 'Greek literature is to me merely words on paper to be juggled with: nothing more.' He had specialised as a textual critic too early, and this had done him 'irremediable harm'.[†] It seems that he had come to regret the obsessive perfectionism which characterised also the approach of Housman, but was unwilling if not unable to change his methodology and broaden his outlook. Despite that, his publications attest an astonishing range of achievements. In only a few years he made a considerable contribution to Greek scholarship, and he left a corpus of written material of which many career-long Greek scholars would be proud.

Note: In writing this chapter I found much useful material in Simon Heffer's biography, *Like the Roman*. A bibliography of Powell's classical writings is contained in R. B. Todd's 'Enoch Powell's Classical Scholarship: A Bibliography', *Quaderni di Storia*, vol. 42 (1995), pp. 89–96. Another article by Todd, 'Enoch Powell as a Classicist: Two Studies', *Quaderni di Storia*, vol. 45 (1997), pp. 81–103, contains an analysis of Powell's introductory lecture at Sydney University and of the classical references in his poetry. Finally, I am indebted to Alan Griffiths and Simon Hornblower for their views on Powell's contribution to Greek scholarship.

---

† Heffer, *Like the Roman*, p. 46.

Enoch Powell and Ulster

Alistair Cooke

A story used to be told in Ulster Unionist circles about one of Enoch Powell's first visits to the province in the 1950s. He was collected at the airport by a staunch Unionist and driven to Portrush in County Antrim, where he was to address a large and enthusiastic meeting. His driver prattled away merrily about a variety of subjects. Eliciting no response, however, he eventually fell silent. As they approached their destination Powell suddenly spoke. 'Tell me,' he said, 'what is the latitude and what is the longitude of this place?' No one could then have foreseen that this distinctly unusual and perplexing Englishman would become one of the greatest of all champions of Northern Ireland's union with Great Britain, inviting comparison with Ulster's most famous hero, Sir Edward Carson himself.

It was Ulster's sudden and unexpected descent into crisis in 1968 which brought the province prominently and permanently into Powell's life. He fell quickly into the habit of making frequent visits to and speeches in Northern Ireland. In June 1972 he reflected on his new-found preoccupation with the province in a speech to Unionists in East Belfast. It had, he said, transformed the life of an English Tory who had 'no ties or connections' with either Ulster or any other part of Ireland:

> I would have been astonished if someone, three years ago, had told me that my thoughts and energies would today be directed to the affairs of this province, beyond almost any other political subject. Yet so it is – so much so that often, at the end of a parliamentary week, it strikes me as somehow incongruous that I do not return, like my Ulster Unionist colleagues, to a constituency in these six counties.

Just over two years later, he *would* find himself returning to an Ulster constituency. Many people in England were greatly taken aback when he decided to re-enter Parliament as MP for South Down in October 1974. In fact it was an entirely unsurprising, though not inevitable, consequence of his absorption in Northern Ireland affairs after 1968, which, he said, led him to feel closer to the Ulster Unionists than to his own party during the course of the Heath government, whose principal Northern Ireland policies he opposed in their company.

The tragic crisis that unfolded in Ulster bore directly and intimately on the fundamental issues of nationhood and identity about which he was then thinking deeply, convinced of their overriding importance in political affairs: everything else was wholly subordinate and secondary. Just before the start of the Ulster crisis he set out the principal results of his prolonged deliberations in a remarkable speech on nationhood at Prestatyn in September 1968 – a speech which no other contemporary Conservative politician could have produced, for it followed in the tradition of the great scholar-statesman Lord Salisbury, of whom Powell was the one remaining powerfully articulate legatee in Tory parliamentary politics. Like Salisbury, he had no easy answers.

> Nationhood is a baffling thing: for it is wholly subjective. They are a nation who think they are: there is no other definition. You cannot discover nations by poring over atlases: for though geography influences nationhood, it does not determine it in any specific way ... Nor will history do your business for you: nations merge with others in the passage of time, while others emerge or re-emerge. Nor again will language or ethnography help: for though, like geography and history, language and race are relevant to nationhood, they are not determinants of it: adjacent nations may speak the same language, yet be fiercely separate, while undoubted nations can comprise those who speak different languages. As for the slippery concept of race, all attempts to match it with nationality are foredoomed to failure.

Nationhood, he continued, was an absolute, indivisible and irreducible:

> There is no such thing as semi-nationhood or semi-nationalism. You cannot try 10 per cent nationhood, and see how you like it ... Nationalism, if it is real, cannot be bought off with less than the

complete article. This is not because the nationalist is less reasonable or more greedy than his fellow men: it is because nationhood is the complete article.

In the United Kingdom, it was through Parliament that British nationhood gained expression, enabling the country to be 'governed and administered as one nation'. 'The essence of a nation is that the parts instinctively view themselves as subordinate to the whole and regard the interest and well-being of the whole as supreme over the interest and well-being of any of the parts.' The establishment of separate, elected law-making institutions in Scotland or Wales would change everything. 'It would be the watershed, the parting of the ways, the sign that a separate nation had been consciously, deliberately and once-for-all admitted to be there.' Only in Ulster was internal self-government compatible with British nationhood, 'for Ulster self-government was the outcome not of nationalism but of the very opposite, of Ulster Unionism ... [which] accepted only with reluctance the unique form of autonomy which emerged [there] ... The motivation of Ulster has remained not nationalist, not separatist, but the opposite.' This view of Ulster's exclusively British nationhood could be maintained only by leaving out of consideration the substantial minority in the province who were motivated by Irish, not British, nationalism.

That is exactly what Powell did in his speech at Prestatyn, delivered a few weeks before the first serious outbreak of violence in Ulster in October 1968. British nationhood in Ulster could not be qualified or diminished by permitting its Irish counterpart (and rival) to occupy a place alongside it. Two diametrically opposed nationalisms could not both be satisfied: one or other of them must prevail. Everywhere nationhood was an absolute.

As Ulster's violence mounted after 1969, Powell took upon himself unhesitatingly the task of defending the province's place in the British nation, of which it was an integral element. It was as if he felt that he had no alternative but to respond repeatedly and forcefully to this severe challenge to British nationhood, on whose preservation the future of his country depended. He became the first senior Westminster politician of Privy Council rank since Andrew Bonar Law in 1911–14 to speak frequently and passionately in the Ulster Unionist cause in and outside Parliament (and he was almost certainly the last such person to do so).

At a time when it became commonplace to insist that Ulster was an immensely complicated subject which few could understand, Powell proclaimed that in essence it was clear to the point of simplicity. The province was the scene of a violent assault on the British nation as a whole which had to be defeated completely. There were other assaults on the nation, no less deadly for being (thus far) largely peaceful in character, from which the struggle in Ulster could not be separated. The British nation must overcome all of them. These were the cardinal points to which he returned repeatedly in speeches in Ulster itself and throughout the rest of the country. He told an audience in Londonderry in January 1971 that 'the issues which have affected the life of Northern Ireland in the last two years are part and parcel of the same great issues which confront the whole of the United Kingdom.' Addressing Conservative women in Beaconsfield two months later, he said:

A part of the United Kingdom has been under attack from an external enemy assisted by detachments operating inside. In Buckinghamshire you have neither seen nor heard: it requires an effort both of understanding and of imagination to realise the fact. Yet it is a fact which concerns Buckinghamshire as it concerns Cornwall or Aberdeenshire or County Down. For when one part of a nation is under attack, the whole is under attack.

In September 1971 he told the Unionists of Omagh that they should harbour no doubts about their British identity: 'The people of this province are part of the British nation, and the soil of the province is British soil, because the great majority of its inhabitants are so minded. As Pericles taught the Athenians, "A nation is not ships nor walls, but people."'

For Powell this was the supreme, all-important fact: he reiterated it continually. But it occupied no place in the lexicon that was used almost universally to depict Ulster's travails. As a result gross error passed as truth – and violence was succoured. He denounced this state of affairs in his Beaconsfield speech of March 1971:

Vocabulary is one of the principal weapons in the enemy's armoury. The campaign in which the British army is engaged, and in which the integrity of this country and the life and liberty of our fellow citizens are at stake, is obligatorily described, reported and discussed in terms designed to deny its real character. The object is to persuade the people of Great Britain that the inhabitants of Ulster are quarrelling among themselves and, unable to refrain from sectarian and internecine violence, are involving in yet another of their everlasting broils the innocent British forces, which are simply attempting to keep the peace between the contending sides and protect them from irreparably damaging themselves. The British public are intended in due course to exclaim: 'If they want to fight, let us leave them to it; Britain never had anything but trouble out of Ireland.' It is the sort of foolish, misguided talk and thought which does the enemy's work for him …

Overshadowing all the other misconceptions sedulously propagated by skilful choice of language is that of 'grievance', 'reform', 'discrimination', 'civil rights'. These terms, which have passed into the orthodox Westminster vocabulary, have turned reality on its head, first by reinterpreting deliberate acts of war as violence provoked by injustice, and then by importing ready made the whole paraphernalia of the 'oppressed minority'. Thus has been built up in the public imagination on this side of St George's Channel the picture of a large and growing (which it is not), oppressed (which it is not), disloyal (which it is not) religious minority in Northern Ireland, whose existence is evidenced by the campaign of violence and thus brings down a deserved retribution on the majority. The propaganda success of the enemy has been brilliant.

If this brilliant and dangerous propaganda was to be effectively combated, Ulster needed to assert its cause and proclaim the truth about its politics and community relations in the assembly of the British nation, the Westminster parliament. In his great speech on nationhood in September 1968, Powell had not suggested that the Stormont regime should be dismantled. But Home Rule had failed to equip Ulster with the means of repelling the furious assault which it faced during its ever-deepening crisis after 1968. It needed to be fully incorporated in the nation as a whole in order to ensure that it had the resources and manpower that could restore its stability and preserve its security in future.

The existence of Stormont also created a dangerously false impression of Northern Ireland's constitutional status, which assisted the advocates of Irish unity. As Powell put it in his Beaconsfield speech:

> The whole vocabulary of three governments, Westminster, Belfast and Dublin, implants the notion that there are somehow three co-ordinate states, and that as two of them are geographically on the same island, Westminster is the 'third man out' … It ought to be the object of Her Majesty's Government to convey, by deed as well as word, the identification of Northern Ireland with the rest of the United Kingdom.

As for reforms to Northern Ireland's institutions, they should never be regarded as providing a basis for the defeat of terrorism:

> I desire no man, if it can be avoided, to be dealt with unfairly or unjustly by the law and public authorities. I hold no brief, on either side of St George's Channel, for injustice. But to imagine that the fixed and settled interest of those whose purpose is to use violence and terror to annex Northern Ireland [to the Irish Republic] could be deflected or appeased by 'reforms' was from the start a belief so patently childish as to raise doubts whether those who professed it could really be in earnest.

Though Powell took strong exception to the way it was done, the summary removal of the Stormont parliament by the Heath government in March 1972 created the opportunity to draw Ulster into the centre of the nation's political life. There, in Powell's view, it should remain for ever represented by its full tally of MPs (up to twenty), which had been reduced to twelve under Home Rule. It was to secure for Ulster such a future that Powell now directed all his efforts on the province's behalf. He explained how it would benefit from a new Unionist constitutional mould in his speech on the legislation which swept Stormont away. He predicted that full participation at Westminster would reorder politics in the province along much the same lines as those elsewhere in the nation:

I have for years advocated the genuine embodiment and parliamentary reunification of the six counties of Northern Ireland with Great Britain, believing that the separate administration and parliament which originally was forced upon the majority in Northern Ireland over fifty years ago, but which over the years they have come to see as a symbol not so much of their independence as of their union with the rest of the United Kingdom ... has nevertheless, in the last three or four years, turned to the opposite effect and become for them a cause of danger and a source of division.

I believe, too, that such true reunification must eventually be the means of healing many of the underlying divisions in the six counties. Mr Callaghan [the future Labour Prime Minister] has often argued that it is essential for Northern Ireland that its people, claiming as they do to belong to the United Kingdom, should participate in the politics of the United Kingdom, and that we are all looking for some way to escape from the exclusive concentration of the politics of the six counties upon the question of union or non-union.

In the greater whole of the parliament of the United Kingdom many of the other political differences which divide citizens in Northern Ireland, as they divide them here, might well come to the surface and gain expression and thus be the means – differences though they are – of nevertheless neutralising the profounder and more irreconcilable antagonisms.

Powell was the first leading British politician to assert that the whole character of Ulster politics would be changed if all the province's affairs were the direct responsibility of the Westminster parliament. He believed that the issues which decided elections in Great Britain would come increasingly to decide them in Ulster too. His conviction would influence a significant body of opinion in the Conservative Party in the years ahead.

'Parliamentary reunification', however, would still leave untouched the greatest source of danger that Ulster faced: the refusal of successive governments since the 1920s, Labour and Conservative alike, to defend its essential interests firmly and unequivocally within the nation of which it was part. British governments had betrayed their duty by treating the citizens of the Irish Republic who resided in the United Kingdom as if they were British, conferring on them the full benefits of that status.† This involved denying what the Republic itself had declared. Nothing could be clearer, Powell said in his 1971 Londonderry speech:

> The inhabitants of the remainder of this island have long ago resolved the question of their national identity to, so far as one can judge, their entire satisfaction: they are not, repeat not, part of the nation which inhabits the rest of the British Isles, nor is the territory which they inhabit part of its national territory. They are Irish, and the rest of the world and its peoples are non-Irish, or, in another word, foreign.

Worse still, the self-declared foreigners who enjoyed wholly unwarranted privileges in Britain belonged to a country which wanted to annex Northern Ireland. 'It is the consistent and settled view and policy of the Irish Republic that this province ought not to be part of the national territory of the United Kingdom but ought to be part of the national territory of the republic.'

Nevertheless, in flagrant breach of their responsibilities to Ulster and the British nation, from 1971 onwards the Heath government and its successors involved the Republic's government in discussions about the future of the province it sought to acquire. That could only have one result, Powell said in his 1971 Omagh speech:

> When the British government is seen taking counsel about peace and security in a part of the United Kingdom with the Prime Minister of the very country which is dedicated to the annexation of that part and cannot fail to approve the objects and consequences of the disorder, what must people think? I will tell you. They think: 'Oho, so the British are wobbling and preparing to get out: else why would they be parleying with the residual beneficiary of their embarrassment?'

It was a line of argument that brought Powell to a remarkable conclusion: that the United Kingdom's government and parliament

---

† Powell was not always opposed to this special treatment. In an interview which he gave in October 1968, he said: 'I just do not think it would be worth the trouble involved to treat the Irish as aliens though that is what they really are. It's not logical, I agree, but then it's Irish.' I am indebted for this reference to David Clarke Shiels of Peterhouse, Cambridge.

bore an even greater share of the responsibility for Ulster's suffering than the terrorists who actually committed it.

> Violence begins, grows and gathers momentum because it is fed by hope of success. It is not, as some foolishly allege, purposeless: alas, it is very purposeful ... Up to the present moment its hope has grown. That hope has been fostered and raised by the actions of the British government, which, in the deeds that speak louder than words, affords encouragement to the enemies of Ulster. The truest, deepest responsibility for the deeds of violence in Ulster does not lie in the back streets of Belfast or Dublin; it does not lie in Northern Ireland, nor in the Republic. It lies at Westminster, it lies with Her Majesty's Government in the United Kingdom and with the Parliament of the United Kingdom. Only when their policies and actions, as well as their professions, bring conviction to friend and foe alike that the realities of this province are understood and that the unity of the realm will be maintained, will the guilt of innocent blood depart from Westminster.

A few years later Powell took his charge against the British government to a final, sensational stage. In its betrayal of British nationhood in Ulster it had not merely been guilty of encouraging violence by giving it hope of success; it had actively conspired to assist progress towards the terrorists' goal, the creation of a united Ireland. Murder was committed along the way in the course of that conspiracy. I found myself numbered among those who were supposed to have knowledge of this conspiracy to destroy Ulster's place in the British nation.

The political crisis which first drew Enoch Powell into Ulster's affairs in 1968 intensified rapidly. The Ulster Unionist Party, which had dominated the province's politics since the 1880s, plunged into turmoil as violence mounted. Personal animosities and disputes exacerbated divisions over policy on security and institutional reform as Northern Ireland's last three Prime Ministers – Terence O'Neill, James Chichester-Clark and Brian Faulkner – strove valiantly, but vainly, to restore peace and stability. The removal of Stormont in March 1972 reunited the Ulster Unionists briefly in protest against the Conservative government's misdeed, as they saw it. Large numbers of them remained implacable in their hostility to Edward Heath and his diligent, newly created Northern Ireland Secretary, Willie Whitelaw, who brimmed with goodwill towards everyone (including, for a few days in June 1972, the IRA).

Whitelaw managed to persuade many moderate Unionists to co-operate with him in his pursuit of a new constitutional order which would create a permanent and guaranteed role in the province's government for the non-Unionist minority (firmly excluding those linked to violence) and would establish a cross-border institution designed to enable Northern Ireland and the Irish Republic to pursue their common interests in close partnership. This was inevitably seen – and not just by diehard Unionists – as a staging post on the road to a united Ireland, which, as Powell continually pointed out, was the declared objective of the Irish Republic, as well as of the IRA. Because of this issue the entire strategy of the British government failed in 1974 – and deserved to fail.

In the summer of 1973 Faulkner, ex-premier but still the Unionist leader, took the fateful decision to share power with elected representatives of the minority, as long as their primary aim was to serve Northern Ireland, not to work for a united Ireland. Miscalculating badly, he also agreed to accept the creation of a Council of Ireland, which would bring together ministers from North and South with a tier composed of members of their two legislatures. The scene was set for a remarkable constitutional experiment: Northern Ireland's first power-sharing executive. It held office for a few short months at the beginning of 1974 before being overthrown by a Province-wide strike organised by 'loyalist' militants with widespread support in the Unionist community as a whole. Faulkner acted in reluctant deference to the fundamental principle that decisions taken by the country's sovereign body, the Crown in Parliament, must ultimately be obeyed. It was a principle which Powell enunciated frequently,[†] but not on this occasion.

---

† For example, in a speech at Kilkeel, County Down, on 6 July 1975, he said: 'To be loyal is, for the Unionist, to accept the will of Parliament as expressed in the law of the land, which is made by the Crown in Parliament ... What, however, no person who calls himself a Unionist can do, without self-contradiction, is to place limits or conditions upon his obedience to the Crown in Parliament.

Powell denounced these far-reaching initiatives with predictable ferocity. They were designed, he said in June 1973, 'to render the constitution acceptable not to those who accept the Union, but to those who fundamentally reject the Union'. Power-sharing was intolerable: it rested on a 'principle totally adverse to any conception of parliamentary or representative government with which we are familiar'. Those who were ill disposed to all or part of Ulster's new constitutional dispensation sought to enlist him prominently in their cause. The group of seven Westminster Ulster Unionist MPs with whom he had acted in close concert for several years wanted him at their helm. In October 1973 it emerged that 'Powell had received, and refused, an offer to become leader of the Ulster Unionists at Westminster.'[†] It was a wise decision since most of the little band ended up standing as pro-Faulkner candidates at the February 1974 general election – and losing ignominiously.

It was at this juncture that Powell first indicated that he had serious leadership ambitions. Faulkner parted company with his deeply divided party at the start of 1974. Powell was available to fill the vacant leadership, having just given up both the Conservative Party and his Wolverhampton seat in sensational circumstances. His closest Ulster Unionist associate, Jim Molyneaux, telephoned him on 10 February 1974. Powell made a note of their conversation. Molyneaux was authorised 'confidentially to state on my behalf in response to enquiries from authoritative sources that only if the "loyal" [i.e. anti-Faulkner] Ulster Unionists invited me to be their leader and to represent them at Westminster, would I be prepared to consider any approach from Northern Ireland', though that should not be taken to imply that 'I would necessarily accept'. He added that he would 'need to be in personal control of the grounds and policy'[‡] on which he sought election. That would be assured if he became party leader. Nothing, however, came of these manoeuvres.

He cannot say: "If Parliament makes laws I do not like, I will not obey them."' This roused the furious anger of other Unionist leaders who insisted that their loyalty was to the Crown alone.

† Simon Heffer, *Like the Roman: The Life of Enoch Powell* (London: Weidenfeld & Nicolson, 1998), p. 680.

‡ Ibid., p. 702.

Between then and his adoption for South Down later in 1974, he was sedulously courted by the Unionists. Molyneaux offered to hand over his seat, the safest in the kingdom, and Harry West, the new leader of the Ulster Unionist Party, from which Faulkner's supporters had departed, coupled an offer of his very unsafe seat with an announcement that 'he would willingly give up the leadership of the Unionists to Powell if he wanted it.'[†] Again, talk was not followed by action.

There was, however, action immediately after Powell's election for South Down in October 1974. West lost his very unsafe seat, and a new leader had to be found for the Unionist contingent at Westminster while West remained in overall charge not just of his own party, but of the United Ulster Unionist Coalition, formed the previous year to secure rejection of power-sharing and the Council of Ireland – a coalition which included the Democratic Unionist leader, Ian Paisley. Powell sought the Westminster post, and lost. Molyneaux later described what happened:

> I wanted Enoch for leader … he had much more experience than any of us, he knew much more about the way government – not just the House of Commons – worked. I thought he would be the right man for our cause. But, when we all got together to talk about it, they decided on me.[‡]

It was an unexpected defeat. 'Powell's closest friends believe he was disappointed not to have become leader.'[§] If he had been chosen, he would almost certainly have gone on to become overall party leader when West's political career ended in failure five years later – as Molyneaux, the Westminster incumbent, then did – as long as adequate trust had been reposed in him by the party as a whole. But he always found that trust difficult to acquire because of the party's strong enduring support for the re-establishment of a devolved parliament, shorn of power-sharing, to which Powell was utterly opposed.

[†] Heffer, *Like the Roman*, p. 718.

[‡] Patrick Cosgrave, *The Lives of Enoch Powell* (London: Bodley Head, 1989), p. 368.

[§] Heffer, *Like the Roman*, p. 738.

If Powell's failure to become the leader of the Unionists at Westminster in 1974 deprived him of a post he wanted to hold, it made absolutely no difference to the policies that were adopted by the group of ten Unionist MPs during the tumultuous years of Labour government that lay ahead. All of the key decisions taken by the Unionists at Westminster bore a firm Powellite stamp. At the time it was widely held that Powell was leader in all but name, imposing his ideas on Molyneaux, who tamely did the bidding of a master of the political craft. There was hardly a journalist or civil servant in the land who did not subscribe to this view. In fact the two men worked together as full political partners; their relationship was based on deep mutual understanding and respect.

For his part Molyneaux was determined that the Unionists should draw fully on Powell's immense political talents. In return 'Powell made it his business to support Molyneaux with utter loyalty, even to the extent of addressing him as "Sir" when a third party was present.'[†] Nevertheless, it was Powell who ensured that their joint endeavours enjoyed great parliamentary success. Without him and his mastery of the political craft the Unionists would not have secured the progress which made this period so significant in their history. This was Powell's finest hour in Ulster politics.

It was made possible by unique parliamentary circumstances. The October 1974 general election gave the Labour Party a slim overall majority which by-election losses and defecting MPs removed within two years. Thereafter, the balance of power lay unprecedentedly not with one minority party, but with three of them: the Liberals, the Scottish Nationalists and the Ulster Unionists – and with a scattering of other MPs unattached to them complicating matters even further. The manner in which they used (or did not use) their votes in parliamentary divisions made the Labour government, of which Jim Callaghan became leader in 1976, one of the most precarious in modern British history.

Under Powell and Molyneaux the Ulster Unionists became Callaghan's most reliable source of support among the minor parties. Expressing great satisfaction in March 1977 that 'he had done a deal with the Ulster Unionists,' Callaghan said he 'could

---

† Ibid.

talk to the Ulster Unionists: they were serious men. He found it difficult to talk to the Liberals. [David] Steel was very adolescent.' He took to the Unionists at once 'because they were his kind of straight, tough old-fashioned conservative people'.[†] In a remarkable political realignment a Party which for nearly a century had acted at Westminster as an appendage to the Tories moved into an alliance with Labour. It was a bold assertion of political independence for which Powell was almost entirely responsible. He alone saw the inestimable value of working with the Party that had for so long supported Irish unity. It too would change its ways. At a secret meeting with Harold Wilson in November 1974 shortly after his election for South Down, Powell confided his view that the 'pacification' of Ulster under a Labour government would bring 'a more secure result' than a settlement reached under the Tories.[‡] Having tasted political freedom, the Ulster Unionists at Westminster were never subsequently tempted to return to their old relationship with the Tories, who had taken them for granted for so long. Powell taught them to decide where their interests lay – and to act accordingly.

Ulster Unionist support for Callaghan was provided through a judicious combination of votes for the government on crucial economic issues, like taxation and public spending, and abstentions on key confidence motions, through which the Conservative Party, under its new leader, Margaret Thatcher, sought to bring down the government and force a general election. Through such adroit tactics, Powell at last overcame Westminster's reluctance to give serious attention to the one policy which in his view (as he had made plain for years) could restore peace and stability: the full integration of the province into the constitutional and political arrangements by which the rest of the nation was governed.

He forced integration on to the political agenda. This was the great prize that he secured from the Unionist alliance with Callaghan. The terms of the alliance were settled at a meeting at 10 Downing Street on 21 March 1977. Callaghan's senior policy adviser, Bernard Donoughue, recorded the event in his diary:

[†]　Bernard Donoughue, *Downing Street Diary: With James Callaghan in No. 10* (London: Jonathan Cape, 2008), p. 168.

[‡]　Heffer, *Like the Roman*, p. 743.

At 2.30 the PM saw the Ulster Unionists who were represented by Molyneaux and Enoch Powell (looking as always like a prosperous barrister) and it went very well. They agreed to support the government *until the end of this Parliament* provided we put Ulster representation at Westminster to a Speaker's Conference and 'consider' giving a new tier of local government to Ulster. On this basis they could offer six abstentions on Wednesday [when a crucial confidence motion was to be debated] and afterwards.[†]

Four years earlier in September 1973 Powell had demanded vainly from the Heath government 'full representation, equal representation, exclusive and sovereign representation – one nation, one parliament'. Now under Callaghan's Labour government he was able to attain his objective. The Speaker's Conference, established by the government, readily accepted Powell's case for full representation. Northern Ireland gained five additional seats, increasing the total number of its MPs from twelve to seventeen, under legislation passed in early 1979. This was Powell's greatest achievement for Ulster.

He was no less determined to secure acceptance of his second principal demand: the creation of a system of local government on the model that existed elsewhere in the country. Callaghan agreed in March 1977 to consider the issue. Having considered it, he showed no willingness to take action. Molyneaux and Powell did what an effective and powerful minority party in highly advantageous parliamentary circumstances should do: they took their demands to the government's main opponent, the Conservative Party. Initially the Tories were far from pleased to hear from them. Thatcher was furious that the Ulster Unionists, once the Tories' most loyal ally, had agreed a pact with Callaghan that blocked her path to power. The imperative need to try and end that pact, however, swiftly overcame her distaste for negotiations with the Unionists, though not her fury at their support for Callaghan.

Powell played no direct part in the discussions that followed. He did not want to exchange views with Thatcher, of whom he had a low opinion before 1979, and she expressed no wish to see him. The secret negotiations were handled with consummate skill by

---

† Donoughue, *Downing Street Diary*, p. 167.

Molyneaux, who loved conspiratorial activity. He was charmed by Thatcher both then and during her premiership, relishing even the shortest of conversations with her: 'I had a great wee chat with Margaret as we walked back from the Cenotaph,' he would say. Molyneaux also got on well with Airey Neave, who had asked for, and been given, responsibility for Northern Ireland in the shadow Cabinet which Thatcher formed after Neave had masterminded her election as Conservative leader in 1975. Neave, a war hero who always cultivated close contacts in the intelligence services, shared Molyneaux's taste for the cloak and dagger.

Their discussions prospered. In the spring of 1978 Neave publicly repudiated the principle of power-sharing as it had operated in 1973–4, and committed the Conservative Party to put all the principal local government services, such as education, health and social services, under the control of one or more elected councils in the province. Thatcher endorsed the new policy on a visit to Northern Ireland in June 1978. Powell seemed to have achieved his second main objective. Devolution would not return. The scene was set for the severance of the Unionists' ties with Callaghan as soon as the legislation to provide for Ulster's extra parliamentary seats had passed (though when the moment came in March 1979, Powell argued strongly that the Unionists should dally a little longer with Callaghan in the (unlikely) hope of getting a gas pipeline linking the province to Britain, but Molyneaux overruled him).

The Tory local government plans, which I helped to devise as Neave's political adviser, were highly controversial. Neave was determined that they should be effectively implemented. He chose as his chief lieutenant Ian Gow, who subsequently made his name as Thatcher's brilliant PPS. Neave constantly told me of his regard for the then rising Tory backbencher, praising his eloquence, vigour and total commitment to the cause of carrying forward Northern Ireland's integration with the rest of the country. Neave's protégé, who was also an ardent Powellite, was earmarked for appointment as minister of state at the Northern Ireland Office under Neave as Secretary of State in a new Conservative government. They would be joined by John Biggs-Davison, a long-standing expert on Ulster who was equally committed to the new policy, and others of like mind. On them now rested Powell's hopes of advancing his cause.

The Tory plans to strengthen the Union had no friends among the Whitehall officials who administered Northern Ireland's affairs. There were sceptics within the Conservative Party itself. Republicans in Ulster had alerted their supporters in Dublin and Washington, who deluged Neave with endless complaints about his policy. He and his group of close colleagues knew they would need resolution, fortitude and a lot of luck if the Conservative Party won power.

It won power in 1979, without Neave. His murder on the eve of the general election campaign changed the course of Conservative Northern Ireland policy. The Heathite principles that Powell detested – power-sharing and all-Ireland institutions – resumed their sway, and the Ulster Unionists, facing a comfortable Tory majority at Westminster, lacked the power to frustrate them.

They appealed to the one person who could rescue their hopes: Margaret Thatcher. At times during the years ahead Powell and Molyneaux convinced themselves that she would eventually insist that a resolute Unionist policy must be followed. No one (not even Powell) felt more strongly than she did that Northern Ireland should remain part of the United Kingdom. But she turned aside from the intellectual challenge of thinking about how that principle might best be put into effect. She devolved policy – first to Neave and after 1979 to a succession of Northern Ireland ministers and officials cast mostly in the completely different mould fashioned in the Heath years.

It has been said that Powell should have directed all his energies to persuading her of the merits of his policy of integration. The opportunity was not missed because of Powell's failure to court her; it never existed. She always refused to devote time to examining and discussing in detail how Northern Ireland should be governed. Powell could not have secured her firm commitment to integration. Another great champion of the cause and ally of Powell, T. E. Utley, tried hard to do so, but she always changed the subject ('I could smack that girl's bottom,' the great Tory journalist said roguishly of the Iron Lady). As Prime Minister she sought policies that would diminish violence swiftly and reduce the often intense international pressure that she faced to ensure that the interests of the non-Unionist minority were fully safeguarded. Powellite integration offered no ready answers to these problems. On the contrary, it could be expected to increase instability in the short

term since it aroused widespread opposition beyond (and, to some
extent, even within) the ranks of the Ulster Unionists. To succeed,
Powellite integration required an absolute conviction that Ulster's
future in the British nation could be secured in no other way.
There was never any possibility that Thatcher would come to share
Powell's conviction.

The Tories' *volte-face* over integration after 1979 intensified Powell's
long-standing suspicion that the means might be found to remove
Ulster from the British nation against its will. He became convinced
that devious officials in Whitehall were working tirelessly to create
a united Ireland, while Parliament was being lulled into believing
that the wishes of the majority of the people in Northern Ireland
would always be respected. Treacherous civil servants thrived above
all in the Foreign Office, which he denounced memorably as 'a nest
of vipers', and in the Northern Ireland Office, which had charge of
all policy relating to the domestic affairs of the province. 'Successive
secretaries of state and the Prime Minister herself', he said in Belfast
in September 1982, 'had been and were the witting or unwitting
executants, stage by stage, of a consistent and continuing process
devised by officials, which was designed to result in an all-Ireland
state embracing Ulster … concealing from Parliament and the
public the true nature of the policies on which they are engaged.'
    He adduced two pieces of evidence in support of his allegations.
The first was a printed briefing note which I had circulated to
Conservative candidates during the 1979 election campaign. It stated
that 'the next Government will come under considerable pressure to
launch a new, high-powered initiative on Northern Ireland, with the
object of establishing another "power-sharing" government in
the Province, which could pave the way for a federal constitution
linking Ulster to the Irish Republic.' These 'remarkable' words,
Powell claimed in October 1983, foretold with uncanny accuracy
what was to come. But the note actually repudiated that view of
the future. It said that Conservatives would not bow to the pressure
for progress towards Irish unity, and concluded by quoting the 1979
manifesto pledge 'to establish one or more regional councils'. Powell
ignored these statements and so created an inaccurate impression of
the note's character and purpose. He became deeply attached to his

misinterpretation. (He may not have seen the full text of the note. Its two paragraphs appeared on separate pages, and it is possible that only the first of them reached him in photocopied form.)

The second document used by Powell to bear out his claims was altogether more significant. It contained an account of two interviews given in 1981 to Geoffrey Sloan, a research student at Keele University, by a knowledgeable, self-confident youngish civil servant at the Northern Ireland Office, Clive Abbott, whom I knew quite well. The document was written by Sloan; Abbott's version of what passed between them never emerged. Sloan's account seemed to provide ample confirmation that a plot was afoot to remove Northern Ireland from the United Kingdom. His document quoted Abbott as saying that the Neave plan for greater integration 'was just not on ... We couldn't break certain undertakings we have given to the Irish government over the constitutional future of Northern Ireland.' Eventually, he predicted, an independent 'confederal Ireland' linking North and South would emerge in which 'Protestant rights would be guaranteed ... A defence agreement would also be made,' bringing the new state into NATO to the great satisfaction of the United States, which had long wanted such a development. Striking a characteristic note of high drama, Powell disclosed the existence of the document and gave an indication of its sensational contents during a Commons debate on legislation to establish a new Northern Ireland assembly, to which he was totally opposed, in 1982.

The government managed to brush these serious allegations aside. Sloan's plausibility was damaged when it emerged that this diligent academic enquirer was also an habitué of the Ulster Unionists' Westminster offices. His document was found to contain factual errors (though this did not impede his career, which has taken him to a post at Reading University and the publication of a study of the geopolitics of Anglo-Irish relations, which omits all reference to these events). The then Cabinet Secretary, Sir Robert (now Lord) Armstrong, was called upon to investigate Powell's claims. His report, written after what Powell regarded as the most perfunctory enquiries, largely exonerated the incautious Northern Ireland civil servant. Yet, years later, Whitehall still remains extremely sensitive about this extraordinary episode. An attempt to elicit the truth in 2004 found that 'serving and retired senior civil servants are edgy about the Sloan–Abbott correspondence, refusing either to talk about it, or claiming that they cannot remember the details.'[†] The full extent to which Abbott's interviews with Sloan reflected official thinking will become clear only when all the relevant confidential government records for this period have been released.

This still unresolved controversy dominated Powell's final years as Ulster's great Unionist champion at Westminster. He quoted repeatedly from Sloan's document and from my 1979 briefing note. In his view they showed conclusively that Thatcher's government looked favourably on Ulster's enemies. Ever greater stress was placed on the unwavering, malign influence exerted by the United States, which, he said at Epsom in October 1982, felt entitled 'to manipulate the internal affairs of the United Kingdom with a view to bringing the island of Ireland within the ambit of the American alliance', overcoming the Irish Republic's commitment to neutrality by presenting it with the territory of Ulster. 'The Northern Ireland Office and the Foreign Office, with American encouragement and connivance, worked unceasingly' to secure their objective, he maintained in a speech at Broughshane, County Antrim, in May 1983.

Two years later in November 1985 the Anglo-Irish Agreement was signed by Margaret Thatcher at Hillsborough, County Down. It gave the Irish Republic a permanent right to express views on some of the main areas of Northern Ireland policy, including the law and the administration of justice. Powell regarded it as a spectacular victory for those engaged in the conspiracy against Ulster. 'This has been done', he said in the Commons, 'because the United States insisted that it should be done.'

Powell came to believe that there were no lengths to which America would not go to achieve its ends. In January 1984 he asserted that the CIA had been responsible for killing the two most important victims of terrorism: Airey Neave, whose support for integration would have thwarted American plans, and Lord Mountbatten, who opposed their nuclear strategy (though two years later, in October 1986, he was to attribute Neave's murder to

---

† Dean Godson, *Himself Alone: David Trimble and the Ordeal of Unionism* (London: HarperCollins, 2004), pp. 73–4.

'MI6 and their friends').[†] Speaking at Coleraine in November 1985, he denounced 'the course of treachery, punctuated by the murders of Neave and Mountbatten, along which the British government's civil service, in collusion with those of the United States and the Irish Republic, have propelled it from stage to stage to the capitulation at Hillsborough'.

Ulster Unionists had every reason to feel profound gloom in the aftermath of these events. 'It is a fearful predicament', he said at Newcastle, County Down, in February 1987 in one of his last speeches as an Ulster MP, 'when our own country is our enemy and in league against us with the most powerful and unscrupulous nation on the face of the earth.' But, he went on, as he surveyed the period of his life in which Ulster had played so great a part, he was still not without hope that the policy which he had espoused since the 1970s would eventually triumph:

> What the terms are I have defined to you before, and I am not afraid to repeat the definition now. They are the Union, the whole Union and nothing but the Union – that is to say, the same rights, civil and political, individual and collective, for all in Northern Ireland, irrespective of politics or religion, as they would possess in any other part of the United Kingdom: British rights for British citizens, under British law made by the British Parliament and administered by British courts. With that programme you are safe.

That was Powell's Ulster creed, from which he never departed – and it remains always his advice to the people he loved so well.

Enoch Powell set out to overturn the assumptions on which British policy towards Ulster rested from the early 1970s onwards. Successive governments insisted, after the removal of Stormont, that the province could be governed successfully only on the basis of power-sharing devolution and a close relationship with the Irish Republic even though it claimed sovereignty over Northern Ireland. This became the firm, unyielding Westminster orthodoxy, the much-vaunted bipartisan approach to Ulster which all

† Heffer, *Like the Roman*, p. 906.

politicians were expected to embrace. Powell rejected it completely. He never deviated from the view that Ulster would enjoy peace and prosperity only if its affairs were settled entirely by the parliament of the nation of which it was part. He gave that alternative policy the name by which it became universally known – integration.

Powell succeeded in halting the onward march of the Westminster orthodoxy in the late 1970s under a minority Labour government. He had the great satisfaction of securing what he described as Ulster's full parliamentary integration through the increase in its representation from twelve seats to seventeen in 1979. If Margaret Thatcher had won only a small majority in 1979 – or been denied an overall majority – Powell might well have changed the course of Ulster's history by securing further integrationist measures.

Through his success in the late 1970s Powell gave fresh heart to the demoralised Unionist people of Ulster, who had been mocked and reviled since the onset of the province's crisis in 1968. He undoubtedly stabilised Unionism at a dangerous moment in its history. A paramilitary force, some 40,000 strong, had come into existence in the early 1970s prepared to defend the interests that Unionist politicians seemed unable to protect. The formidable partnership between Powell and Jim Molyneaux at Westminster restored Unionist faith in constitutional politics. 'The most loyal and least understood' subjects of Her Majesty felt more secure, thanks to them.

The 1980s brought Powell little except setbacks and reverses. He was no longer able to challenge the entrenched Westminster orthodoxy successfully. He looked to Thatcher to keep the pretensions of the Dublin government in check. She failed him, signing the Anglo-Irish Agreement in 1985. That was the nadir of his career in Ulster politics. He was criticised by his colleagues for misreading all the signs, insisting until the last that Thatcher, whom he had come to admire, would not let him down. His influence waned. He did himself no good by dwelling at great length on conspiracy theories which gave bitter expression to his deep-seated anti-Americanism.

Northern Ireland today is governed by an extraordinary ramshackle coalition of opposites which Powell would never have expected to survive for more than a few weeks. It was made possible by his old political foe, Ian Paisley, whom he once described 'as the most resourceful, inveterate and powerful enemy of the Union' which he professed to support. But the end of the Union is not firmly in sight. Rather Ulster's latest political dispensation appears to indicate that within the Union a *modus vivendi* has been reached between the two starkly opposed nationhoods that exist on Ulster's narrow ground. In 1968 Powell warned that the people of Ulster 'cannot forever like the Laodiceans halt between two opinions'. It seems after all that they can, at least for now if not for ever.

Note on sources and acknowledgements

Powell's speeches have provided the principal source material used here – as published in two collected editions, *Still to Decide* (1972) and *A Nation or No Nation? Six Years in British Politics* (1978) for the period before 1979, and as preserved in the Powell Archive for subsequent years. I have drawn extensively on Simon Heffer's monumental biography and on other books about Powell. My own substantial records on Ulster, including a large file on Powell, were destroyed after I left the Conservative Research Department in 1997. I have relied chiefly on memory for the accounts of events in which I was personally involved. I have learnt much from my conversations over the years with Frank Millar, a leading commentator and writer on Ulster affairs. Grateful thanks are due to David Clarke Shiels of Peterhouse, Cambridge for kindly allowing the relevant sections of his forthcoming Ph.D. thesis on Powell to be consulted.

The Poetry of Enoch Powell

The poetic muse left Enoch Powell with the passing of youth, but she returned regularly each year for one single occasion. On 2 January 1953, and on every 2 January thereafter until his death, Enoch Powell composed a short poem as an anniversary gift for his wife, accompanied by a bunch of roses (one for every year that they had been married, until this became impractical!). The first eight poems in this book are a small selection published here for the first time, including the poem written at the start of 1969, which acknowledges the tumultuous previous year through which Enoch and Pam Powell had just passed.

Also included are three unpublished early poems written before the war, and only recently discovered. One of these commemorates King George V's Silver Jubilee of 1935.

XII

There's no such prize
To win again
So great as this;
No choice so wise
Can now remain
Of so much bliss,
So sure before
Yet surer after,
As these twelve years
Confirm it more,
So void of tears,
So full of laughter.
Let's not then haste
The gift to waste,
But lingering taste
What's ne'er replaced.

2.1.1964

XVII

Sweet seventeen the poets sing
The sunlit years of youth,
That line the pathway, bright and brief,
From birth to wedding ring.
But sweeter than sweet seventeen
The years that thence descend
Through toil and danger, joy and grief,
Towards the dark, have been.

2.1.1969

XIX

Still, when the bleak winds bluster
Through January's night,
These roses thicken, cluster,
And bid the snow despite.
So, when this long year closes
And we to earth shall go,
Red still shall these our roses
Be flowering in the snow.

2.1.1971

XXV

Midwinter's roses – are they first or last,
Foretaste of summers that are yet to be
Or afterthought of summers that are past?
Neither; for they, nor hope nor memory,
Live only now, and like all living things
The proof of touch, smell, taste and sight abide
The buried years no Orphean magic brings
Back to the light; no sorceries provide
Assurance of what shall and shall not be.
Here, and here only, past and future stay,
Each present instant holds eternity,
Each dawn precludes an everlasting day,
And in the red heart of a winter's rose
Our souls' immortal motion has repose.

2.1.1977

XXVI

Do not the tribute of this year despise:
Two single blooms, one large, one small – no more!
Man is a counting creature, who descries
His life in numbers round. When one is o'er,
He starts afresh, and images therein
His mortal immortality. So here
The five times five – a Silver Jubilee –
Complete one age, another age begin.
Think then the larger rose's hue to be
All silver, which some Rosenkavalier
Has brought for presage of the times of gold,
Which the red bud shall presently unfold.

2.1.1978

XXVII

Thrice three times three, the perfect numeral,
Cubic, symmetrie, every way the same,
Although the seasons pass and petals fall,
Shall stand for symbol of that lasting frame
Within which each the other holds secure,
Likeness on earth of that all-knowing love
That keeps invisibly fixed and sure
In their respective place the spheres above.

2.1.1979

XXXVII

We never could at first have thought
What all the years between have brought,
Nor seen ourselves with flustering posies
Composed of thirty-seven roses;
And goodness knows what still remains
Of such unconventional gains.
No cause then to begrudge the years
Where always something new appears,
Or with the passing time disclose
The pleasure that we had before.
The only thing that does get worse,
It seems, is quality of verse.

2.1.1989

XL

In that far land
Outside the realm of hope
Through which I wend,
I wonder that your hand
Still stretches from the past
To hold me fast
And guide me down the slope
That reaches to the end.

2.1.1992

An ODE on the Silver Jubilee of his Majesty King George V
Thou, mighty poet of the Empress Queen,
Thou, Tennyson, assist! No less a song
Than aught of thine should grace a nobler scene
Than any from her glorious reign and long:
For now, when five and twenty years have seen
George our defence, four Heralds homage bring
From four free nations to the English king –
Four, and not five! But England's chivalry,
Best in the person of her sovereign found,
Disdain to heed the taunt, and patiently,
Content meanwhile within a narrower bound,
Waits till that Isle in willing loyalty
With brother Celt and Saxon foe shall kneel
Before a common throne for common weal.
Nor far behind, perhaps, in that glad day
Shall India be found – but us beseems
Much less, alas, to prophesy than pray,
Where dark the future sits, and schemes on schemes
Falling might fill the wisest with dismay!
Our hope is still with him that calm has reigned
In confidence and quiet, by strife unstained.
Who, when the great Dominions snarl and brawl
For lucre, cut their brothers' throats like thieves
For bales of merchandise, corrupt with gall
The sacrament of common blood, believes
That what is great shall not by meanness fall,
And 'mid the chaff of loyalty for gain,
Forgets not how to see and prize the grain
Of honourable will. When late the might
Of slumbering Britain, long provoked, arose
And with alliance shrewd, by stubborn fight,
Destroyed great Germany (whence issued woes
To others, but on us shone peace and light),
He was our strength; his throne, while all around
were dashed in pieces on the blood-red ground,
Unmoved remained. And now against a sea
Of other, blacker perils he shall stand
The rock and ward of English liberty.
Through him, while others are enslaved, our land
May work and live in freedom; wherefore we
With grateful mind spontaneously will bring
The fruits of freedom to the English King.

The Swallows

In younger years the swallows on the wing
That autumn warned to cross the sea
Before the winter's deepening,
But swallows were to me.
But these I watch with unaccustomed ruth;
Far other now their flight appears:
They seem the thoughts of fleeting youth
That fly before the years.
They wheel, they fly, they shun my chiller clime,
They seek in haste a kinder shore:
Others will know them in their time –
To me they come no more.
Sept 1936 7.28 London Bridge to Tun. Wells

HYMN

The crackle of a bursting pod,
A shrill cicada's cricket-whirr,
And silence, brooding in the calm
Effulgence of the noonday sun
That sears the uncomplaining clod –
Silence; and yet there is a sound,
Not cricket-whirr, nor murmuring flow
Of bloodstream coursing through the head;
A faint vibration of the ground,
Distant and low, but like the tread
Of countless feet that fall as one.
So still it is, the branches stir
As in a breeze, and back and fro
Ripple the leaves of fern and palm.
Eight thousand miles below this place
The armies march. In swelling tide
The endless grey-green columns roll
Westward and east across the face
Of Europe. Earth beneath that stride
Shakes till a tremor as of fear
Runs through from pole to antipole
And issuing spells its message here.

Vale
Some Reflections on Thirty-seven Years in the House of Commons

Delivered at a dinner of the Salisbury Group
at Hatfield House, 12 October 1987

This speech was perhaps the closest Enoch Powell ever came to answering the question posed throughout this book. As such, it seems appropriate to allow Enoch Powell the last word.

I imagine it has been the common experience of everyone who spent a great part of a lifetime in politics that at the end he was like some traveller who, having journeyed on from day to day, finds himself at last in a strange country, where the landscape is no longer recognisable and the people speak a foreign tongue. Reflecting upon how to come to terms with thirty-seven years in the House of Commons, I decided to ask myself a question. Of all that has come to pass in those thirty-seven years, what is it that you would not have been able to believe if, when you first took the oath in 1950, you had been told that you would live to see it?

I begin by identifying something that would not have been incredible to me. In 1950, though the former Indian Raj was no longer ruled from Westminster, the remainder of the Empire which Britain had taken with her into the Second World War in 1939 remained as before. Yet if I had been told in 1950 that, long before I ceased to be an MP, nothing would be left of all that but a dozen tiny specks here and there on the globe, I could have believed it. I was to vote in 1954 against the treaty with Egypt under which Britain evacuated the Suez Canal Zone, not because I believed our foothold there was tenable but because of the hollowness of the pretence that we would be able to re-occupy it. I had already attained to the insight that Britain, parliamentary Britain, could no longer control territories with any appreciable populations of their own; but even the residual notion of a ring of strategic positions round the world had become unsustainable if we could not stay at the Isthmus of Suez. I consequently found myself startled and mystified by our disastrous reaction to the nationalisation of the Suez Canal by Nasser in 1956. What else, I wondered, had been expected?

The speed with which the remainder of the Empire was dismantled also did not surprise me. Indeed, I remember, when Iain Macleod was Colonial Secretary, discussing with him, and not jocularly, whether it might not be possible to confer independence on batches of half a dozen colonies at a time. What did surprise me but ought not to have done was to discover, when opposition spokesman for the Conservative Party on defence in the mid-1960s, that Kipling's 'East of Suez' was alive and kicking in so much of popular and, apparently, official imagination. Didn't people realise yet, I wondered, that Britain was now the United Kingdom of Great Britain and Northern Ireland, fullstop?

I was not, however, utterly blind to the almost unlimited capacity of my fellow countrymen for self-delusion. Anyone would have been dismissed as raving mad who in 1950 told the people of Britain that by the end of the century approaching one-third of the population of Inner London and of certain other areas of England would be negro or asiatic. It was by drawing attention to that prospect more than a decade and a half later that I was to alter the course of my own political life and arguably the course of British politics. Yet, for all that, if a voice from heaven had told me in 1950 that Britain would do such a thing to itself, I would have found the prophecy horrific but not incomprehensible.

I already knew that the British, or at least those whom the British permitted to speak for them, were compulsively, besottedly, gripped by the delusion that something called The Commonwealth somehow was making them 'mightier yet'. I had vainly tried in 1948 from a desk in the Conservative Parliamentary Secretariat to brief the Conservative Party to resist Labour's British Nationality Bill, which defied political reality by divorcing nationality from allegiance and which was to make possible the immigration into Britain from asiatic and other Commonwealth countries that subsequently took place. When able to speak in my own person, I protested alone in

1953 against the consequential alteration in the titles and the status of the monarchy. That, in the cause of the Commonwealth delusion, the British might allow irreparable damage to be inflicted upon themselves at home and that anyone who told them so would be knocked down and trampled underfoot would not therefore have been an event beyond the range of my comprehension if what in fact happened had been prophesied to me when I first took my seat in the House. Enough, however, of what I might have believed. Let me come to what I could by no means have believed and yet have had to watch come to pass.

When I contemplate, with benefit of hindsight, the one great central and agonising astonishment and incredulity in which the later years of my political life have been lived, I sometimes think that, if I could have looked deeper after the Suez catastrophe, I might have discerned the seeds of a future which was already contained in the sunset delusions of Empire and their sublimation into the delusions of Commonwealth.

The Suez fiasco cut deep into the consciousness of the British people. It had the same sort of effect as a nervous breakdown, similar to what America experienced after the Vietnam war but more severe. They no longer felt sure of themselves. They disbelieved that they could any longer be a nation, with all that meant in terms of independence, pride and self-confidence. It was at this point that British defence policy was wholly re-cast.

The revolution pivoted upon the nuclear deterrent and the power and will of the United States. The British decided they were henceforward secured against war and shielded from mortal attack by America's assumed monopoly or supremacy in nuclear weapons. The one condition was that Britain would be an integral part of that European alliance which the United States embraced with its decisive military underwriting. American hegemony was accepted as inescapable necessity. Britain must needs be the faithful ally, which entailed conformity, as of necessity, with the aims, methods and philosophy of America's foreign policy and strategy. Disobedience would spell the forfeiture of security and exposure to the nameless perils, to say nothing of the economic consequences of providing for the defence of the British Isles.

In this comfortable frame of mind, Britain brought conscription to an end and halved the proportion of its gross national product that was devoted to defence. More was involved, however, than the subordination of British defence and foreign policy to those of the United States and the adoption of the American world-view as obligatory in British political thought and discourse. The United States believed, and believes, that its commitment to shield its European allies cannot be expected to be honoured unless it has sufficient assurance of their solidarity. The nuclear guarantee demanded the existence and the integrity of something called 'Europe': it could not logically be extended to a collection of numerous, politically independent and deeply differentiated states, even though all of them might formally be parties to the alliance. The 'Europe' whose liberty America guaranteed must be not less recognisably an entity than America itself.

Thus the ruling and official classes in Britain became committed to the political unification of the states which belonged to the American alliance on this side of the Atlantic. Public sentiment was in a condition which permitted this purpose, however cautiously, to be pursued. Britain, it seemed axiomatic, was no longer an island; Britain, since it could no longer defend itself, was no longer independent. It followed that Britain was no longer a nation: it was a part and not a whole; its only logical and intelligible destiny was to be absorbed into the new political entity which would conform with the scope and conditions of the American guarantee. This was the new, the final surrogate for lost empire; and if the British liked to tell themselves that they were going to 'lead Europe' in a 'special relationship' with the United States, the necessary bromides were obtainable on prescription.

The chosen instrument of political unification was the European Economic Community, as Prime Minister Edward Heath confirmed when in October 1972 after the passage by Parliament of the European Communities Act he declared there would be political unity by 1980. Adherence to the Community involved the most comprehensive possible renunciation by the United Kingdom Parliament of its exclusive power to tax and to make law and of the exclusive right of the Queen's courts to declare the law, and the express acknowledgment that those powers were to be exercisable in future by the institutions of the Community.

I have now arrived at what would have been to me in 1950 incredible and still in 1987 remains incomprehensible, namely, that any House of Commons could pass such legislation or that the British people would tolerate it. I have been mistaken. The House of Commons did transfer its powers to an authority outside the realm, and the people of Britain not only did not care but continued to give their support and approval to those who had done this thing.

What then is a person to do, for whom political independence and parliamentary self-government are integral to his understanding of his own country and who cannot understand how the Crown in Parliament of the United Kingdom can be other than sovereign over all persons, things and causes within the realm? It is not a matter of an elected Parliament adopting policies or laws with which he disagrees. The Parliament which he thought he knew and the country which he thought was his have changed into something else. Where does he go?

I have found no answer to that question. He can choose not to belong to the altered Parliament. That choice at first I took. But his own country a man can no more renounce than he can decide not to be the son of the parents who brought him into the world. I persuaded myself that it was defensible to seek to sit in Parliament as a member of a party which remained opposed to Britain's act of abdication. It was my punishment to be forced to witness the Parliament of the United Kingdom consent to share with a foreign state responsibility for the government of a part of the realm, and that, the part for which I was elected to sit. I ought to have known better and realised that a Parliament and a country so sunk in their own estimation that they had transferred to an external authority the right to make their laws, impose their taxes and judge their judgments were not likely to be squeamish about doing the same to a small and helpless minority within.

I believe the philosopher C. M. Broad once demonstrated to his satisfaction that in a country at war the pacifist is in a predicament from which only one logical exit exists. The exit, he argued, was suicide. It may be so; but what if one's duty remains intact to a nation which by its own actions has declared itself no longer to exist? There is no way out then, not even by desertion.

Interview with Mrs Pam Powell

Pam Powell was married to Enoch Powell for forty-six years. She has never before spoken publicly about her marriage or his career and the controversies which surrounded them. This is a transcript of conversations held early in 2012 between her and Richard Ritchie, who for many years was Enoch Powell's archivist. The interview began by asking Mrs Powell about herself, how she met Mr Powell and her first impressions of him.

How did you come to work in the Conservative Research Department?

It was all down to the socialist government's dollar shortage in 1947! I was working in New York at the UK delegation of the Military Staff Committee of the United Nations. We had a lovely set of offices on the ninetieth floor of the Empire State Building, and we were paid for by the Ministry of Defence and Cabinet Office. I had originally joined the War Cabinet Offices and Ministry of Defence in May 1944 as a temporary shorthand typist Grade 2 at £2 10s. a week. As a consequence, I had already signed and was subject to the Official Secrets Act. The dollar crisis meant that Captain Coleridge RN, whom I worked for in New York, was told that he must get rid of all his trained English-based girls. Of course our bosses complained like mad, because they didn't want to get rid of us. Twenty-two officers and six girls! We had a lovely time as you can imagine, and I had a lovely boss! Captain Coleridge tried to keep me but it didn't work, so I had to return home on my own on the *Queen Elizabeth*.

I had already decided that I did not want to remain in the civil service and had told Captain Coleridge to make sure that the civil servants in the MoD knew that I was going to leave – I had only been hired on a temporary basis at the end of the war. Once I was back, I went to Mrs Hoster's, which is where I had been trained as a shorthand typing secretary, and they said, 'Well, you had better go and work for the Conservatives' and I said, 'Yes, I think I better had.'

What was the name of that secretarial place?
Mrs Hoster's; it was very well known then. They used to provide very highly trained secretaries for No. 10 and political jobs generally.

Did she suggest the Conservative Research Department because she knew you had some political experience?
She knew I had good references, obviously, and she knew I was furious about being returned to the UK when I was happy in my job in New York and enjoying life there. So I went along for an interview at the Conservative Parliamentary Secretariat – I think it was called that in those days – and it was Enoch who interviewed me.

And when you were hired, were you hired to work for him personally or for the officers as a whole?
No, for him because it was his secretary who had just left. I think he asked the establishment officer at the Conservative Parliamentary Secretariat about me, saying, 'What sort of a secretary is this?' She said, 'A good secretary, good references'; he said, 'All that a bachelor might want?' and she said, 'Yes, all that a bachelor might want.' Apparently this really is what they said – anyway, it's what I have always grown up with, and I don't see any reason why they should have made it up.

Do you think your fellow secretaries thought Mr Powell would be easy to work for, or was in any way unusual?
No, no, they just said, 'I bet it will take some time before you call him anything other than Brigadier Powell' and I said, 'Yes, probably.' But I thought it sounded a good job and of course the other secretaries were working for excellent people too – such as Iain Macleod, Reggie Maudling and Henry Hopkinson. The first thing I ever did for Enoch was to type his resignation letter to Mr Churchill as secretary to the India Committee.

Was it a collegiate atmosphere at the office or did you all work quite independently?

We were broadly independent. We all had occasional lunches together, but not often. Our bosses liked each other. They were together in one small room so, although they covered different subjects, they often talked to each other, of course. It was a fantastically interesting office and we all had our own officer to work for, briefing the opposition front bench. Those three [*i.e. Powell, Maudling and Macleod*] were supplying briefs all the time to a new opposition front bench accustomed to having civil servants at their disposal. So the officers in the Research Department had to churn out briefs, sometimes up to three a day. It really was terrific. And then, as secretaries, we would sometimes take the briefs to the opposition spokesmen, and on occasions work for them too ourselves. When I worked for Enoch in Research, for example, I sometimes did work for Mr Eden. He was a charming man to work for. If it was a Saturday and you had a wedding to go to – in those days we were young and had weddings to go to – Mr Eden would always let us.

I remember that your husband had a great deal of respect for Eden too. He told me that he was extremely effective in the House, really commanded the chamber.

After Suez, and when he had ceased to be Prime Minister, Anthony Eden was being painted by Andrew Freeth, who was a great friend of Enoch's and godfather to Jennifer [*their younger daughter*]. Eden said to Freeth something like 'I have been thinking about it since and I now understand what your friend Enoch Powell was trying to tell me.' I suppose Andrew must have then said, 'Oh, what?', or something like that. And Eden told him that after having been briefed by Enoch on something to do with housing, Enoch had said, 'I have just finished briefing you on a subject which I know a lot about. May I now say something to you on a subject which *you* know a great deal about?' Eden said, 'Yes' and Enoch went on to warn him about the Americans and not to trust them. I can't remember the exact words, but on those lines anyway. Eden didn't agree with him at the time, but after Suez I think he sympathised more with the point Enoch was trying to make.

How did your work for Mr Powell in the Research Department develop into a friendship and eventually marriage?
Enoch was first elected in 1950 with a majority of 691, and during that election I was secretary of the Questionnaire Committee under Lord Woolton. By the way, this led to the one and only time I worked for Mr Churchill, the greatest thrill of all. I went to his house at 28 Hyde Park Gate to take dictation for the Conservative Party manifesto for the general election [*of 1950*]. After the general election I went to a job in the Council of Europe in Strasbourg. But I had always wanted to know what it was like to work in an ordinary constituency during a general election campaign. I had seen Enoch once or twice in the meantime – he had taken me to the theatre, but nothing more than that. And so when the 1951 election came along, he asked, 'Can you work for me?' and I said, 'You bet I can', and he organised it.

So up to then, had you taken much interest in Mr Powell's personal life, or was it a fairly formal relationship between you?
Fairly formal. I had got to know him a little through helping him do some of the index for his *History of the House of Lords in the Middle Ages*, but that was in the recesses when we weren't so busy.

Do you think outside the office he led a solitary life at that time?
Fairly, I think, fairly – although he met people out hunting! He lived in a pretty spartan flat in Earls Court Square, which is where we started life after marriage.

You married him very shortly after the 1951 election on 2 January 1952.
Yes.

When did it become clear that you had married someone who wasn't going to pursue a conventional political career – that it would be an 'up and down ride'?
Exactly at the time when he asked me to marry him, absolutely, because I can remember entirely what was said in the bachelor pad in Earls Court, bought by his gratuity when leaving the army.

When he asked me to marry him he said, 'It will be...' – hang on a minute, I shall remember correctly in a moment – 'It will be grinding poverty and a life on the back benches.' So that was the condition. I just laughed, of course, and said, 'Yes!'

Up to that moment, he had reached the top of almost everything he had set his hand to: what made him think then that he was going to stay on the back benches, rather than become Prime Minister?

I don't think it had been as easy as all that in his previous pre-war life. He found it very difficult for instance to get a university chair, because he was considered much too young. When he finally got one – in 1937, I think it was, in Sydney – he hadn't got all that much self-confidence, particularly not at the beginning. Also, remember that he had always assumed that, for him, politics meant India; that is what he had always wanted, and why he wanted to go into politics in the first place, as you know.

For the sake of posterity, tell the story of Enoch looking for you in the Central Lobby.

That was after we got married. We had had our honeymoon, I saw him going around the Central Lobby and he couldn't remember which of the women there he had been on a honeymoon with as everybody was wearing a hat.

What was your reaction?

I thought it was jolly funny.

Some people might have been annoyed.

I wasn't annoyed, I thought it was jolly funny. It was different because, having worked for two and a half years for someone, you knew them as a friend whom you totally trusted. Love came in 1951 during the election campaign in Wolverhampton.

Let's turn then to his early years in Parliament. You've just said he had no expectation of being anything other than a backbench MP.

Yes, but that was a prospectus of marriage. Don't forget he also had a lot of ambition later on. After quite a few elections when the

Conservatives won, he would often say, 'Well, that's no good for us' because he didn't expect it to lead to promotion.

Would it be correct to say that the first setback politically was when his friend Iain Macleod joined Churchill's government before he did?
It was, exactly. That was a very great disappointment, particularly about that time, when Iain was actually living with us in the small flat in Earls Court Square – when his wife Eve had polio – and we had got to know him very well. At that point, we were good friends and yes, Enoch was jealous. But the actual friendship with Iain still survived because they had been in the same room in the Conservative Research Department – sometimes with Reggie Maudling – and those three *were* friends, as far as any friends in politics are friends. Iain was actually extremely disappointed when we didn't make him Susan's godfather in 1954 [*Susan was their elder child*].

When he was eventually offered a job, he turned it down.
Yes, he did.

Did that surprise you? Why exactly did he say no?
Because he didn't want Wales, he wanted something different. I think he thought he was offered Wales because he had in fact written the Welsh Charter.

But it was quite a thing to say to Churchill, 'I am not going to accept a job from you as it is not the one I want'!
Yes, but I do remember afterwards at a tea party in No. 10 – and Churchill invited the wives as well – I do remember when we shook hands, and when he shook hands with Enoch, Churchill said, 'I quite understand, young man, that you refused' and that must have been very shortly after he had turned down the job.

So in a way this was the first manifestation of his backbench prediction coming true, but also an inconsistency. He expects to remain on the back benches; is jealous when a friend gets promoted; but turns down a job from one of the greatest Prime Ministers even when it is offered.

Yes, I know. He did turn it down – and luckily for Churchill, because apparently, according to John Colville's memoirs, they had already exceeded the quota for ministers from the House of Commons.

So at the start, it was life as a backbench MP and a constituency MP. Did he enjoy the constituency side, or just regard it as a chore, as it was in those days for some MPs?
Oh, he enjoyed it.

How often did you visit Wolverhampton during a year?
Well, we had the house up there, as you know. He did a fortnight's canvassing in January, which always paid off in the following general election. We went up Easter and summer with the children and they learnt to ride in Shropshire and that sort of thing. He went up a great deal more than I did. Most of the constituency things when I first married Enoch were about housing and 'demob' issues.

Nowadays, MPs visit their constituency virtually every weekend; you wouldn't have done that!
No, wouldn't have dreamt of it. Transport was very different in those days. Wolverhampton is 150 miles from London. When you consider what it's like today, I suppose it's interesting to remember that when Susan was born, we said we would take her up to meet the mayor *just once*; and then we told the chairman of the ladies' committee we would come to just *one* coffee meeting with the baby, because it was too cold in our house up there for us to bring her until she was a bit older. I mean you wouldn't get away with that now, would you? But they were nice people in Wolverhampton. Early on, there was one major row – there is always one major row in any constituency, and that happened before we got married. But they were a decent set of people; they were much nicer than the Birmingham ones, I thought.

Eventually, his first job came in December 1955 when he was appointed parliamentary secretary to Duncan Sandys at the Ministry of Housing. But his first high-profile job came in January 1957 when he was appointed Financial Secretary to the Treasury, often described then as the most important job outside

the Cabinet. Did you feel at that moment that his career was taking off and that he might become very important in politics?
Not at that stage. But don't forget, we got married in 1952 and Susan came along in 1954 and Jennifer in 1956. So all my thoughts and energies were on the children, and managing our two houses in South Eaton Place and Wolverhampton.

Were you left to look after the family side of life by yourself?
He always had a major say in everything, and he always came back home at the end of the working day. There wasn't an awful lot of difference between being a backbencher and in government, although he was away more and of course he was always speaking at weekends, always, always.

Even before he was famous?
Even before he was famous. I am sure it was because he wanted to make himself well known in the Conservative Party, and he was known to be a good speaker and kept the engagements he had made.

You must have wondered occasionally whether it was conceivable that you might become the wife of a Prime Minister. And if it happened, whether you would like it.
Oh yes, indeed I did, of course I did. I would have been mad not to have done, having been interested in politics all my life. But I never thought it was likely. There were moments when I thought that if he had done one or two things differently, it might have happened. I often used to say to him, long before 1968, that perhaps we ought to be entertaining people more, because that was to some extent expected of you in those days, especially if you wanted to get on and be noticed. But he said, 'No, I have a different approach', or words to that effect, and that was that. He just wasn't interested in that side of it.

Well, in any case, before we discuss his political ambitions further, we should perhaps deal with his first major resignation, and which actually – contrary to what is often supposed – was his only principled resignation from government over a matter of policy, in this case the level of government spending.

The three of them [*Peter Thorneycroft, Enoch Powell and Nigel Birch*] resigned, exactly. The press thought the row was about Cyprus, and had no inkling of what was going on. It was definitely a joint decision. It wasn't Enoch pushing Peter Thorneycroft; they were three very different people and he remained friends with all three of them.

It has often been suggested that it was Enoch who pushed them all into it.
No, it really wasn't.

A general impression would be that your husband was a more formidable character than Thorneycroft.
I suppose Enoch was more academic, but then Peter had very many skills; he was a lawyer and had a great deal more political experience.

But it's hard to think of your husband playing second or third fiddle to him in terms of economics.
Nobody ever knew what happened with those three. None of us did. Enoch always said that they approached every problem from three different perspectives but always arrived at the same answer. And although the press said that their resignation was all because of Enoch, in fact Nigel was a very smart cookie and just as influential. He was the one who coined, 'Never glad confident morning again.' It was a great friendship among the three.

Some people say that they hoped their resignation would bring down Macmillan.
No, I don't think they thought they had a hope of doing that. I dare say they might have thought it would be nice if it happened, but they really genuinely thought they were printing too much money.

But do you think Enoch was disappointed that it didn't cause a bigger row? If the whole of the Treasury team resigned today, it would be a major crisis…
Because there wasn't any modern technology, you see, there was no 24-hour television or anything like that; lots of people didn't have a television, even then. We didn't have television until 1965, and that was only because Jennifer was recuperating at home after

her appendix was removed. No, Macmillan went on his trip to wherever it was [*a tour of the Commonwealth*], having just described the resignations as 'a little local difficulty' – and that put the kibosh on it.

Your husband returned to government in July 1960 as Minister of Health.
Yes, although only after having refused an earlier offer to return, because Thorneycroft wasn't given office at the same time.

A highly principled refusal.
Yes, I suppose so. I often thought his principles got in the way half of the time.

Did you say that to him sometimes?
Oh, you bet I did.

Did you sometimes think he was sacrificing family interests almost pigheadedly?
No, not family because—

Well, it would have meant more money, more promotion.
Yes, but we didn't expect to have more money. 'A life of grinding poverty'; that is what he said, 'grinding poverty', and we were very strapped for cash.

But generally were you disappointed when he resigned from a job or refused to accept a job?
Yes, I was disappointed but I saw the reason why he did it. Actually, I don't think I was very fussed about his saying 'No' to Mr Churchill, but that's only because of what Mr Churchill said to Enoch, when we went afterwards to the tea and when he shook hands. It was such a thrill.

Anyway, he returns to government and for the first time at the head of a major department – Health – which leads eventually to his joining the Cabinet. Do you think he was happy at the Ministry of Health and did he enjoy being in the Cabinet?

He enjoyed being in the Cabinet, but Health wasn't the job he wanted. What he always wanted was Defence. That's why, when Ted was dishing out shadow posts, Enoch asked to be shadow Defence and Ted said, 'OK, you can have it.' But he enjoyed Health too, in the end. As you know, he was most interested in mental health. Macmillan gave a lot more money to the Health Service and Enoch put most of it towards mental health. Did you know that we stopped having cigarettes in the house about that time?

Why, because he thought it looked bad for the Minister of Health to have cigarettes in his house?
Yes. He and I never did smoke anyway, but we did think it was bad to have cigarettes because the press would be on to us. My mother was, if you remember, a chain smoker!

An early example of concern for both 'health and safety' and the media!
Yes, but he did enjoy Health, and he really got dug into it. He did wonder whether he would ever get anything else.

Oh, did he? What made him wonder that, do you think?
Well, because everybody changed jobs regularly, and he stayed put.

Some people thought he might resign over the Profumo crisis. How well did you know Profumo?
Not well, but Enoch got on with him fine as a colleague. He had been in the army, he was very much a womaniser; he loved women, we knew that. The press at that moment was very interested in how Enoch was going to react. Of all the Cabinet, he was thought to be the most likely member to resign over the Profumo scandal – 'Sea-green incorruptible' the press called him. But Enoch was not in any way tempted to do so. The only reason he stayed silent on the issue for as long as he did was that he had been told to say nothing until the very end, because this was the time when his intervention would be most helpful and Macmillan needed backing. He was happy to do this 100 per cent. He genuinely, absolutely believed Macmillan was not at fault, because of the Galbraith thing; you know about the Galbraith thing?

No.

Well, Tam Galbraith [*Hon. Thomas Galbraith*] had been a junior minister at the Admiralty before moving to the Scottish Office. His Private Secretary was John Vassall, who was arrested for espionage in 1962. Galbraith was forced by Macmillan into resigning from the government. Enoch thought to his dying day that the reason Macmillan didn't sack Profumo was because he, Macmillan, reckoned he had been much too hard, and too soon, on Galbraith.

We are now approaching the next occasion when Enoch turned down high office and left the government: his refusal to serve under Alec Douglas-Home after Macmillan's resignation and because of his support for Rab Butler. This is an episode in British politics which has been written about at length; but how did it seem to you at the time? First of all, was Enoch personally close to Butler by this time?

Rab had been head of the Conservative Research Department and was close politically to Enoch. But he wasn't personally close – he was much too high up for us.

Even then, was he?

Oh, yes. Enoch thought he was a very good chairman of Committee, he always said that, but we didn't often mix with him socially.

Many people say one of the reasons Butler didn't get the leadership was because a large part of the Conservative Party disliked him for his attitude towards appeasement and his conduct during the war when he was suspected of favouring a deal with Germany. There was also the term 'Butskellism', which implied that Butler and Gaitskell were too similar in their beliefs, and that the Tory Party wasn't distinctive enough, particularly on economic policy. Why then was Enoch so enthusiastic for Butler?

Enoch thought at that time that Butler would have made a good Prime Minister. And of course, if Butler had become Prime Minister, Enoch would have remained in government, would almost certainly have been offered a very senior post and a conventional route to the top might have opened up.

So he and Iain Macleod thought Butler deserved it; it wasn't just self-serving?

Yes, they did, they genuinely thought he was the best of the contenders, and that he deserved it. I think afterwards Enoch *did* wonder what Butler would have been like as Prime Minister. But at the time, he had no doubt that Butler was the candidate whom it was right to support. And of course both Enoch and Iain were constitutionally affronted by 'this man who has blasted from the Lords'. However, the inner circle went to see Macmillan in hospital, and Alec got it. But of course, and this is the point, Macmillan didn't ask all of his Cabinet for their views. Enoch and I didn't know if Iain was sent for, but Enoch certainly wasn't. The Butlers were having their house done up, so they were staying in St Ermine's Hotel in Caxton Street, and both Enoch and Iain went round to see Butler separately. But they didn't convince him to fight for the job; he caved in, saying, 'No, I will join Douglas-Home.' Enoch was then sent for by Alec twice, but Enoch told Alec that – after all that he had said – he wouldn't be able to look at himself in the mirror if he joined his Cabinet. But he also told Alec, 'Don't think I don't like you, and I hope we can continue to be friends.' And we did, we had them to dinner and they had us.

You knew Douglas-Home quite well then, already?

Slightly, I mean it was much more of a hierarchy in the Tory Party in those days, the higher up you were, the more you mixed. But I always found that, when working for people as a secretary, the higher up they are, the nicer they are to work for and Alec was a very, very nice, lovely man.

Why didn't Butler fight for it, do you think?

Those who knew Butler from the days of the Research Department thought that if his first wife Sydney had been alive, he would have been a tougher man. Sydney was a very, very tough lady. I myself never met her, but apparently he was totally bereft when she died. His second wife, Mollie, was a friend of ours and a much softer character. There is no doubt that Rab wanted to become leader. Rab always had an eye open for that and would have been thinking about it, 100 per cent of the time. But of course, we all know what happened.

And that was when Enoch said to you, 'Our lives are never going to be the same again'?
Yes, he did, when Rab didn't get the leadership for the second time. It was an absolute watershed. Nothing changed our political life more than Butler's failure to be Prime Minister, and Enoch's immigration speech of 1968. Nothing changed our life more than those two events.

When both Enoch and Iain Macleod refused to serve under Alec Douglas-Home, did that make them closer again?
Yes, it did.

If Enoch had known then that he would never again return to office, would he have acted differently?
No, but he would have been very, very disappointed. He *was* disappointed that it turned out as it did. But he would always say right up until quite late on in his political career with the Conservatives, 'Enoch the Cork.' That is what his phrase was; he often said it. For example when I would be saying to him, 'Oh God, what is going to happen now?' he would reply, 'Don't worry; Enoch the Cork.'

You mean he believed he would always come 'bobbing up' again?
Bobbing up somehow. And of course, as you know, his other favourite saying was 'The Lord will provide.'

Well, once Edward Heath became leader, your husband got the job he wanted, shadow Secretary of State for Defence. So this is when we must begin to discuss his relations with Heath in the lead up to the Birmingham immigration speech of 1968. First, before their major row over immigration, do you think your husband wanted Heath's job? He had after all contested Heath for leadership of the Conservative Party.
At the beginning, definitely no. Yes, he stood in the leadership election [*of 1965*] mainly with the intention of expressing interest and reminding people that he was a future contender – 'leaving

his calling card', as he put it. But that doesn't mean he intended to challenge Heath again. He probably wouldn't have stood in the first place had he expected to receive so few votes. A lot of people 'dropped off', which is what happens in politics. He understood it, he didn't mind, and he ended up with a job he really wanted – shadow Defence – and which he was loving.

Do you think Mr Heath perceived him as a threat?
Yes, but he shouldn't have done. I remember that we were having drinks with friends on the day that the 1966 election was announced, and Ted was there. I was deputed by Enoch to tell him, which was true, that Enoch didn't have any intention of trying to depose him. Heath was paranoid about that sort of thing…

Right from the start?
Oh, yes, right from the start. I was sitting, talking, telling him all this, as agreed by Enoch. I had just said all this when the wife of the editor of the *Daily Express* came in and said, 'There is going to be an election.' Heath buzzed off, leaving me stranded. Neither polite nor sensible politically, because I was in the middle of all this. Enoch told me to tell him that he didn't have any ambition to get his job, he wasn't going to try and get his job. He told me that.

But you also told me once that in those days you thought an eventual bust-up with Heath over something – you didn't know what – was inevitable!
That's true too!

Okay, so now we come to the next watershed which you've already mentioned. Can you remember – before he became famous for his immigration speech – whether you often spoke about immigration at home or because of what you were experiencing in Wolverhampton?
You didn't need to talk about it, we could see it all around us because Wolverhampton was becoming totally, totally different. I mean, look at what actually happened: we bought our house in 1954 for £1,300 – semi-detached, five bedrooms, very cold as you remember, didn't have a telephone – and we sold it in 1975, using a different

name, and got exactly the same money we paid for it after twenty-
one years because all around had so greatly changed.

**Early in 1968 he made a major speech on immigration in Walsall.
It received a lot of attention but it is claimed Enoch was surprised
that there wasn't more of a reaction.**
Yes, yes, he expected there to be a bigger reaction in terms of publicity – not controversy – and that is why he decided he would have to
do it again. Enoch wanted to make people in the country at large
understand what was going on in constituencies like ours.

**As you know, it was often said afterwards that he was naive or
duplicitous in assuming that Quintin Hogg, as shadow Home
Secretary, wouldn't object to his talking on this subject. How did
you both feel about that at the time?**
Enoch thought they were all in agreement. I don't know in what
order they left the shadow Cabinet room on the day they decided
not to support Labour's race relations legislation. I think it was the
last time they met before Easter. Enoch went out of the room, he
told me this afterwards, and because he thought his line was shared
by the shadow Cabinet, he intended to mention to Hogg the fact
that he was going to make an immigration speech, but he couldn't
catch him up. He had tried to speak to him, but of course that doesn't
mean he anticipated the scale of the reaction. None of us did.

**Okay, so he does the next one, the famous one in April; but this
time you are surprised because the reaction is so enormous. When
did you first hear that this speech had caused such convulsions?**
It was the holiday time so the children were with us in
Wolverhampton. Outside church on Sunday morning there were
journalists surrounding us, so that was clearly a sign. But I suppose
it was Robin Pollard [*the agent for the Wolverhampton South West
Conservative Association*] coming round to our house to tell us that
Mr Heath wanted to speak to Enoch on the phone that really
indicated something momentous. We didn't have a telephone in
Wolverhampton, so Robin said first, 'You will have to borrow a
phone' or something like that, but they decided in the end to go
round to the office and take the call there. Robin went with him

and opened up the office, because it was the weekend. Then Enoch returned to the house and said, 'We have got to go.' We didn't have a television in Wolverhampton either, we knew we faced a crisis and therefore we had to return to London. So we bundled the children into the car and drove off.

What were your feelings on the drive back?
I was worried. He was pleased that the speech had been noticed. But then he was sacked.

What was his reaction then?
Surprised, he was very surprised and he thought what a bloody fool Ted Heath had been.

The content of the speech will always be a matter of deep controversy, but there is one thing I wanted to ask you about – namely the veracity of the letter he quoted from which came to be known as the 'little old lady' letter: did she exist?
The letter most certainly did exist. I did see it, but I don't know where it went. We couldn't find it, but I do remember. It did exist. There was a specific letter, and also one of the papers claimed they had got hold of the little old lady – whether that is true I don't know – but no, I saw that letter and probably put it somewhere so safe that we could never find it again. Whatever happened to it I don't know, I wish I did; we all turned the place upside down, everybody did, and we couldn't find it. I wish to God we could have found that letter.

People would still have argued that the existence of the letter did not prove the existence of the person it was talking about.
They might well have said that, but it would have been a lot easier if we had been able to find it and we all tried.

This relates to your libel action against the *Sunday Times* in 1969–70?
Oh, yes, now that is an interesting point. The law suit we launched against the *Sunday Times* was because they called him 'a racist' and didn't believe the letters he quoted from were typical of those

he had received. The case had to be dropped because to continue with it would have meant announcing to the world in general the names and details of all the constituents and correspondents who had written to him similar letters to those quoted in his speeches. That was a thing he would never, ever do and that is why we had to stop the case and settle for a draw. And we were very strapped for money.

Was there anything about this speech that he thought privately was to be regretted or that he said just to you, 'Perhaps I did go too far there'?
Not really, no, because he was quite sure he was repeating what he had been told by his constituents and what was common knowledge in the areas affected.

You have told me on other occasions that you used to feel sick when there was an immigration speech.
Yes. Always after April 1968.

Did you ever feel it was unfair his putting you and family through such anxiety and controversy?
No, it wasn't unfair, because this was his career. I didn't feel it unfair, but I wished to God sometimes that it wasn't happening.

Do you think he would feel he had got it right, if he were alive today?
I think he would be very thankful that it hasn't got as bad as it might have been. I heard him say that one day perhaps – and it will be a long time after we are dead and gone – there will be a lot of intermarriage which would help to reduce the risks. He thought that might happen.

He often implied that the British people wouldn't accept the situation which exists today.
They have accepted it, because they have got no option.

But an important question is whether the issue has developed in the way he predicted. My feeling is that this country has experienced less physical violence than he predicted, but if alive today

he would still have argued that the character of the country has changed every bit as fundamentally as he expected.
I think he would have agreed with everything you have just said. I think he would have agreed with that.

Something which is often said – even by people well disposed to him and who acknowledged the problem at the time – is that his speeches were counterproductive and made it more difficult for others to raise the subject of immigration.
That is exactly what Bill Deedes[†] always thought, I remember that. It was very stupid to think that, but that is what a lot of them thought. They said Enoch's speech prevented anyone else from speaking on immigration.

What was your and Enoch's reaction to that when people like Bill Deedes said it?
He thought it was absurd, and so did I. Enoch was speaking about what was happening all around us, in the middle of the West Midlands and in the constituency. He felt it was his duty to point it out.

And then there is the accusation that Enoch was a racist and didn't like foreigners.
Well, I always think of his friend General Cariappa, when people say that. Nowadays, what I'm about to say sounds completely normal and unexceptional, but at that time in India, it certainly wasn't. Enoch was secretary of the All Indian Army Committee, and he and the general were going around most of India – this was after the war, after August 1945 until he was demobbed in 1946, I think. They were stopping at various places to take note of whatever was going on in the Indian Army in those days. They stopped at the Byculla Club, in Pune, and the club said that the Indian gentleman, who was General Cariappa, couldn't come in because they didn't have anybody except white people here. So Enoch said, 'Take my baggage out of this club, I am going to stay with my friend General

---

† Conservative Member of Parliament for Ashford (1950–74) and later Editor of the *Daily Telegraph*.

Cariappa', and he did. One would expect nothing else today, but in those days in India the club's rules were normal, accepted and to be obeyed. Subsequently, he came to see us in England and we had him to a meal at home and he had us to whatever club he was staying at in England. Very charming man.

And then of course before the war there were instances of your husband helping to get Jewish refugees out of Germany...
Yes, indeed, Paul Maas, and we saw Paul Maas until he died.

He was one of Enoch's best friends?
Yes, it was largely through Enoch he got out of Germany before the war, and got a post in Oxford. Enoch helped him as much as he could when he came here. A very charming, very frail old gentleman.

So, the rupture with the Conservatives has occurred, he is now a household name, never out of the newspapers, highly contro-versial and his motives are called into question. Did any of this upset him?
After he had been sacked, his biggest disappointment was when he had been invited to make a speech to the Army in Germany. Denis Healey was Secretary of State for Defence and refused him permis-sion to go to Germany to make the speech to the Army because he was a 'racist'. He was more upset by that than anything else, because he loved the Army. That hurt him more than any other single thing.

After 1968, I suppose it's fair to say that, save in a national emer-gency, the chance of his ever becoming Prime Minister or return-ing to high office had completely disappeared.
Absolutely, that is exactly what Peter Thorneycroft said long after the resignation in 1958. He said this to me when we were having a meal, just the four of us. He said, 'The only way that Enoch is going to get anywhere near the top, Pam, is if there is another war' and I said, 'Well, we don't want that', but that is what I thought too. I think, incidentally, that he would have been a jolly good Prime Minister, had we had a war, which thank God we did not have. I have always thought that and that is obviously what Peter Thorneycroft thought.

I think it is generally acknowledged that Enoch helped Heath and the Conservatives to win the general election of 1970 when, in the final days, he urged the country to 'vote Tory' even though personally he had nothing to gain from a Tory victory. However, I don't think he expected this to work in the way it did. My recollection is that you both assumed Heath would lose the election.
Yes, we did, we most definitely wanted him to.

You wanted him to?
Oh, yes. But in the end, and on the other hand, people were ringing us up all the time, MPs and others saying, 'For God's sake, make a "helpful" speech', so he made the 'vote Tory' speech, you know, 'The man with a boat, or the man with a pipe'. To be honest, I think his feeling was 'I don't think you are going to win, but nobody is going to accuse me of having lost it for you'. Also, whatever it meant to him personally, it was hard to argue that the continuation of the Labour government was in the public interest. At least on the economy, we thought Heath would be okay.

What broke all the calculations was that his speech actually worked in some key marginal seats! So despite your overwhelming victory in Wolverhampton South West it was actually a pretty low moment for you both.
After the 1970 election, he knew it wouldn't happen, becoming Prime Minister. If the Conservatives had lost in 1970, it is conceivable that there would have been moves to bring Enoch back into a shadow Cabinet led by someone other than Heath. It probably wouldn't have happened, but it might have done. But once Heath won the election which everyone thought he was going to lose, we knew that we had absolutely nothing to hope for in terms of office unless there was an overwhelming crisis. So after 1970, he thought that the overriding thing was the Common Market, and he would devote everything he had to preventing it from happening. He thought he would renew his partnership with people like Michael Foot and repeat the success they had had in derailing the reform of the House of Lords. And of course, when that failed, he also thought he would help win the referendum which eventually Wilson called. He got that absolutely wrong.

What do you feel when people suggest that Enoch was an example of those really clever people who sometimes miss the obvious and lack judgement?
Do you mean, was he too clever for his own good in a way? Yes, if you put it like that… What he always regretted was that he didn't go – and it wasn't his fault, it wasn't for want of trying – but he always regretted enormously that he didn't see proper active service in the war. Of course, as he once or twice said, 'They used the best bit of me, the head'! But he resented it, regretted that he hadn't been in the proper war. I think he did feel that there were a lot of people whom he knew who were killed, they didn't come back, and that he should have been one of them.

Enoch did once say to me also that one of the worst things he could have imagined happening to him was being taken a prisoner of war, as my father was.
In the Far East?

Well, that's what happened to my father, but not just in the Far East. I think he felt being taken prisoner was the worst thing that could happen to anyone, full stop. He would rather have been killed than taken prisoner.
Yes, I am sure he would.

It wasn't a view universally shared!
No, but I think that certainly would have been Enoch's view.

Who would you say were your husband's closest friends in politics?
The first thing he used to say was that there are no real friends in politics, and certainly not on one's own side! But that's not quite true. On the Conservative side, he was of course very friendly with John Biffen. He was probably the closest. But he was very friendly too with Nick Ridley, Ronald Bell and John Hay, who I think acted as his sort of 'whip' when he stood for the leadership of the Conservative Party.

There were a number of people on the left whom Enoch got on well with too, weren't there?

Oh, yes. He got on with Richard Crossman very well, and of course with Tony Benn.

He broke with Tony Benn, though, over the 'black flag of Dachau' speech in the 1970 election.[†]
Oh, yes, but then he came to Enoch's funeral, do you remember?

Yes, but to be honest the impression I had at the time was that Tony Benn went to almost everybody's funeral! However, I think they became closer again over the issue of the European Union.
Enoch got on all right with Jim Callaghan too. I remember, ages after 1968, when he was Prime Minister, Callaghan came up to us and said, 'Oh Enoch, you would like my job, it's a jolly good job, you know, you would like it.' I remember him saying that and we all laughed.

And Michael Foot of course was the one he liked best.
And who he knew best. And of course they had this terrific partnership – well, you know all about that – stopping the reform of the House of Lords.

The issue of friendship is important because it was tested to the hilt after the 'vote Labour' speech of February 1974. How did you feel about that speech?
Desperate, it was the worst time of my political life, the worst of everything for me, because I thought the party mattered so much, I really did. I hated it and of course so many people with whom we were friends, who had stuck with us in 1968 and whom we considered our 'barometers' – people like John Hall, who sat for High Wycombe – they didn't understand either. 1974 was much worse for losing friends than those we lost in 1968. There were MPs after 1968 who thought Enoch would return to office and who agreed with him. But not after 1974.

---

† This refers to the speech made by Tony Benn during the 1970 General Election when he said, 'The flag hoisted at Wolverhampton is beginning to look like the one that fluttered over Dachau and Belsen.'

Do you think that he felt the same, that there would never be a way back after urging people to 'vote Labour'?
Correct. That is what I remember him telling me. He didn't, he really, really didn't.

So it was one of those rare events where a politician knowingly commits political suicide for the sake of a principle?
I think that would be fair.

And it did help secure the 1975 referendum on whether or not Britain should remain in the EEC, although I don't think Enoch would have stood as a Conservative anyway by that stage because of everything else the Heath government had done.
Remember that as far back as 1972, he went around with an application for the Chiltern Hundreds in his pocket [*the device through which an MP voluntarily relinquishes his seat during a parliament*].

I had forgotten that.
He had it in his waistcoat pocket for ages. He had it in his pocket, I remember, all one holiday in France. Nobody knew it. It was because of the controversy in 1972 caused by the expulsion of the Ugandan Asians.

Anyway, it wasn't the end. Within eight months, your husband returned to the House of Commons in the October 1974 election as the MP for South Down in Northern Ireland. What was your reaction? Did you have mixed feelings?
He had given a lot of help to the Ulster Unionists but we were surprised when we came back from a holiday in Italy, and they wanted to see him.

Oh, so you were surprised?
Totally surprised, totally, totally.

Did it take a lot of thought on the advisability of standing for Parliament again, this time for Ulster?
No, we came back from a holiday and we then went to stay in Sussex and I think there was a telephone call and he said, 'I have

been asked if I would like to stand and they think they could fix it in Northern Ireland.' I said, 'Good gracious, Ulster, why, what...' and he said, 'Well, I don't know, but I think I have got to do it.' And then by the time we came back to London, he said, 'I know I have got to do it. I have been helping them as far as I could as an MP for Wolverhampton, I think I must do it.' That was that.

Did *you* express any doubts at that moment about it?
He always said publicly – and to me – 'Well, I have helped them in divisions so many times in Parliament, I can't not go.' He felt genuinely it was a duty, he felt he ought to do it; but let's face it, he also wanted to go back to the House.

Were you content or did you say to yourself, 'Oh Lord, do I have to go through this again?' when it became clear that actually he might re-enter politics?
In a way I thought, 'Do I have to go through with this?' because I could see what it would involve in terms of time and commitment and I had hardly ever been to Ulster and I didn't know anything about it and in those days it was quite alarming. Not that I was in any way frightened to be in Ulster. You have heard the story about my wisdom tooth?

Tell me again.
Our first visit to South Down, there was a great set of people to meet us at Aldergrove[†] and we got into a car, several cars in a procession, and suddenly they all said, 'Get out.' So we all had to get out and we went behind the shop front because there was a possible bomb just over there – and my wisdom tooth was hurting so much, I was living on brandy and painkillers. It hurt so much I thought, 'I don't care if the damned thing does go off, it will stop this awful pain.' And after that in Ulster, they all thought Mrs Powell was so brave not worrying about a bomb: but I wasn't brave, I was just horribly in pain with a wisdom tooth and couldn't think of anything else. But from then on, I had this reputation for bravery! I absolutely didn't deserve it at all.

---

† Belfast's airport.

Did you come to like the new constituency?

I thought they were marvellous. Enoch used to call on every priest, Church of Ireland, Roman Catholic, whatever, and they were terribly nice too. I think they must have thought for a time, 'Oh, we have got an odd Englishman here!' At our first election, they used to ask me to speak at every election meeting – I think because they wondered if I could talk at all. I was very careful to say very little as I knew then so little about Ulster politics, but we made a lot of friends there. They expected me to go and make the sandwiches at election meetings. I did it once and I thought, 'No, I want to go in and hear what they are saying and what questions they are asking.' Well, I had to: I wasn't going to be making sandwiches after he had just finished the speech!

I never could imagine anybody less at home in a Masonic, or Orange, lodge than your husband.

I know.

He wasn't the sort of person that liked regalia, he didn't like dressing up.

No, he never did.

And although he was an Anglican, he certainly wasn't a Bible-thumping Protestant.

Gosh, no. Oh yes, don't put this in, but no cross on the altar did seem very different to me.

Some people will find that interesting; no reason not to mention it...

Oh, all right.

So he must have felt sometimes like a fish out of water? But it didn't seem to change his view as to whether or not he should have done it.

No, he thought far more of the fact that he must try and keep Ulster inside the Union. I think it was that and put up with whatever else sprang from it.

Do you think he ever expected to lead the Ulster Unionists?
It was right that he didn't, because he wasn't an Ulsterman.

But at one stage I'm sure Enoch thought that it might have been part of the plan for him to become leader. It was also discussed in the press.
He thought he might be invited to be leader, but he could see once he got there how they were and he was neither surprised nor disappointed. He had taken that road and that was that; he loved South Down and it was a jolly nice place.

And through this, he began again to have high-level contacts with the Conservative Party. I haven't asked you yet about how your husband regarded Mrs Thatcher. I remember that he was very critical of her when she was elected as opposition leader and remained critical of her right up until the end of the Falkland War. It was the Falklands that changed his view of her, wasn't it?
Yes, it was. Before that I think he was fairly distant and very critical of her over Northern Ireland. But he absolutely changed, and funnily enough, I dug all this up by accident recently: there was a press statement by Thatcher, from No. 10, saying: 'Following the talks which the PM had on 4 May 1982 with the parliamentary leaders of the Social Democratic and Liberal parties to discuss the Falkland Islands, the PM had a meeting on 5 May with Mr Enoch Powell, he being the only Privy Counsellor representing a Northern Ireland constituency.' They managed to bring off the meeting on that basis. And I recorded at the time, because Enoch told me, that Mrs Thatcher had said at 9.30 p.m. on 5 May 1982 on arrival, 'I would trust you with the life of my child.' And at the end, she said, I put this down when he came back, 'It is a relief to be able to talk to you, there is nobody else I can talk to like this.' She said this in the PM's room in the House. Enoch told me she had said it and it was very gratifying.

There are still those who question your husband's commitment to Ulster.
All of Enoch's being centred upon Northern Ireland remaining in the United Kingdom. He was absolutely a patriot first and

foremost, and he said that he hadn't done six years in the Army just to chuck it all away. He thought the Ulster people deserved to remain part of the UK. That is why he went on to become an MP for Ulster when he left in February 1974, because he had been voting with the Ulster lot in the House of Commons already for quite a long time.

I have always believed that your husband is a very great challenge for biographers because he never kept a diary – he described it as 'regurgitating one's own vomit' – and his correspondence was seldom other than short and to the point. His speeches tell one everything there is to know about his political views, but they don't tell one much about him as a person. So, let's conclude on a personal note. At the end of the day did you ever feel that Enoch was being selfish about his career and not thinking enough about what he was putting you and the family through, especially when he was so controversial on the issue of immigration?

No, I've never felt that. After all, I've always been a political animal. I thought sometimes that what he did was a damned nuisance and I did say once or twice, 'Are you really going to say that?' Occasionally, he might take a little bit of notice of what I said about an odd bit of a speech if I saw it, but not on a significant point. My only violent disagreement with him on a political subject was on capital punishment, which as you know he disapproved of. I have changed my mind now, I have completely changed my mind. But going back to your question about the family, you know of course he never accepted an increase in the parliamentary salary, at least not until after a general election?

Did that annoy you?

Oh, yes, oh, yes it did, it did annoy me. Do you know what I did? I rang up the Fees Office and I said, 'Look, I hope when it comes to a pension it won't make any difference' and they said, 'No'. Well, wouldn't a wife do that?

Absolutely right, he should have thought about it.

He possibly did, but I mean money was tight.

He didn't seem to have many self-doubts.
I only heard him once – and that was years ago after we had lost the seat – I only once heard him musing, 'Perhaps I should have stood as an Independent and taken up another seat': that would have been one of the seats which were offered to him as an Independent Conservative after 'Vote Labour'. I heard him say that, but not in any serious way...

I actually heard him wonder whether it wouldn't have been better never to have returned to the House of Commons at all after February 1974...
And not stand in Northern Ireland?

Correct. But not because of anything to do with Ulster. It was because of the European issue. He did once say, 'You know, maybe I should have stuck to my original decision never to belong to a parliament which was no longer sovereign.'
Yes, I know, I can remember...

One of the things that he also said was that he didn't think he would have made a very good diplomat. Do you remember?
Oh, yes, I remember him saying that and I am sure that is true, I think that is very true, don't you?

Yes, but it is one of the very few occasions when he conceded that he might not have been good at something!
I don't think he was good at ball games. I have got a medal that he got for gym at school, we all laughed at that; I have still got it in the study. That is almost unthinkable, isn't it?

He had no interest in sport at all, did he?
No, he even refused Billy Wright to go to Wolverhampton Wanderers. They were very big people in the football world. But they didn't mind. I think he may have gone to dinner but he excused himself having to watch anything, he probably said he was busy elsewhere.

So we conclude on one of the themes of this book. Do you think he considered that his political life ended in failure?

Enoch always said the two most important things you could get were a VC and a 'Rt Hon.'. Those are the two things he would have liked most and he got one of them. And he was resilient. When he became ill, and fell downstairs and lost his mobility through Parkinson's, he still thought that there was plenty he could do because he could read and he could write. He didn't give up, but he knew that life would be different.

Enoch Powell left Parliament in 1987. While still in demand as a speaker and commentator on political events, his energies turned increasingly to religion, culminating in 1994 with the publication of his major transla-tion of St Matthew's Gospel entitled The Evolution of the Gospel: A New Translation of the First Gospel, with Commentary and Introductory Essay. *In asserting the primacy of Matthew, he was again demonstrating his propensity for controversy, although others have argued the same both before and since. He was working on a similar study of St John's Gospel at the time of his death. He was buried dressed in his brigadier's uniform.*